Latin American Women's Writing

Latin American Women's Writing

*Feminist Readings
in Theory and Crisis*

EDITED BY
ANNY BROOKSBANK JONES
AND
CATHERINE DAVIES

CLARENDON PRESS · OXFORD
1996

Oxford University Press, Walton Street, Oxford OX2 6DP

Oxford New York
Athens Auckland Bangkok Bombay
Calcutta Cape Town Dar es Salaam Delhi
Florence Hong Kong Istanbul Karachi
Kuala Lumpur Madras Madrid Melbourne
Mexico City Nairobi Paris Singapore
Taipei Tokyo Toronto
and associated companies in
Berlin Ibadan

Oxford is a trade mark of Oxford University Press

Published in the United States
by Oxford University Press Inc., New York

© Anny Brooksbank Janes and Catherine Davies 1996.

British Library Cataloguing in Publication Data
Data available

Library of Congress Cataloging in Publication Data
Latin American women's writing : feminist readings in theory and
crisis / edited by Anny Brooksbank Jones and Catherine Davies.
Includes bibliographical references and index.
1. Spanish American literature—Women authors—History and
criticism. 2. Spanish American literature—20th century—History
and criticism. 3. Feminism and literature. I. Jones, Anny
Brooksbank. II. Davies, Catherine, 1952–
PQ7081.A1L36 1996
860.9'9287'098—dc20   96–16383
ISBN 0–19–871513–7. (Pbk)
ISBN 0–19–871512–9

1 3 5 7 9 10 8 6 4 2

Typeset by Graphicraft Typesetters Ltd., Hong Kong
Printed in Great Britain
on acid-free paper by
Biddles Ltd.
Guildford and King's Lynn

For our families

Oxford Hispanic Studies

General Editor: Paul Julian Smith

The last twenty years have seen a revolution in the humanities. On the one hand, there has been a massive influence on literary studies of other disciplines: philosophy, psychoanalysis, and anthropology. On the other, there has been a displacement of the boundaries of literary studies, an opening out on to other forms of expression: cinema, popular culture, and historical documentation.

The new *Oxford Hispanic Studies* series reflects the fact that Hispanic studies are particularly well placed to take advantage of this revolution. Unlike those working in French or English studies, Hispanists have little reason to genuflect to a canon of European culture which has tended to exclude them. Historically, moreover, Hispanic societies tend to exhibit plurality and difference: thus Medieval Spain was the product of the three cultures of Jew, Moslem, and Christian; modern Spain is a federation of discrete autonomous regions; and Spanish America is a continent in which cultural identity must always be brought into question, can never be taken for granted.

The incursion of new models of critical theory into Spanish-speaking countries has been uneven. And while cultural studies in other language areas have moved through post-structuralism (Lacan, Derrida, Foucault) to create new disciplines focusing on gender, ethnicity, and homosexuality, it is only recently that Hispanists have contributed to the latest fields of enquiry. Now, however, there is an upsurge of exciting new work in both Europe and the Americas. *Oxford Hispanic Studies* is intended to provide a medium for writing engaged in and taking account of these developments. It will serve both as a vehicle and a stimulus for innovative and challenging work in an important and rapidly changing field. The series aims to facilitate both the development of new approaches in Hispanic studies and the awareness of Hispanic studies in other subject areas. It will embrace discussions of literary and non-literary cultural forms, and focus on the publication of illuminating original research and theory.

Contents

Notes on Contributors

SUSAN BASSNETT is Professor of Comparative Literary Theory at the University of Warwick, and Director of the Centre for British and Comparative Cultural Studies. She is a leading authority in Translation Studies and Comparative Literature, in British Cultural Studies, and Women's Theatre Studies. Her publications include *Sylvia Plath* (Macmillan, 1986), *Feminist Experiences: The Women's Movement in Four Cultures* (Allen and Unwin, 1986) and *Comparative Literature: A Critical Introduction* (Blackwell, 1993). She has edited *Knives and Angels: Latin American Women's Writing* (Zed, 1990) and her many translations include Margo Glantz's *Family Tree* (Serpent's Tail, 1991). She is currently researching travel writing and nineteenth-century imperialist texts.

ANNY BROOKSBANK JONES is currently Senior Lecturer and Head of Spanish at Nottingham Trent University, where she specializes in Latin American and Spanish cultural and political studies, feminism, and post-colonial theory. She has published numerous essays on Latin American and Spanish writers, and feminist theorists, including Ana María Moix, García Márquez, Luce Irigaray, and Julia Kristeva. Her current research focuses on women and politics in Spain and Latin America. She is currently completing a book entitled *Women in Spain* for Manchester University Press.

DEBRA CASTILLO is Professor of Romance Studies and Comparative Literature at Cornell University, where she specializes in contemporary Hispanic literature, women's studies, and post-colonial literary theory. She is author of *The Translated World: A Postmodern Tour of Libraries in Literature* (Florida State University Press, 1984) and *Talking Back: Toward a Latin American Feminist Literary Criticism* (Cornell University Press, 1992), and translator of Federico Cambell's *Tijuana: Studies of the Border* (University of California Press, 1994). She has published numerous essays on contemporary Latin American, Spanish, US Latino/a, and British Commonwealth fiction. She is a member of the *Diacritics* editorial board and book review editor of *Letras femeninas*.

CATHERINE DAVIES is Senior Lecturer in Hispanic Studies at Queen Mary and Westfield College, University of London. She is author of

Rosalía de Castro no seu tempo (Galaxia, 1987), *Rosalía de Castro e Follas Novas* (Galaxia, 1990), and *Contemporary Feminist Fiction in Spain: Montserrat Roig and Rosa Montero* (Berg, 1994), and editor of *Women Writers in Spain and Spanish America* (Mellen Press, 1993). She has published numerous essays on Spanish and Spanish American literature and is currently completing a book on women writers in Cuba. She is a member of the editorial boards of *Journal of Hispanic Studies, Tamesis,* and Grant and Cutler *Critical Guides.*

NORA DOMÍNGUEZ completed her studies at the Universities of Salvador and Buenos Aires before taking up a lecturing post in the Facultad de Filosofía y Letras in Buenos Aires, where she is currently Co-ordinator for Interdisciplinary Women's Studies. She has lectured and published widely in Latin America, France, Germany, and the US on issues around gender/genre and Argentinian literature. Her book *Guillermo Cabrera Infante: tres tristes tigres* is currently in press with Hachette.

JEAN FRANCO is Emeritus Professor at Columbia University, New York. Her more recent publications include *Plotting Women: Gender and Representation in Mexico* (Columbia University Press, 1989) and a co-edited book (with Juan Flores and George Yúdice), *On Edge: The Crisis of Contemporary Latin American Culture* (Minnesota University Press, 1992). She is currently co-editing (with Juan Flores and George Yúdice) a series on cultural studies for the University of Minnesota and is general editor of a series of translations of nineteenth-century Latin American texts to be published by Oxford University Press, funded by the Lampadia Foundation. She is also preparing a book on cultural relations between the US and Latin America for Harvard University.

SUSAN FRENK lectures in Modern Spanish and Latin American Studies at the University of Durham. She has published articles on Latin American writing, is one of the joint authors of *Women's Voices from the Rainforest* (Routledge, 1995), and a contributor to *Spanish Cultural Studies: An Introduction* (Oxford University Press).

LINDA GOULD LEVINE is Professor of Spanish at Montclair State College, where she also teaches Women's Studies. Her publications include: *Juan Goytisolo: la destrucción creadora* (Joaquín Mortiz, 1976); *Feminismo ante el Franquismo* (with G. Waldman, Ediciones Universal, 1980); a critical edition of *Reivindicación del Conde Don Julián* by Juan Goytisolo (Ediciones Cátedra, 1985); and *Spanish Women Writers: A Bio-bibliographical Source Book* (with E. Marson and G. Waldman (Greenwood Press, 1994). She has also published over sixty articles and papers on aspects of Latin American and Spanish literature, feminism, and women's writing.

JO LABANYI is Reader in Modern Spanish and Latin American Literature at Birkbeck College, University of London. In addition to various articles on modern Spanish and Latin American fiction, she has published two books on the contemporary Spanish novel, edited a book on Galdós, and co-edited *Culture and Gender in Nineteenth-Century Spain* and *Spanish Cultural Studies: An Introduction*. Her translations include works by Galdós and Marta Traba, and she is currently preparing *The Politics of the Family in the Spanish Realist Novel* and a book on Spanish cinema in the 1940s.

LUIZA LOBO is Professor of Comparative Literature and Literary Theory, and Chair of the Department of Science of Literature at the Federal University of Rio de Janeiro, Brazil. She is author of *Epica e modernidade em Sousândrade* (EDUSP and Presença, 1986), *Teorias poéticas do Romantismo* (UFRJ and Mercado Alberto, 1987), *Crítica sem Juizo* (Francisco Alves, 1993), *O haikai e a crise da metafísica* (Numen, 1993), and three collections of short stories. She has contributed to *The Bloomsbury Guide to Women's Literature*, ed. Claire Buck (Bloomsbury, 1992), *Clarice Lispector: a Bio-bibliography*, ed. Diane Marting (Greenwood Press, 1993), and *Dictionary of Brazilian Literature*, ed. Irwin Stern (Greenwood Press, 1988).

SHARON MAGNARELLI is Professor of Spanish in the Department of Fine Arts, Languages and Philosophy of Quinnipiac College, Connecticut. Her publications include *The Lost Rib: Female Characters in the Spanish American Novel* (Bucknell University Press, 1985); *Reflections/Refractions: Reading Luisa Valenzuela* (Peter Lang, 1988); and *Understanding José Donoso* (University of South Carolina Press, 1992). She has also published over fifty articles on aspects of Latin American literature and women's writing and is on the editorial boards of: *The Forum*; *Antípodas*; *Latin American Theatre Review*; *Siglo XX*, and the *Instituto Internacional de Teoría y Crítica del Teatro Latinoamericano*.

ADRIANA MÉNDEZ RODENAS is Associate Professor in the Department of Spanish and Portuguese and Comparative Literature at the University of Iowa. She is author of 'Tradition and Women's Writing', in *Engendering the Word: Feminist Essays in Psychosexual Poetics*, ed. Temma F. Berg *et al.* (University of Illinois, 1990), and 'Elena Garro', in *Dictionary of Literary Biography*, ed. William Luis and Ann González (Brucoli, Clark, and Layman, 1994). She has also published essays on Latin American Literature in leading journals and is currently working on a book entitled *La Condesa de Merlín: Gender and Nationalism in Colonial Cuba.*

DORIS MEYER is Roman S. and Tatiana Weller Professor of Hispanic Studies at Connecticut College, New London, Conn. She is author of *Victoria Ocampo: Against the Wind and the Tide* (Braziller, 1979), and has also edited *Contemporary Women Authors of Latin America* (Brooklyn College Press, 1983), *Lives on the Line: The Testimony of Contemporary Latin American Authors* (University of California Press, 1988), and *Reinterpreting the Spanish American Essay: Women Writers of the 19th and 20th Centuries* (University of Texas Press, 1995). She is currently completing a book, *Speaking for Themselves: Neomexicano Cultural Identity and the Spanish Language Press* (University of New Mexico Press).

Introduction

ANNY BROOKSBANK JONES AND
CATHERINE DAVIES

> uno no puede verse a sí mismo sino en un espejo
> (one can only see oneself in a mirror)
>
> Victoria Ocampo

THE common root of crisis and criticism in a moment of decision is by now familiar. However, the juxtaposition of crisis and theory in our title invokes a more telling and timely relation, and a more decisive way of looking at both. It acknowledges theory's central but contested place in contemporary academic writing and it recognizes that in Latin American studies these tensions are compounded when theory declares itself feminist.

Each of the essays in this volume addresses different feminist inflections of theory and crisis. The volume is organized around the triple articulation of theory's own contested status as politics, the crisis of feminist theory, and theory as a discursive field in which social crisis is registered and played out. Theory as micropolitics is put increasingly into question in Latin America by the macropolitics of cultural change, as women emerge as innovative protagonists of the new social movements. But theory is also the field or theatre in which critical transformations are discursively produced and performed. It is in particular a theatre of contention. Broadly speaking, feminism finds itself caught between postmodern critiques of universality and objectivity on the one hand and humanist narratives of justice and progress on the other, while literature strains between the sweep of grand theory and the particularity of historically grounded texts. Although Latin America has not been proof against such conflicting concerns, critical emphasis has tended to fall on materialist discourses of causation. As a result, to forgo these discourses in favour of postmodern conceptions of the material is effectively to reject much of Latin American cultural theory. Many male cultural critics in particular have preferred to approach writing as a more or less transparent window on to the relations and events it describes. They view the key feminist assumption that analytic and representational categories are not transparent or universal as unengaged. By comparison feminist critics have tended to be more open to the text's status as representation of gender and other relations, and more prepared to engage with those relations *as words*.[1]

This volume was not conceived as an overview of such tensions in Latin American feminist critical practice or theory, nor as a field in which the articulations that sustain practice and theory could be teased out. It is predicated on the assumption that neither completeness nor separation are options in this context. Instead it offers very specific readings which foreground the unsettling and powerfully productive potential of the crisis in and around theory. In the process it intervenes in debates which are helping to reposition feminist critical discourse within Latin American studies and the academy at large. For this purpose it appropriates the work of theorists not generally thought of as feminist—including Bakhtin, Baudrillard, Freud—as well as others—like Irigaray, Spivak, and Butler—who usually are. But if, as we have argued, theory can no longer be ignored, neither can it be unquestioningly celebrated or rejected. Instead contributors to this volume concentrate on what particular theories can and cannot do. Theory in a Latin American frame is seen as invoking a range of analytic strategies oriented towards a critique of institutional and other orthodoxies. For feminist theorists these strategies might include: engaging with common sense, gender-neutrality, and objectivity as patriarchally determined constructs; reassessing institutionally privileged notions of gendered and cultural identity and their relation to the social; analysing the founding conditions of the discourses that perpetuate institutional orthodoxies. As the essays in this volume inflect these and related concerns they engage with decisive moments in the discourse of politics and the material, of identity and subjectivity, of race and ethnicity. They trace crises at home, in the city, in genre, and in gender as performance, and they exploit theory's own difficult moments.

---

[1] As in any statement about 'Latin America', there are many exceptions to these broad tendencies. See essays by Anny Brooksbank Jones and Debra Castillo in this volume.

Questions of gender/genre and its links with performance and crisis are addressed from a range of perspectives. Sharon Magnarelli's essay focuses on Griselda Gambaro's 'theatre of crisis', and specifically on how in *El despojamiento* the Argentinian challenges women's conventional misrepresentation by appropriating and remotivating certain conventions of femininity. The audience witnesses the process by which the woman character, Mujer, comes to recognize herself as at once subject and object, seer and scene. Denied access to power, she self-consciously assumes the effects of non-power: she responds complicitously to the forms of erotic and economic oppression thrown up in the play, and acts out the cultural ideal of the erotic in order to arouse the desire of the young male Muchacho. The manifest failure of Mujer's efforts highlights the emptiness of the erotic ideal itself, in Magnarelli's view. By indicating that the dispossession of the title extends beyond the play's ending, Gambaro evokes the extent of this denial of power, and in particular its disregard for the supposed boundaries of public and private space. As a result this particular power asymmetry becomes in some sense paradigmatic. At different points in the play it recalls life under a totalitarian government, the empty and repeatedly deferred markers of consumerism and economic exchange, and the degradation of theatre itself (which is itself linked for Gambaro to a consumer-led concern to please rather than challenge).

Like Magnarelli, Nora Domínguez looks at gender's relation to performance, this time in the work of Argentinian writer Norah Lange. Domínguez explores the construction of the family imaginary, the dissonances that disrupt it, and the gender performances through which its strength and resilience are nevertheless reaffirmed. Lange's writing between 1937 and 1956 is read as a single, overarching novel of apprenticeship (the narrative of a gendered subjectivity in process) and a space in which the hegemonic family narrative can be resistingly assumed and rewritten. For Lange's first-person narrators—women trapped in private spaces or who repeatedly adopt disguises—each resisting performance is different, according to context and audience perspective. By the end of the 'macro-novel', however, the accrued experience of gender, family, and writing as cultural constructs forms the ground for a theory of writing and reading. At which point the writing subject moves on to a new phase.

While Domínguez offers a reading of gender performance, Doris Meyer's essay approaches Nellie Campobello's account of the Mexican Revolution, *Cartucho*, as genre performance, and as an example of the resistance literature that has recharacterized the articulation of literature, politics, and gender in Latin America. Meyer's feminist appropriation of Bakhtinian dialogics enables her to explore the counter-hegemonic possibilities of autobiographical narrative and dialogized testimony in a moment of national upheaval. Campobello, she contends, challenges master discourse and official versions of Mexican history in a semi-fictionalized life-writing which questions the generic boundaries of novel, autobiography, and *testimonio*. Campobello (who as a young girl lived through the Mexican Revolution) can thus be seen as the unacknowledged precursor of more recent Mexican writers such as Rosario Castellanos and Elena Poniatowska who, like her, undermine authoritative discourses by representing in their writings orality, polyphony, and the 'transgressive, subaltern perspective' of the questioning girl-child. Although Sylvia Molloy's concept of autobiography in Latin America as a public story is relevant here (to the extent that the autobiographical act in *Cartucho* is not that of the private self but of the collective memory) the public story in question belongs to the oppressed and rebellious few.

Meyer's is one of three essays in the collection which engage with the discursive effects of political crisis. In her study of *La casa de los espíritus* and *Eva Luna*, Susan Frenk traces the narrative of bodily/discursive pleasure through which Isabel Allende challenges the discursive oppression of the Chilean dictatorship. In this timely reassessment of the political importance of Latin America's most popular woman writer Frenk challenges unfavourable comparisons of Allende's formal conservatism with the neo-avant-garde productions of (among others) fellow Chilean Diamela Eltit. For Frenk it is precisely the familiarity of her narrative modes that empowers Allende's readers. The 'readability' of these texts, it is argued, is not an escape from the social but one element in an exploration of the political, ethical, and discursive possibilities of romance.

Partly because it is concerned primarily with horror rather than pleasure, Jo Labanyi's essay is particularly resonant when read alongside that of Frenk. Their contrasting approaches are underlined by Labanyi's use of Eltit in her discussion of the equation of political horror with the unbounded female body. Reading Eltit's *Vaca sagrada* with Julia Kristeva and Mary Douglas, Labanyi explores the use of the female body as a focus for sado-masochistic impulses and as an image of horror for both men and women. While men are able successfully to abject this horror, she argues, women are obliged to identify with it, and to replicate with their body the horror outside. For Labanyi, '*Vaca sagrada* is a political novel but it cannot be called a committed novel . . . for it argues that both men and women must recognize their need for, and complicity with, horror'. For Eltit, to attempt to order experience in writing is to risk an encounter with this horror, and Labanyi concludes by suggesting that to acknowledge this displacement process may itself provide a form of salvation.

Labanyi's is not the only essay in the collection to reflect the growing importance in a Latin American frame of feminist appropriations of psychoanalytic theory. Adriana Méndez Rodenas again uses Kristeva, although very differently, to explore the crisis that underlies the emergence of the desiring subject in contemporary Mexican narrative. She contrasts the representation of a stunted and autistic 'manic' Eros in Juan Rulfo's *Pedro Páramo* with the 'love in the feminine' that figures in María Luisa Bombal's *La amortajada*. The 'impossibility' of Rulfo's and Bombal's narratives has to do with their depiction of the tense interrelations of Eros and Thanatos, love and death. Méndez reads the sublimation of love inscribed in these novels through the Narcissus myth, as interpreted by Plotinus, Freud, and Kristeva. While Rulfo represents the 'objectless eroticism of the classical Narcissus', she suggests, Bombal depicts the curtailment of women's desire by patriarchal prohibition. Unlike Rulfo's, however, Bombal's protagonist is able to achieve the sublimation of her desire in death; she is reabsorbed into the earth in a bodily fusion with primeval matter, becoming a flower (Narcissus) in bloom. By contrast, Rulfo's protagonist is alienated from the land, dies like crumbling stone, and returns to an inanimate state. The juxtaposition of these two narratives reflects a powerful comparative strategy in Latin American feminist criticism and one which has produced perceptive rereadings of (often male-authored) canonical texts.

Turning to Argentina, Susan Bassnett's study of the work of Alejandra Pizarnik uses psychoanalytic theory to address questions of power, horror, and the discourse of madness. Her chapter reads the figure of the Bloody Countess and a selection of Pizarnik's poetry through Luce Irigaray's work on women's language, the repressed female imaginary, and productive mimesis. Bassnett suggests a reading of Pizarnik's novel which relates the melancholia that emerges from the author's diary entries to that of the legendary Erzebet Bathory. The novel offers a disturbing depiction of a woman's violence towards other women in which the Countess transgresses all moral and social restrictions. The result is something quite different from the 'freedom through excess' associated with the writings of the Marquis de Sade. Bassnett notes that, for Pizarnik, the act of writing and of using language is at once destructive and life sustaining and goes on to explore the extent to which poetry, in particular, is seen as an act of mourning. Adapting Gilbert and Gubar's notion of female creativity as the creation of 'a dark double' unleashed on patriarchal society, she reads some of Pizarnik's key poems as instances in which the rage of the woman writer is translated into visions of madness and violent death. This doubling, Bassnett concludes, is evoked most explicitly in the mirrors in which the Countess endlessly seeks herself and into which Pizarnik finally disappears.

In her study of Cristina Peri Rossi's *Solitario de amor*, Linda Gould Levine draws primarily on the work of Judith Butler. The essay focuses on the Uruguayan's allusive and enigmatic contribution to the elaboration of transgressive gender definitions and sexual roles. The novel is read as an 'anatomy of passion', part of Peri Rossi's ongoing project to reconfigure male and female sexuality. Here, specifically, she proposes to displace the phallocentric erotic economy in favour of the possibilities of sexual multiplicity. In this remapped terrain, Gould Levine argues, human sexuality no longer figures as a conventionally circumscribed imposition, but as fluid, free, and open at last to an androgynous subjectivity. This subjectivity can be inferred through intensely erotic descriptions of the female body which, Gould Levine suggests, evoke the paradisical pre-Oedipal moment in which lack can figure as a characteristic of male rather than female sexuality.

Decisive moments in the status and representation of the home are the focus of essays by Luiza Lobo and Catherine Davies. Lobo traces Sonia Coutinho's representation of women's emergence from the narcissistic enclosure of domestic space into the Brazilian postmodern city street. Following Lyotard, the female *flâneur* is represented as forgoing dichotomous systems of thought for new topographies of the mind. By taking the female protagonist out of the home and into the maze of city streets, Lobo argues, Coutinho shows how the postmodern city can enable women writers to step out of traditional generic constraints and allow female characters to 'read' the city and assume agency and independence. Contrasting Coutinho's *flâneur* with those of Baudelaire and Virginia Woolf, Lobo explores female characters' epic voyage or 'periplus' through endlessly unfolding city streets. This movement, she suggests, reproduces the enigma of the detective novel, which represents the greatest generic innovation of Brazil's women writers. Lobo goes on to trace the metafictional and stream-of-consciousness techniques used to offer psychological insight into the minds of these women. Coutinho's reading of the self and the cityscape, she concludes, opens up the possibility of a very different imaginative geography for women.

By contrast, Davies highlights the figuring of the unhomely and the uncanny in the poetry of Excilia Saldaña. Her postcolonialist analysis examines tersely complex articulations of gender, race, class, and economics and their implications for a particular black female subjectivity in post-revolutionary Cuba. Developing the concepts of the 'split' writer and the 'two-toned' text, Davies argues that neither mainstream Caribbean nor African American criticism can account for the complexity of the work of black women writers in socialist Cuba. In an attempt to plot a path between black essentialism and black deconstruction she refers to the work of Homi Bhabha in her study of Saldaña's long autobiographical poem. Saldaña is seen to articulate the 'unhomely moment', the lack of a sense of belonging, both in the context of the extended Caribbean family and its post-revolutionary Cuban formulations, and from the point of view of Freud's account of 'das Unheimlich' (the uncanny). Saldaña's poem, charting the dramatic process of black, female self-representation in a moment of social crisis, is 'writing the body' as much as 'writing from a sense of place'.

Anny Brooksbank Jones's essay and Debra Castillo's response both examine how theory and politics are increasingly called into question in Latin America by the consequences of socio-

cultural difference. Jones begins by recalling some of the feminist critics who have worked to open up Latin American texts
and have, in the process, challenged some of the founding
assumptions of critical theory. To this end she traces selected
moments in a very particular history of Latin American feminist criticism. Touching on the different feminist assumptions
they invoke, she focuses increasingly on what are loosely termed
their micro- and macropolitical dimensions. The closing section considers current attempts to bring these two orientations
together, and the theoretical and practical difficulties implied
in this project.

Castillo focuses on a rather different aspect of the crisis in
cultural—and particularly cross-cultural—theory. She begins
with (what is characterized as) the West's relation to Third World
crisis at a time when oppositional criticism is increasingly made
to substitute for oppositional action. Acutely aware as she is of
the necessity for, and the limitations of, cross-cultural dialogue,
Castillo also knows that these limitations are not restricted to
cross-hemispherical exchange. This point is tellingly illustrated
in an analysis of María Luisa Puga's experience of 'an absolute
lack of a common ground for discussion' with the young Yaqui
Indian audience she encounters on a lecture tour in rural
Mexico. From this analysis are derived some timely insights on
the constructed nature of ethics and agency. In the process
they call into question the supposedly universal value systems
which ground notions of agent, process, and object, and on
which certain dominant conceptions of the political depend.

The last word on the politics of writing, however, goes to
Jean Franco, whose Afterword contrasts the rise of the Latin
American art romance with the emergence of a 'more refractory aesthetic'. Her tracking of this aesthetic in the neo-avant-
garde production of Tununa Mercado and Diamela Eltit is
particularly resonant when read in conjunction with the essays
of Jo Labanyi and Susan Frenk, and represents an important
contribution to one of the key debates in current Latin American cultural studies. Franco is less persuaded than is Frenk by
the claims of the art romance, although she concedes that the
term is not necessarily a negative one. Instead she notes a move
on the part of neo-avant-garde writers like Tununa Mercado and
Diamela Eltit away from popular texts (like those of Allende)
which are premised on the desirability of forms of equality

feminism. For avant-garde writers, Franco suggests, the pluralist traditional narrative of these mass sellers reproduces the seductions of neo-liberal commodity culture. In its place they advocate a new and more resistant aesthetic, one that is genuinely revolutionary in its ability to bring older forms to crisis and to organize meanings along new lines. At the same time, Franco claims, these writers seek to expose the limits of a system in which gender has been implicated in forms of social control, and to demonstrate that feminism's possibilities need not be exhausted by the familiar binary of equality/difference.

The contributors' shared concern—as readers, teachers, and researchers—for Latin American women's writing emerges clearly from this collection. It is evident in the fresh readings of some of Latin America's best-known women writers, as well as in innovative approaches to those like Diamela Eltit who are only now making their name. Beyond this common concern, however, readers will inevitably find some conflicting assumptions. As a discursive field produced (in part) by and for the negotiation of socio-cultural change, we have argued that theory is an index and precipitator of such conflict. While it questions and challenges, therefore, it cannot be relied upon to generate solutions. Instead it offers something like the possibility of dialogue with Latin American writers or a bridge through and across the texts discussed here—a possibility which nevertheless acknowledges that no dialogue is symmetrically powered and that bridges are not always distinguishable from bridgeheads.

As editors we are aware that bringing together a disparate group of people from Latin America, the US, and Europe, all working within their own very different sets of constraints, has not been the least of this volume's achievements. We have made many new friends without whose patience, and prompt, positive responses our task would have been a good deal less congenial. We should also like to thank Evelyn Fishburn, Paul Julian Smith, and other colleagues and friends in the UK for their generous support during the preparation of this volume, as well as Nottingham Trent University and Queen Mary and Westfield College, University of London, for the research funding which enabled the project to be completed.

1

Acting/Seeing Woman
Griselda Gambaro's *El despojamiento*

SHARON MAGNARELLI

ONE of Argentina's best-known and most highly respected contemporary playwrights, Griselda Gambaro (b. 1928), has written more than two dozen plays and numerous narrative works. Labelled theatre of the absurd, theatre of the grotesque, theatre of cruelty, and, more recently, theatre of crisis, Gambaro's works focus on oppression, both political and interpersonal.[1] Ironically, although Gambaro's early works were highly acclaimed, they were also criticized for her apparent indifference to feminist concerns. As might be expected, these criticisms did not appear until the 1980s when feminist theory began influencing Latin American literary analysis. Paradoxically, this was also the decade in which Gambaro's own growing awareness of feminist issues was already becoming apparent in her works. In fact, many of her plays from the 1980s focus on the oppression of women, and in them it is often a female character, rather than a male, who represents 'everyperson'. Still, one could argue that female characters are not abundant in Gambaro's early plays, and that, when she does include some females, they are generally peripheral.[2] None the less, I would argue that at least one play from the 1970s brings women to centre stage and spotlights some of the issues raised by feminism: *El*

---

[1] Taylor (1989*b*; 1991) has analysed Gambaro's work as theatre of crisis, as has Feitlowitz (Dauster and Feitlowitz 1990). These and other recent critics (e.g. Scott 1993) have challenged some of the other labels for Gambaro's work. Significantly, Gambaro herself does not necessarily agree with the labels.

[2] Although Emma is a major character in *El campo*, it could be argued that the fact that she is female is not essential to Gambaro's message. For Nigro this lack of female characters has led critics to study Gambaro's works almost exclusively in asexual or transsexual contexts (1989: 65), which is the opposite of what I intend to do here.

despojamiento (*The Dispossession*, 1974), a work that might also be viewed as a prototype of Gambaro's early and late works in so far as it exhibits the multiple, interrelated thematic threads or referents we have learned to expect from the playwright.[3]

Those threads include the historical (tensions leading to the Argentine military regime of 1976),[4] the socio-political (oppression in all its forms and the complicity of the victim in that oppression), and, more recently, as indicated, the feminist (the oppression of women in both economic and erotic terms). *El despojamiento*, however, adds a thematic thread not frequently conspicuous in Gambaro, particularly in her early plays—the theatrical.[5] This thread in turn encompasses several additional facets: the notion of woman as an actress by definition, compelled to assume the various roles assigned her; the voyeuristic relation of the audience, male or female, to the performance; and the generally unacknowledged position of the theatrical institution *per se*, as simultaneous exploitation (economic or sexual) and imposition of the values of the *status quo*.

Many of these elements are readily apparent in even the most cursory synopsis of this one-act play. The protagonist,

[3] *El despojamiento* was published in 1981 in *Tramoya* and in 1983 in *Escandalar*. It has since been published by Ediciones de la Flor, in *Teatro 3*, which dates the play from 1974. Although I used the *Escandalar* edition for this study, quotations and page references come from the more accessible Ediciones de la Flor version. Where relevant, I have indicated the discrepancies between the two versions. Although 'despojamiento' might be translated several ways (stripping, robbing, plundering, despoliation, dispossession), I shall emphasize the latter because of the etymological implications of the term. According to Corominas (1954), *despojar* derives from the Latin *spoliare*, to strip the hide or the skin from an animal. Although the text has been read as a stripping/striptease, a removal of clothing (Boling 1987), etymologically the verb implies a far more serious loss than that of clothing, indeed a mortal loss. Also, the fact that an animal is generally the object of the Latin verb accentuates the dehumanization of the subject which Gambaro graphically portrays.

[4] With regard to Argentina's tumultuous political history, Taylor notes, 'The rampant political violence of the 1960s developed into the orchestrated terrorism of the 1970s' (1991: 97).

[5] As will become apparent, I agree with Feitlowitz, whose article came into my hands as I completed this study. She notes that Gambaro 'uses blatant artifice in her plays to probe the nature of theatricality and our responses to it, not only in art but in daily life' (Dauster and Feitlowitz, 1990: 34). Taylor reads Gambaro's theatre of the 1970s as a warning against theatricality (1989*b*: 16). Similarly, in *Theatre of Crisis* Taylor notes, 'Griselda Gambaro . . . scrutinizes the role of theatre and theatricality in Argentina's criminalized society of the 1960s and 1970s' (1991: 96). None the less, *El despojamiento* is one of the few Gambaro plays that deals with theatre *per se*, in a self-conscious manner.

designated only as Mujer (Woman) waits alone in a room for
unspecified people, presumably men, who will interview her
for an undefined job involving either acting or modelling. While
she waits, the other character, Muchacho (Boy), enters several
times and appropriates, sometimes forcibly, a number of her
possessions and articles of clothing (that covering which defines us as human beings). Although he never says a word and
often fails to acknowledge her existence, she chatters on in an
absurd rationalization of her situation, assuring herself that 'no
hay papel que no pueda encarar con . . . talento' (there is no role
I can't meet with . . . talent) (Gambaro 1989: 179). During her
incessant prattle, she looks at herself several times in her pocket
mirror (thereby converting herself into both spectator and
spectacle) and inadvertently provides information about her
private life, worrying that Pepe will abuse her again for being
late or not having his shirts ironed and his lunch ready. By
minimizing both the set and the characters and by having
spectators witness what appears to be unusual (but not incomprehensible) behaviour on the part of the characters, Gambaro
has accomplished what Brecht and the Russian Formalists
sought—to defamiliarize the familiar so that we might see and
judge it differently. What the playwright defamiliarizes here is
woman, object of the gaze, theatrical (re)production. At the
same time, Gambaro has underscored (as her plays so often
do) the parallels between our public and private spheres, for
the protagonist's monologue prompts the audience to recognize that the dispossession Mujer experiences in public, on
stage, mirrors what she has suffered at home, at the hands of
Pepe, suggesting that the theatre does not cease when the
actress leaves the stage recognized as such. On the contrary,
as Butler has posited in a different context, 'Her/his performance destabilizes the very distinctions between the natural and
the artificial, depth and surface, inner and outer through which
discourse about genders almost always operates' (1990: p. x).

Written as it was during a decade of escalating political turmoil
and violence in Argentina, *El despojamiento* unquestionably proffers an allegory of totalitarian government.[6] The protagonist's

[6] The play was written after the end of the military regime established by a *coup*
in 1966. According to Skidmore and Smith, during the regime, 'There was also a
shocking rise in political violence, such as clandestine torture and execution by
the military government and kidnapping and assassination by the revolutionary
left' (1984: 102).

situation metaphorizes that of the Argentine people during the 1970s. Denied access to both power and the powerful, who are always off-stage, out of sight, Mujer waits in an anteroom, outside the centre of power. She interacts only with Muchacho, the agent of that invisible entity whose omnipotence may well be predicated on its invisibility.[7] In addition, as is typical of many Gambaro works, the play dramatizes the extent to which victims are conditioned to be complicitous in their own victimization so that eventually the totaliarian demands need no articulation.

On the most universal level, then, *El despojamiento* is about oppression. But at the same time, it is also about theatre and acting, and, more important, about the roles we assume in our everyday life—roles that also facilitate oppression, ours or others'. Someone has to assume the role of oppressor, someone that of oppressed, or the 'play' cannot go on. In the public sphere, we, as audience, would be denied the spectacle we have come to see were it not for the power/oppression of the invisible director (both inside and outside the fiction in this case). Within the fiction, that director keeps Mujer waiting and thus generates the drama we watch. Outside the fiction, some director, also ever invisible, has organized the spectacle we observe. In the private sphere (and again within the fiction), Pepe, as invisible to the audience as the director is, also oppresses Mujer, assigning her diverse roles, some more overtly theatrical than others: servant, *ingénue*, one who presents the 'aquí-no-pasa-nada' (nothing-is-wrong) face to the police after he has beaten her, etc.

Thus, the thematic threads of theatre and oppression merge in the subject of woman, for the play specifically examines the oppression of generic woman and her (en)forced status as endless role player. Luce Irigaray has posited that the only path historically assigned to the feminine is that of mimicry (1985: 76). In the words of the French thinker, ' "femininity" is a role, an image, a value, imposed upon women by male systems of representation. In this masquerade of femininity, the woman loses herself' (1985: 84). Further highlighting the questions of economics and desire, which to my mind are central to the

---

[7] The fact that she is in view, in some sense under surveillance, at least by the audience, also evokes the situation of the Argentine public during the military regime.

play, Irigaray continues, 'this masquerade requires an *effort* on her part for which she is not compensated. Unless her pleasure comes simply from being chosen as an object of consumption or of desire by masculine "subjects"' (Irigaray's emphasis, 1985: 84).

Specifically, Gambaro dramatizes both the loss and the masquerade by appropriating the conventions of femininity and subverting their customary usages. By denying us the illusionism of naturalistic theatre, she demonstrates that femininity itself is theatre, a play scripted by and for the invisible other. As a result, the audience is induced to reconsider the structures that have framed women (in both senses of the word 'frame'). Yet if, as John Berger (1977) posits, seeing is what establishes our place in the surrounding world, Gambaro also demonstrates that traditionally woman has always already lost herself, for she has seen and been seen as a function of the (usually, *but not necessarily* male) spectator/director, whose desires she continually tries to anticipate. That is, she has been taught to see herself as he would see her, as other (whether in the mirror or in the photographs), in a role, prospective object of his desire. Yet, that spectatorial other (be it the director or Pepe or even us as audience) is never seen in this play, never staged. Instead he parallels what Berger has designated as the principal protagonist of the European oil painting of the nude, the one to whom everything is addressed—the implied male spectator, outside the frame, in front of the painting, or, I would add in this case, in front of the spectacle of which he is the master(ing) eye/I.[8]

Furthermore, in *El despojamiento* Gambaro demonstrates that, when the male spectator is absent, the woman assumes his role as well as her own and *over*sees herself, converting herself into both seer and seen/scene as she tries to imagine how he would like to see her.[9] From the beginning we watch Mujer monitor

---

[8] 'Mastering eye/I' (without the parenthesis) is a term borrowed from Griselda Pollock (1988: 64).

[9] Taylor has noted that the victims of Gambaro's plays are themselves often 'spectators watching the unthinkable happen as well as actors experiencing it' (1991: 105). In addition, Kappeler has suggested that at the root of sexism 'is the way men see women, is Seeing' (1986: 61). Here and at other points in this essay, when I refer to the protagonist assuming a role or wearing a mask, I do not mean to suggest the existence of an essential being or stable identity apart from the mask and discourse. On the contrary, the sense of self-identity simultaneously produces and is produced by discourse and role playing. Mujer changes roles frequently, but she never stops playing a role.

herself. When she enters, the scene is set with only a small sofa, a chair, and a small table with magazines. Surely we are meant to perceive those magazines synecdochically as the 'source' of the image Mujer is trying to mirror. Thus, she frequently looks at herself (and, I suggest, for herself) in her pocket mirror, in search of a reflection that would comply with the magazine images. In other words, as the play opens the woman is already spectacle, specular reproduction, one who has tried to mould herself to the appearance or role that invisible others have deemed pleasing/desirable. Like any woman, as Irigaray has argued, Mujer 'can "appear" and circulate only when enveloped in the needs/desires/fantasies of others' (1985: 134). But here, as throughout the play, Gambaro calls attention to the fact that the copy is a failure. Indeed, *El despojamiento* repeatedly dramatizes the seams in Mujer's identity, the discontinuities, the gaps and slippage from the cultural ideal.[10] Mujer has not reached the goal and cannot mirror the images from the magazines, in part (but only in part) because of her economic plight. As an unpaid labourer in the home, she lacks the cash to purchase the commodities that magazines present as the means to desire and pleasure.

But it is important to note that even if money were not an issue, the ideal as presented by those magazines would still be unattainable. And it is designed to be so, for the consumer must never reach the projected goal and stop buying. Yet Gambaro takes this notion one step further and proposes that theatre, like all art forms, functions in a similar manner when it proffers unrealizable goals: characters we cannot be, pleasures we cannot experience.[11] At the same time, Gambaro seems to suggest that the positing of impossible goals is prompted by an even more perverse, political motive: impossible goals assure that the subjects (like Mujer) will fail, internalize their failure, and read it as inadequacy on their part. In this way other socio-

[10] Butler (1990) sees all gender acts as failed copies and imitations of what is already not original, as imitations without origins.

[11] In her discussion of film, Silverman alludes to the insufficiency the female spectator is likely to experience when faced with ideal images of exceptional women on the screen (1988: 174–6). However, Butler has posited that 'heterosexuality offers normative sexual positions that are intrinsically impossible to embody, and the persistent failure to identify fully and without incoherence with these positions reveals heterosexuality itself not only as a compulsory law, but as an inevitable comedy' (1990: 122).

political problems (such as unequal distribution of wealth, sexism, and racism) are obscured. In the process, those in power are implicitly exonerated: society places the blame on the individual and individual inadequacy rather than the socio-political structure or the abuse of power. Here, as in advertising, were any of the idealized goals to be reached, the game/play as we know it would cease; the charade could not go on.

In the Gambaro play that charade is highlighted from the beginning. Mujer's first words of submission, 'Sí, sí, sé que llegué temprano. No tengo apuro, esperaré' (Yes, yes, I know I arrived early. I'm in no hurry, I'll wait) are followed by words of rebellion, 'Cretinos! . . . Disponen del tiempo de una como si fuera de ellos' (Cretins! . . . They dispose of one's time as if it were their own) (Gambaro 1989: 171).[12] Although the rebellious words are spoken in the absence of an interlocutor, they mark still another role, that of 'making oneself respected', a role in which Mujer also fails dismally. Gertainly no one respects her on stage just as no one respected her when, after Pepe had beaten her, she told the police that she had fallen down the stairs.[13] Her 'fine performance' that time pleased the spectator, Pepe, the master(ing) eye/I, who rewarded her with a kiss. With this as her paradigm and in search of another metaphoric kiss from her audience, she tries on various roles, attempting to discover the one for which she will implicitly be rewarded with a kiss: '¿Qué es lo que quieren?' (What is it they want?) (Gambaro 1989: 178); 'A mí me dan las indicaciones, el guión y ¡allá voy!, con mi talento, mi ductilidad' (They give me instructions, the script, and there I go! with my talent, my malleability) (Gambaro 1989: 180).[14] But herein lies her problem: she is so malleable that she exists primarily (or perhaps

[12] The *Escandalar* version of the play (Gambaro 1983) does not include the words, 'I know I arrived early'. The addition of these words highlights the protagonist's insecurity in so far as later in the play she notes, antithetically, that she always arrives late for everything. Thus the play demonstrates, first, that the goal is unattainable for the woman (she is always either too late or to early) and, second, that she has internalized the responsibility for her failure.

[13] This concern with 'making oneself respected' is somewhat more apparent in the *Escandalar* version of the play, which adds the words, 'Siempre tuve en cuenta esto: ¡nada de rebajarse!' (I always kept that in mind: no lowering oneself!) (Gambaro 1983: 21).

[14] The *Escandalar* version states, 'con mi talento, *mis ganas de trabajar*, mi ductilidad' (with my talent, *my desire to work*, my malleability) (Gambaro 1983: 22, emphasis added).

only) as role, as a mirror reflection of someone else's desires, for, as Irigaray has suggested, 'in the masquerade, [she has submitted] to the dominant economy of desire in an attempt to remain "on the market" in spite of everything' (1985: 133).[15] Yet Mujer fails to recognize the mirror reflection since she has been taught not to see it and says of herself on more than one occasion that she improves a script: 'Enriquezco un guión, si me dejan lo . . . redondeo' (I enrich a script, if they let me . . . I round it out) (Gambaro 1989: 180). As is so often the case throughout the play, Mujer's words contradict what seems apparent to the audience (that she adds nothing to the pre-existing script of femininity). Gambaro dramatizes this discrepancy by having the protagonist use terms that have one meaning for her, one intended to shore up her preferred self-image, and quite a different one for the audience. Like all else in this play her words are simultaneously performative and generative. In this particular case two of the terms at issue are *enriquecer* (to enrich) and *redondear* (to round out). Although Mujer thinks she can improve a script, her 'rounding out' leads to a circular entrapment of the self. She has been taught to make the role round so that it encircles her; it has no beginning and no end, and, most important, no exit. She is entrapped by it and has no stable identity apart from the role(s). And her notion of 'enriching' is equally equivocal. Indeed, the example she provides of her capacity to 'enrich' was the time when she modified a script, changing it from the traditional one (where girl meets poor boy, love triumphs, and they live happily ever after) to one in which the girl marries a millionaire who abandons 'all' for her (all but his money, which paradoxically translates into abandoning nothing). Revealingly, however, her 'new' ending is the same: love still triumphs, and they live happily ever after in a fairy-tale world that contrasts sharply with her own life. Although she calls those who believe that love triumphs 'idiots', her script effectively follows the same paradigm. The only difference is that in her version they 'live happily ever after' with money. Product of a consumer society (and often the product 'consumed'), she has failed to comprehend that the issue is less money itself than the absurd myth that money

---

[15] Boling has noted that Mujer is oblivious to the fact that 'desire is determined by a patriarchal system and is not inherent. She attempts to conform to an image of desirability constructed and sanctioned by the dominant culture' (1987: 63).

can be exchanged for power or love—that is, pleasure, if indeed someone else's. Still her belief that money will make a difference has brought her to this waiting room in search of yet another fairy-tale script and will lead her to debase herself to (literal or metaphoric) prostitution.

What is particularly interesting about the roles Mujer is prepared to perform is that they are all defined by eroticism: *ingénue*, show girl, prostitute. Furthermore, they are marked by an increasing visibility of the erotic as well as a progressive hardening of the role on the part of the 'actress'. The *ingénue*, whose eroticism is the most veiled, naïvely believes that she has the power to seduce and control the male other. Furthermore she imagines, first, that her seductive/erotic powers are inherent to, and emanate from, her and, second, that her 'knight in shining armour' will spend his life pleasing her. At the other extreme, the prostitute recognizes her lack of power and expects to please rather than be pleased. In each case what is at issue is the body, the body erotic, but Gambaro's point is that the body erotic is ultimately inseparable from the body politic or the body economic, for, as presented, that body erotic is a masquerade, always already a creation for the spectator/possessor, and one which allows the master(ing) eye/I to empower itself and see itself in a favourable light.

In this sense Muchacho functions as a synecdoche of the larger picture, oppressing Mujer not out of eroticism, although she has been taught to perceive it as such, but as part of a play of power. Let us recall that Muchacho begins by appropriating the photographs of herself Mujer has brought with her. That is, at first he touches only her image, although as we shall see each item he purloins does inform her image. For Mujer those pictures function as a fantasy mirror, showing her as she has been told she should look. As she says after looking at herself in a literal mirror, 'en las fotografías no se ven las arrugas, no se ven los dolores' (in the photographs you don't see the wrinkles, you don't see the grief/pain) (Gambaro 1989: 171). That is, the photographs efface the wear and tear of life and time. In so far as her photographs hail back to a former time, they also mimic Mujer's earlier role as *ingénue*, one which simultaneously, if indeed paradoxically, points to the present and her current inadequacy to the part coupled with her continuing ingenuousness. The fact that in some sense Mujer continues to play the role of innocent throughout (her performance is marked by her credulousness), underlines Gambaro's point that one cannot remain untouched by the role(s) one plays and that the role becomes the self. As Mujer notes, '¡La ingenuidad es lo último que se pierde!' (Naïvety is the last thing one loses) (Gambaro 1989: 180–1). Thus, once again, because the role is simultaneously performative and generative, it encircles her, and she 'sees' in the photographs and elsewhere what (and as) the dominant discourse has taught her to see and fails to comprehend that what she perceives as eroticism is merely oppression.

None the less, like her pocket mirror, her photographs signal her dual status as the seer and the seen/scene while they provide Gambaro with the technical means to draw the audience's attention to language's capacity for 'double speak'; that is, while seeming to communicate one message, the pictures communicate another (like Mujer's words). Having established that the photographs portray a more favourable and youthful image, Mujer then contradicts herself and acknowledges they do show her wrinkles. The invisible photographer did not frame her properly or show her in her best light. Thus, again Mujer has assumed a role, seen and been seen (if only by herself), as she imagined would be pleasing to the other, while Gambaro highlights the question of framing, the invisible artist's decision regarding what will be seen and how it will be seen. As a result, spectators are reminded not to be completely credulous but to seek a contradictory subtext, to look beneath the would-be mirrors of art and discourse (and beyond their artistic frames) in search of the gaps or slippage. Or, perhaps better expressed, spectators are encouraged to ask why the mirrors of art and discourse reflect and frame what and as they do? Whose master(ing) eye/I benefits?

Thus, the audience is encouraged to recognize the fiction as such and the 'reflection' as constructed. By repeatedly shattering the (verbal) play world after it has been so laboriously constructed, Gambaro (in good Brechtian fashion) precludes spectator identification to a large degree. We may be able to identify with the looker but not with the 'looked at' (which is where identification traditionally occurs), for Gambaro presents the play world as just that (a play world) and the mirror of art as unreliable, inevitably manipulated by an (often invisible) other. As spectators (female spectators, at least), we are prompted to question and analyse the role, the femininity, with which we might otherwise have readily identified, if not complicitously authorized and/or assumed.[16] We are encouraged to consider how much of our own role playing is created by someone else's discourse of oppression, disguised as eroticism. Just as throughout the play Mujer is barred from finding an image that 'fits' her, the audience is precluded from finding a nice, comfortable mirror of fiction here in which to situate ourselves. But, and equally important, we are also spared the unrealizable model we so often find in theatre and film—the woman with whom we might like to identify but who we can never be.

The second time the boy enters the room he takes nothing, but he treats Mujer like an object, walking by her without responding to her smile or words. Later, he returns and successively dispossesses her of her cape, a shoe, an earring, and her skirt, which he tries to wrench from her but which she eventually removes and gives to him. Paradoxically, the objects themselves, even before they are taken from her, already mark her dispossession or degradation. Her shoes are worn, her earrings imitation gold. Her cape is not her own but borrowed. In this respect the title of the play is ironic or misleading and subtly undermines the authority implicit in the theatrical paratext, in all that frames a theatrical production (titles, programme information, criticism—that is, prior discourse). Although the word *despojamiento* suggests that what the audience will witness on stage is a dispossession, in many ways Mujer is already dispossessed before she appears on stage. Thus, if the audience, influenced by the title, believes that the woman has something left of which to be 'dispossessed', it is perhaps placed in the same position of ingenuousness that Mujer so often occupies—one of uncritical acceptance of someone else's words. On the other hand, if she is to be further dispossessed, the only 'possession' left is her sense of self, yet even that identity is destabilized before the end of the play. As she queries and answers, '¿cómo

[16] Male spectators might react differently since they might not be unable to identify with the protagonist. Let me state the obvious, however, and note that the difference in reaction between male and female spectators is not a product of their biological differences but rather of their gender training: because of society's response to their genders, they have probably had different experiences and been taught to 'see' differently. Judith Butler (1990) takes this notion one step further and reminds us that even what we perceive as biological differences are culturally determined, that they are factors that have been discursively framed so that we see them in a certain way.

tiene que estar una adentro para ciertos trabajos? Una tiene que estar rota o muerta' (how does one have to be inside for certain work/roles? One has to be broken or dead) (Gambaro 1989: 181). But, having come too close to the dangerous truth that she is metaphorically dead or broken before she begins, she backs away and refutes the facts: '¡Yo no! Yo: ¡margaritas adentro!' (Not me! Me: pearls/daisies inside!).

But let us consider more specifically the possessions Muchacho purloins. Significantly, he takes one shoe, leaving the other behind, which, as Mujer later acknowledges, hurts her foot because it is too small. Presumably, she has forced her foot into a shoe that does not fit in order to comply with some external model. Muchacho's subsequent appropriation of her earring is similarly meaningful. First, it immediately follows his only humane gesture toward her, when it *seems* he is about to caress her. Instead, he yanks the earring from her ear in a gesture reminiscent of the many times in Gambaro's works the cruellest acts follow the kindest. Second, while this is the only act of physical harm portrayed, it evokes others that have occurred off stage—Pepe's abuse, for example. Of course, the physical pain Mujer suffers in both arenas is not coincidental; on the contrary, it induces her to be more 'co-operative', more complicitous in her own oppression, and to internalize more completely the assigned role(s), just as she has internalized others' words.[17] At the same time, just as Mujer has forced her foot into a shoe that is too small, she has mutilated (pierced) her ears. Furthermore, in the case of the earring, as in that of the shoe, Muchacho leaves behind the mate and thus signals the objects' lack of intrinsic or extrinsic value for him. If he were appropriating them for their use or exchange value, he would need the pair.

When Muchacho returns for the penultimate time, Mujer has already removed her stockings, presumably in erotic preparation, but, unexpectedly, he takes the small table instead. He apparently has no desire to strip Mujer in the erotic sense, that is, to see the naked body. He has stripped possessions from her only to dehumanize her and, as one would strip the hide from an animal, with complete disinterest—and this in spite of his

---

[17] Kappeler notes that in prostitution the powerful buy or force the compliance of the other (1986: 157). Here Mujer's compliance is both bought (potentially at least) and forced.

youth. Let us not forget, he is designated Muchacho not Hombre (Man), which would be the logical counterpart to Mujer.
The fact that he is immature evokes the question of role, for, unlike an adult, a boy is still learning how to behave in a socially
acceptable manner and 'act like a man'. Thus, like Mujer,
Muchacho plays a role that is no longer perceived as such—
that of the macho *par excellence*, the not disempowered—and
has become his own spectator, seer and seen/scene.[18] None
the less, the fact that he is an adolescent underscores Gambaro's
point that this is not eroticism; although he is an adolescent in
a period of reputed heightened erotic curiosity, the table holds
as much interest for him as the body erotic. The removal of
furniture, destined as it is to convert Mujer's surroundings into
a site bereft of all signs of humanity, points away from the
erotic potential and towards her dehumanization.[19]

For his final entrance, Mujer has unbuttoned her blouse,
opened it, and sits with her legs apart in what is labelled '*un
gesto patéticamente provocativo*' (*a pathetically provocative gesture*)
(Gambaro 1989: 181). At the end the woman waits passively,
ready to be possessed in the erotic sense, believing that this is
what he seeks, his pleasure; this is what makes her valuable.
But this is not what has been asked of her. Are we then to view
Mujer as an actress who is inadequate to the script? Or is his
reaction merely another phase of the 'play' of oppression, another form of degradation and of convincing her of her failure
to meet the model and become an object of desire? So, again
ignoring her, Muchacho now removes the sofa from the room,
in visual confirmation of the earlier stage directions that she is
an object to him (but clearly not of desire). Thus, mirroring
her life off-stage, the woman on stage passes in turn through
the roles of *ingénue*, show girl, and prostitute, still to the apparent indifference of the dramatized spectator, who, for all her
efforts to please him, is '*desprovisto de carga emotiva*' (*lacking an
emotional charge*) (Gambaro 1989: 175).

But Gambaro's point is that Mujer cannot please; not only
does pleasure come from within rather than from the outside,

---

[18] While my focus is the roles women are compelled to play, I would certainly
argue that men too are required to play specific (and limited) roles within society.

[19] Boling has read his removal of the furniture as the destruction of the theatrical image and notes that 'the action of the play involves the dismantling of the
stage' (1987: 60).

but by definition the circle of desire is such that desire would cease to exist were fulfilment attained.[20] Nor does Mujer recognize that she cannot win this perverse game whose rules she has misunderstood by not distinguishing between eroticism and oppression, or perhaps more important, between seer and seen/ scene. Her confusion is apparent in her words, 'la gente no mira a uno en la cara persiguiendo los moretones, mira los ojos . . . y entonces, con estos ojos . . . ¡yo tengo la batalla ganada!' (people don't look one in the face, seeking bruises, they look at one's eyes . . . and then, with these eyes . . . I have the battle won!) (Gambaro 1989: 174). She continues, 'todavía dispongo de un par de ojos que . . . Cuando vuelva ese infeliz, lo miraré . . . seductora y . . . *lo dejo duro*' (I still have a pair of eyes that . . . When that wretch comes back, I'll look at him . . . seductively and . . . *I'll leave him hard*) (emphasis added, Gambaro 1989: 174). In addition to the oblique reference here to the socio-political events in Argentina in the 1970s and the general public's unwillingness or inability to see the 'bruises', Mujer expresses the belief, often held by the oppressed, that she wields significant power. No doubt she is not completely powerless, but, because of what she has been taught, she believes her power to be erotic and located in the eyes. The terminology here, with its erotic connotation, is well chosen, but it is important to recognize that it is she, not he, who has been 'seduced', seduced not by what she has seen but by the illusion of her erotic power. It is she who has been looked at, by herself and by us, and it is she who has been left 'dura' (hard/hardened): '*se endurece en la pose*' (*she becomes hardened in the pose*) (Gambaro 1989: 173); '*se le petrifica la sonrisa*' (*her smile petrifies on her*) (Gambaro 1989: 181). Her learned, theatrical, erotic pose leaves not him hard/hardened but her.

On some level, then, the woman's role as prostitute(d) in this script might also be read as a metaphor for the social degradation of theatre, the attempt to project an image that will please the passive, complacent audience, letting it see itself in a favourable light, (thereby promoting the *status quo*) rather than shocking it into action (albeit political, not erotic). In this regard

[20] Riffaterre notes, 'For desire to exist subjects must project their libidos onto the object and the predication expressing this projection must be negated or postponed. Otherwise, fulfilment would be attained and desire would cease to exist' (1990: 86–7).

Gambaro seems to be criticizing all those involved in theatre
who sell out, who try to please those invisible, economic, or
socio-political powers, and suggests that they may well be left
as hard and hardened as Mujer.[21]

But what about us as audience? What about our passive and
yet also complicitous role as spectators? Are we not in the same
position as Mujer—spectators left hard/hardened by the spectacle, encircled by or entrapped in it? Remember there is no
role playing without an audience of some type. I have already
noted that the invisible oppressors both inside and outside the
fiction provide us with the spectacle we have come to see.
However, in *El despojamiento* the audience is not seduced into
identification, for Gambaro withholds the model or mirror in
which we may have liked to have seen ourselves reflected. On
the contrary we are alienated by both Mujer and Muchacho.
We are denied that self-delusion to which Mujer so frequently
resorts and are encouraged to perceive it as such. Indeed the
playwright refuses to frame or arrange the theatrical mirror so
that it will reflect positive images of ourselves. Like Mujer, who
does occasionally see the discontinuity, the slippage and gaps
rather than what she would like (or has been taught) to see,
we too are forced to see the seams in what we thought was a
seamless identity, to see what we would not like to see or be,
as well as the incongruities between what words have told us is
there and what our eyes witness.

None the less, if we accept the definition of the spectator as
a type of voyeur, one who would see without being seen, there
can be little doubt that we too are complicitous in the exploi-
tation/dispossession of the role player. Ultimately, our position
is precariously close to that of the invisible, off-stage director/
viewer whose desires the actress believes she must fulfil. And
surely, while leading us to recognize this negative image of ourselves, Gambaro simultaneously frustrates any voyeuristic desire we might experience. Although the play has been labelled
a striptease,[22] in fact, as Robert Stam has said of Buñuel's *That
Obscure Object of Desire, El despojamiento* is 'a narrative striptease

---

[21] No doubt Gambaro also criticizes those in the arts who failed to speak out
against the military regime.
[22] See the Boling article (1987). I would also note that while I disagree with
Boling about the use of the term 'striptease', our readings of the play are generally
compatible.

that refuses to strip. It refuses to let us see what we want to see'
(be it, in Gambaro's case, a positive, coherent image of ourselves or the naked body) (1992: 66). The play 'scrutinizes . . .
our phantasmatic relation to the spectacle, exposing desire as
a cultural and (artistic/theatrical) construct' (1992: 66). I have
already discussed the question of desire as the cultural/theat-
rical construct of a consumer-oriented society, but it is essential
to note that the erotic/seductive potential of *El despojamiento* is
consistently defused, and in that sense the play is anything but
a striptease. First, Muchacho's appropriation of Mujer's clothing
provides no titillation and leads less to nudity than to incompleteness: no outer wrap, one shoe, one earring, etc.[23] Furthermore, the spectatorial pleasure generally associated with the
striptease is glaringly absent here; as I have noted, the boy's
confiscation of her clothing is impressively non-erotic. The
clothes are removed from the room just as the furniture is—
with complete indifference. And, I would insist that Mujer does
not strip; her clothes are taken from her, albeit with her co-
operation, but it is a co-operation that reflects her internalization of the oppression, her acquiescence to the role (just as
the clothing itself does). Finally, the removal of clothing does
not lead to a display of the woman, the body erotic, as it would
in a striptease, even if, as Butler (1990) posits, the body erotic
itself is only another socio-political construct. If spectators leave
the theatre thinking they have seen a striptease or the naked
body, that is only their projection. The audience has seen
dehumanization but certainly not eroticism. Etymologically the
word *despojamiento* refers to the skinning of the hide from an
animal, and there can be little doubt that Mujer has been
'skinned' of her identity as a human being. While that 'skinning' surely serves socio-political, economic, and theatrical ends,
it is anything but erotic. Thus, the 'stripping' that spectators
may believe they have seen parallels what Mujer thinks she has
seen: something other (and far more dangerous) than what we
wanted (or had been led) to believe it was.

Metaphorically, too, theatricality and femininity as theatricality are stripped or deconstructed in this play. Boling (1987) is
correct to suggest that the dismantling of the set highlights the

---

[23] Her skirt is taken, but her undergarments would still cover her, leaving her
incompletely attired but not naked.

theatrical artifice *per se*. And if, as Kappeler posits in *The Porno-graphy of Representation*, 'the aim of realism is to obliterate our awareness of the medium and its conventions and to make us take what is represented for a reflection of a natural reality' (1986: 2), then Gambaro underscores the theatrical underpin-nings of what we label 'reality' while showing the mask of femin-inity to be theatrical representation, that is, not natural. Indeed, she has accomplished what Griselda Pollock has asked of femin-ist critical strategies: that they critique 'dominant realist modes which "naturalize" bourgeois and masculinist ideologies' (1988: 171). Surely *El despojamiento* underlines how unnatural (how artificially created, theatrical) those ideologies are and how de-pendent they are on the dominant discourses (and the discourses of dominance), which (re)image 'reality' for us. As Pollock fur-ther recommends, 'If the dominant pacification of populations takes place through passive consumption of meanings natural-ized through realist modes of representation, feminist critical practice must resist such specularity . . . It has to create an en-tirely new kind of spectator as part and parcel of its represen-tational strategies' (1988: 181). Gambaro begins to create that 'new spectator' by encouraging us to question our relation to the spectacle and by obliquely prompting us to ask of theatre the questions that Kappeler asks of pornography: who is holding the mirror of 'nature', for whose benefit, and from what angle? (1986: 2).[24] As Kappeler also notes, 'Represen-tations are not just a matter of mirrors, reflections, key-holes. Somebody is making them, and somebody is looking at them' (1986: 3).

Although I have quoted Kappeler's study on pornography, which to my mind is most apropos here, my references to her work are not intended to suggest that *El despojamiento* is porno-graphic. Quite the contrary. First, *El despojamiento* implicitly encourages spectators to ask those questions that pornography would silence. Second, while the relationship between Mujer and Muchacho, and by implication between her and the invis-ible director(s), marks the site of the exploitative, pornographic relation as defined by Kappeler (1986), Gambaro deconstructs,

---

[24] Kappeler's questions echo those earlier asked by Said in his discussion of the politics of interpretation: 'Who writes? For whom is the writing being done? In what circumstances?' (1983: 7).

in some sense invalidates, that relation by marking it as such and dramatizing (making visible) the implicit (invisible) power plays. *El despojamiento* exposes the mechanisms of representation; it is in those mechanisms of representation that the pornographic lies, in the fact of representation here represented, not in the play itself. Furthermore, Gambaro's play defies the complicity between author and audience, a complicity based on superiority and dominance, which Kappeler defines as fundamental to the pornography of representation. In the final moments, Mujer may be offering herself but, unlike in pornography, the audience will never see the naked body or the penetration.

Thus, *El despojamiento* is doubly subversive. It not only refuses to let us see, it also subverts the potential love story (preferred plot line in much theatre and film) and refuses narrative closure by denying the audience the pleasure of a reconciliatory ending in which the actress escapes the exploitation of theatre. In the traditional tale she would be rescued by the loving man who would take her away from 'all this', marry her, and care for her ever after. Significantly, because that 'ever after' always occurs off-stage, we never see it (it consists only of words); nor do we ask if it might not parallel the earlier exploitation we did see. Thus, Gambaro subverts the happy ending by taking us beyond the 'ever after'. In this case, Mujer's role as *ingénue* has already led her to 'ever after' and the promised land/man. Yet that 'promised man' directly informs her dispossession. As her monologue indicates, rather than providing safe haven, he oppresses her at home as she is oppressed in the theatre, forcing her into roles that do not fit her. Significantly, however, those roles that do not fit her do accommodate his own and allow him to see himself as he would like to see himself rather than as he is. Her roles allow him not to see his own economic failures and to see only hers. But she must not let him see too much of her humiliation, for it may reflect back on him: 'iSi Pepe me ve, me achura. . . . Me mata' (If Pepe sees me, he'll butcher me. . . . He'll kill me) (Gambaro 1989: 178). The imagined spectator must see only what will flatter his self-image, and he certainly must never be allowed to suspect that his self-image is a construct. If the image does not please him, she will be rewarded with brutality or erasure rather than a kiss.

LIST OF WORKS CITED

BERGER, J. (1977), *Ways of Seeing* (New York).

BOLING, B. (1987), 'From Pin-Ups to Striptease in Gambaro's *El despojamiento*', *Latin American Theatre Review*, 20 (Spring), 59–65.

BUTLER, J. (1990), *Gender Trouble: Feminism and the Subversion of Identity* (London).

COROMINAS, J. (1954), *Diccionario crítico etimológico de la lengua castellana*, 4 vols. (Madrid).

CYPESS, S. M. (1975), 'Physical Imagery in the Works of Griselda Gambaro', *Modern Drama*, 18: 357–64.

—— 'The Plays of Griselda Gambaro', in Lyday and Woodyard (1976), 95–109.

DAUSTER, F. *et al.* (1979) (eds.), *9 dramaturgos hispanoamericanos*, ii (Ottawa).

—— and FEITLOWITZ, M. (1990), 'Crisis, Terror, Disappearance: The Theater of Griselda Gambaro', *Theater*, 21 (Summer/Fall), 34–8.

GAMBARO, G. (1981), *El despojamiento*, *Tramoya*, 21 and 22: 119–27.

—— (1983), *El despojamiento*, *Escandalar*, 6 (January to June), 17–22.

—— (1989), *El despojamiento*, in *Teatro 3* (Buenos Aires), 169–81.

GIELLA, M. A. (1987), 'El victimario como víctima en *Los siameses* de Griselda Gambaro', *Gestos*, 3 (April), 77–86.

HOLZAPFEL, T. (1970), 'Griselda Gambaro's Theatre of the Absurd', *Latin American Theatre Review*, 4 (Fall), 5–11.

IRIGARAY, L. (1985), *This Sex Which Is Not One*, trans. Catherine Porter (Ithaca, NY).

KAPPELER, S. (1986), *The Pornography of Representation* (Minneapolis).

LYDAY, L. 'Introducción al teatro de Griselda Gambaro', in Dauster (1979), 89–91.

—— and WOODYARD, G. W. (1976), (eds.), *Dramatists in Revolt* (Austin, Tex.).

MITCHELL, W. J. T. (1983), (ed.), *The Politics of Interpretation*, (Chicago).

NIGRO, K. (1989), 'Discurso femenino y el teatro de Griselda Gambaro', in Taylor (1989*a*), 65–73.

POLLOCK, G. (1988), *Vision and Difference: Femininity, Feminism, and the Histories of Art* (London).

RIFFATERRE, M. (1990), *Fictional Truth* (Baltimore).

SAID, E. W. (1983), 'Opponents, Audiences, Constituencies, and Community', in Mitchell (1983), 7–32.

SCOTT, J. (1993), 'Griselda Gambaro's *Antígona Furiosa*: Loco(ex)centrism for "jouissan(SA)"', *Gestos*, 8: 99–110.

SILVERMAN, K. (1988), *The Acoustic Mirror: The Female Voice in Psychoanalysis and Cinema* (Bloomington, Ind.).

SKIDMORE, T. E., and SMITH, P. H. (1984), *Modern Latin America* (Oxford).

STAM, R. (1992), *Reflexivity in Film and Literature: From Don Quixote to Jean-Luc Godard* (New York).

TAYLOR, D. (1989*a*) (ed.), *En busca de una imagen: ensayos críticos sobre Griselda Gambaro y José Triana* (Ottawa).

—— (1989*b*), 'Paradigmas de crisis: la obra dramática de Griselda Gambaro', in Taylor (1989*a*), 11–23.

—— (1991), *Theatre of Crisis: Drama and Politics in Latin America* (Lexington, Mass.).

ZALACAÍN, D. (1980), 'El personaje fuera del juego en el teatro de Griselda Gambaro', *Revista de Estudios Hispánicos*, 14: 59–71.

ZAYAS DE LIMA, P. (1983), 'El teatro de la vanguardia, de Eduardo Pavlovasky a Griselda Gambaro', in *Relevamiento del teatro argentino (1943–1975)* (Buenos Aires), 131–3.

2

Literary Constructions and Gender Performance in the Novels of Norah Lange

---

FEW Argentinian women have written more compellingly on the family than has Norah Lange.[1] Her narrative reveals precisely how the modern family imaginary is constructed, and its

---

[1] Norah Lange (1906–72) was the fourth daughter of a family of four girls and, finally, a boy. Her father was a Norwegian engineer and technical geographer and her mother was of Irish/Norwegian descent. She was born in Buenos Aires and spent her childhood in Mendoza. On the death of her father the family returned to the Belgrano quarter, to a house in Tronador Street already famous for its literary gatherings. Guests included the young Jorge Luis Borges, Horacio Quiroga, Alfonsina Storni, and Leopoldo Marechal. These social and family contacts drew Lange to poetry and encouraged her participation in the early vanguardist experiments of the 1920s. She founded the journal *Prisma* and later *Proa*, with Borges and González Lanuza. In 1924 the first edition of the journal *Martín Fierro* appeared, bearing its famous manifesto by the man who was to become Lange's companion and one of Argentina's most important poets, Oliverio Girondo. The magazine opposed all forms of symbolism and modernism, and encouraged the lively vanguardist spirit of modern Argentina both in its content and in the literary and social movement that grew up around it. Norah Lange was considered its muse: in Néstor Ibarra's famous phrase: 'el ultraísmo necesitaba una mujer y la tuvo' (Ultraism needed a woman and it had her). Borges wrote the prologue for her first book of poetry, *La calle de la tarde* (1925). This was followed by *Los días y las noches* (1926) and in 1930 *El rumbo de la rosa*. In 1927 (the year in which the magazine *Martín Fierro* closed) she met Oliverio, and in that same year her first novel *Voz de la vida* was published. In 1928, at the age of 22, Norah travelled to Norway in a cargo boat with 30 sailors. As a result of this experience she wrote her novel *45 días y treinta marineros* (1933). Thereafter she worked as a translator, leaving the writing of poetry to Oliverio. Many members of the Martín Fierro group referred to Lange in exalted amatory language and she became the regular speaker at its entertainments and meetings. This was a period of late nights and heavy drinking, visits by famous poets (Pablo Neruda and Federico García Lorca, among others), scandalous scenes in the street, travel, masquerades, prizes, and recognition. It came to an end in 1967 with Oliverio's death, and she died herself five years later.

crucial role in the definition of a writing project.[2] Each of her
novels registers the strength and resilience of the family model.
They also demonstrate its complexity and diversity, and the
process by which family and narrative articulate, condense, and
manipulate material from the socio-political and subjective
spheres. From *Cuadernos de infancia* (1937) onwards, Lange
reworks these concerns until, with *Los dos retratos* (1956), the
model breaks down. Each reformulation supports and inflects
the family model, enabling Lange to create a very personal
articulation of literature and gender. In *Los dos retratos*, where
she stretches this model to its limits, the family is a representation (in this case a photograph), a text partially and obliquely
reproduced in other representational systems. Like the modern
family, the photo-text is a reproduction of a lost original, but
one on which a discursive apparatus of power and supporting
practices has been erected. As a result, the novel's photo-text
and the idea of the modern family both figure as originals to
be attained and recuperated, but also interrogated. By positing
the family as text Lange reveals its status as construct, a construct
which may be expanded, transformed, or adapted in accordance with subject positions, meanings generated in different
contexts, and the actions of subjects who produce and receive
those meanings. In the process she casts new light on her
earlier writings and reveals how the various literary forms of
the family 'construct' are generated in accordance with diverse
but specific literary rules. Literature thus figures as a space in
which it is possible to question the hegemonic narrative of the
modern family while experimenting with the family imaginary.
This imaginary is sustained by the repetition of certain stories,
generating a hegemonic narrative which, in turn, reproduces
the binary opposition of gender. Norah Lange's literature tries
to empty out and expose the workings of this narrative. To this
end she makes its site of enunciation the first-person voice of
a young woman, who adopts the model more or less resistingly
and in the process rewrites it.

Francine Masiello has linked Norah Lange's representation
of the family to the search for a structure of meaning able to
evade state control (Masiello 1992: 150). Although Lange

[2] I use the term 'imaginary' to refer to the set of social myths and beliefs that
form social meaning and individual attitudes and actions.

restricts her literature unequivocally to representations of the family, women and houses, this isolation of private experience is nevertheless projected outwards. Her model of the modern family required the creation of two distinct spheres, one of which had to be constructed as the privileged site in which a certain type of woman might deploy a different power, but a power stripped of political content (Armstrong 1987).[3] The exaggerated importance of the private sphere in Lange's texts should thus be read as an effect of this separation of spheres, but also as a sign of her mistrust. When the moment came to define her writing project Lange linked the importance of the family imaginary to a specific type of aesthetic proposition, which had to be realized through a series of personal negotiations between public and family morality, cultural site, and literary materials.

Lange linked these negotiations to two voices. One is that of a woman trapped in the private, family sphere: the other, its counterpart in the social-literary sphere, is that of a woman whose body is repeatedly disguised.[4] The criticism of the period persistently foregrounded Lange's status as female—as a 15-year-old girl, for example, or a young woman—and she came to interpret this as an accusation or slur.[5] Her first narrative

[3] This may not be the only idea from Nancy Armstrong to find its way into my essay. Her powerful and fascinating book changed my way of thinking about the family, sexuality, and the novel.

[4] For the presentation of *45 días y treinta marineros* Oliverio Girondo made her a mermaid costume. A photograph of the occasion shows her long, reclining mermaid's body surrounded by 30 sailors, with Oliverio in captain's uniform alongside Pablo Neruda, Nalé Roxlo, and other poets and painters. Lange played a key role in the many festivities of the period and when the time appointed for toasts and speeches arrived she generally presided. According to María Esther de Miguel 'Norah preparaba tales discursos con anticipación, consultaba, se documentaba (acerca de las personas y sus hábitos) y luego los decía, los interpretaba, subida a una mesa, desde el podio que podía ofrecerle un cajón, erguida su magra figura, llameante su cabellera desmelenada, brillante los ojos claros' (Norah looked forward to preparing her speeches. She consulted people, researched the person in question and their habits, and then delivered or rather performed the speech standing on a table, with a box as her makeshift podium, the slim body upright, with her mane of gleaming hair and bright shining eyes) (de Miguel 1991: 169). In 1942 she collected these speeches and in 1968 they were published, together with some additional material, as *Estimados congéneres*. In 1961 Oliverio was hit by a car and operated on. When she recovered Lange organized a party in which she appeared in a nurse's uniform and gave a speech thanking all those who had helped her. We return later to the subject of disguises.

[5] Borges wrote the prologue for *La calle de la tarde* (Lange 1925). In it he declares: '¡Cuánta eficacia limpia en esos versos de chica de quince años!' (How

texts (*Voz de la vida* (1927) and *45 días y treinta marineros* (1933)) both concern women at odds with the respectable prudishness of contemporary Argentinian society. The first is an adulteress, and the second a young woman travelling to Europe unchaperoned and surrounded by men. These two stories challenged the hegemonic gender narrative which women were obliged to reproduce, the penalty for non-compliance being exclusion as women or writers.[6] Lange must have recognized the inflexibility of this narrative, the power it exercised over subjects, and its regulation of their practices. She doubtless also recognized that this narrative was rooted deep in the literary institution. Women writers were obliged to wield without question the authority vested in them to articulate the feminine. Lange soon learned that women in modern society had special knowledge which had to be made clearly and consistently explicit, that she had to write respectable fiction, and that her heroines had to be tamed. She therefore assumed a different type of commitment, ceasing to concern herself with heterosexual relations, or tales of courtship and marriage. From *Cuadernos de infancia* onwards she embarked on a new literary project. She built worlds without men, where women were shut up alone in their houses and those who wrote did so not in order to earn money but secretly, for the pleasure of it.

It is my contention that this writing project lasted for twenty years, from the appearance of *Cuadernos de infancia* (1937) to the publication of her last novel, *Los dos retratos* (1956), and

pure and effective are this fifteen year old girl's verses!). Ramón Doll's fascinating critique of *Voz de la vida* makes clear what was expected of women writers: conformity with the morality of the day and a direct relation between heroine and writer. He warns against the risk to society of sexual freedom, and characterizes woman's suffrage (which was not introduced in Argentina until much later) as liable to devalue social and political life (Doll 1928: 88–90).

[6] By hegemonic gender narrative I understand the cultural construction which presents itself as a type of original, a set of mandates, a model which predicts and prescribes bodies, sexualities, behaviours, roles, capacities, ways of feeling, thinking, producing, and types of relations which subjects must form in accordance with their sex. The hegemonic narrative circulates socially, it constitutes discourses, passes through them, and produces varying degrees of respect and obedience in subjects. This characterization was produced by the research group I lead at the University of Buenos Aires. It is made up of myself and Professors Marcela Castro, Diana París, Silvana Daszuk, and Silvia Jurovietzky. Our objective is to investigate gender constructions and narratives in various areas of 20th-cent. Argentine literature. This theoretical work is indebted to the reflections of Judith Butler (1990a) and Teresa de Lauretis (1984 and 1987).

that it can be read in its totality as a novel of initiation—even though the genre's key figures, the tutor and the young apprentice ready for initiation, do not appear until *Los dos retratos*.[7] This 'macro' text has a first-person narrator throughout: first, a child (*Cuadernos de infancia*), then an adolescent (*Personas en la sala* and *Antes que mueran*), and finally the adolescent who becomes a writer and receives a bequest in *Los dos retratos*. This single voice assumes different forms and tones, and by the final text is able to formulate a theory of writing and reading. Novels of apprenticeship always articulate a subjectivity in process, and in Lange's case this process continues from one novel to another. They also reveal that all initiation is an initiation into writing. In her novels the adolescent learns to be a woman in women's worlds, sampling and confronting different gender stories; entering and leaving the world of the family becomes a literary issue, and she learns to represent both the family and herself. I shall develop this thesis with particular reference to the first and last novels of this period—while gesturing occasionally towards the others—in order to demonstrate how a literary genre can be built up through a set of texts, and how its textual organization can articulate an experience of gender and writing as they appear in the process of construction.

In her interrogation of gender forms Lange uses infantilized narrators ready to recognize and understand a rule-governed world and to begin their apprenticeship in it. These women are enclosed in spaces which are at once constructed and performed, and this enclosure isolates and protects them. They acquiesce to this space and time, turning their solitude to social account. The opposition inside/outside is explored in detail, not only as the object of persistent questioning in the fictional world but as the very condition of its existence. Inside and outside articulate different types of practices, each designed to give coherence to these spaces and to the subjects who move through them. Women's activities within these spaces must maintain this coherence, protecting it and ensuring its cultural stability.

The first two vignettes of Lange's *Cuadernos de infancia* offer two images of women: the first is the familiar image of the mother; the other is stranger, that of the strongest woman in the world, who shares the family's dining-room in a provincial

---

[7] Lange left her last text, *El cuarto de vidrio*, unfinished and as yet unpublished.

hotel. Both spheres demand powerful women—for if mother-hood is a necessary condition for attaining power in the pri-vate sphere, the woman who manages to leave this sphere must also be powerful. Characterized by a deformed body, the woman in the public sphere enacts the female gender each night, in a circus ring. The coherence and stability of the private world thus depends on an oblique and hyperbolic transformation of the woman in the public world.

This inscription of gender as performance enables other such inscriptions to be conceived as acts of repetition and per-formance (Butler 1990a: 140). There is a sense in which they operate discursively to keep gender within a binary framework while simultaneously shaking its stability. Lange initiates a pro-cess which destabilizes the category's frozen forms while filling them with new meanings. For example, the narrator's mother maintains a natural and coherent notion of maternity. Yet in dialogue with this representation is a scene in which, in her parents' absence, the older sister consoles her crying younger brother by attempting to breast-feed him. Observed through a crack in the door by the rest of the girls, this scene has all the power and fascination of spectacle:

Sentada en la cama, en una actitud de sacrificio y misterio, Irene mantenía a Eduardito entre los brazos. El camisón desabrochado descubría su pecho desnudo. . . . Estupefactas, comprobamos que introducía una mano en la misma forma que lo hacía su madre y levantaba un poco la pequeña redondez de su seno contra el cual se hallaba apoyada la boca de Eduardito. (Lange 1979: 39)

Sitting on the bed in an attitude of sacrificial mystery, Irene held Eduardito in her arms. Through the open nightdress her naked bosom was visible. . . . We watched astonished as, just like mother, she reached inside and raised very slightly the small round breast against which Eduardito's mouth was pressed.

Once constructed as spectacle this private, intimate, action becomes ritualized and made public, and gender's conventional status in thrown into question.

Another group of scenes underlines this process. The story of tragic and lonely women starts here, and continues in Lange's other novels.

En esa época me hallaba convencida de que las mujeres debían ser muy débiles, fisícamente, y que una especie de languidez, una perpetua convalescencia constituía la característica de la verdadera feminidad. Segura de que una mujer capaz de desmayarse a menudo era perfecta, una noche me acosté con una mano cerca de la garganta, imaginándome desmayada. Ansiosa por llegar a ser una mujer ideal, me abstuve de respirar. (Lange 1979: 54)

During this period I became convinced that women had to be physically very weak and that a kind of languidness or perpetual convalescence was the mark of true femininity. Convinced that regular fainting was the mark of the perfect woman, I went to bed one night with my hand by my throat, imagining that I had fainted away. Desperate to become an ideal woman, I stopped breathing.[8]

The adolescent narrator needs to prove the effectiveness of this story by acting it out. *Cuadernos de infancia* thus rehearses a gender narrative which becomes a productive and effective literary contribution to Lange's later efforts.[9]

The question of seeing or being seen circulates throughout this set of novels. In *Los dos retratos* the female narrator overcomes her terror of being watched; in *Cuadernos de infancia* she uses disguises to position herself as the object of the gaze. In one of the final scenes of *Cuadernos de infancia* the female narrator stands on the roof of her house. Clad in a man's hat and poncho, gesticulating and roaring with laughter, she shouts in a variety of languages and insults her neighbours. By acting and speaking as a man and wearing men's clothes she is able to objectify herself. This disguise exposes the other gender, the one that tries to hide itself, while the gender that tries to represent itself is being watched. What is fascinating is perhaps not so much the gaze as it shuttles between one gender and another, but the disguise itself: the object in which both co-exist (Garber 1992).[10] This reconfiguration of the original gender pair questions identities previously conceived as stable and

---

[8] This tale of tragic women can be found in episodes 18, 21, 25, and 29 of *Cuadernos de infancia*.

[9] This gender narrative is realized chiefly in *Personas en la sala*, but also figures in some fragments of *Antes que mueran*. In *Los dos retratos* it dissolves in the course of the narration. The character of Elena—the great-aunt who does not marry, and did not become what she had hoped because of family commitments—marks the abandoning of this story as a productive resource. Elena represents the outbreak of a long-suppressed hatred.

[10] For Marjorie Garber this questions the binary thought of gender duality by introducing a third term. It represents not another sex but a mode of articulation, a way of describing the space of a possibility. Judith Butler advances a similar view of the travesty (Butler 1990*b*).

unchanging. As it fades away, the performance itself constitutes the fleeting inscription of a subject, an inscription critical
of sexual binarism. It is this binarism that the text seeks to
dissolve (173–4). This play suspends the idea of a sexual identity but only momentarily. For although the text presents different constructions of the female gender its representation
of the family retains the notion of a given and stable original,
a point of return (Molloy 1991).[11]

In episode 15 the narrator is at the centre of what promises
to be a happy family scene. The father, a distant figure who is
absent from most of the scenes, takes her in his arms and sets
her down on the table, his eyes gleaming with pleasure. The
object of everyone's gaze is completely unaware of what they
have planned for her. The happy moment when her new clothes
arrive from Buenos Aires becomes instead a harsh lesson, a humiliation at the hands of her family. They dress her up in men's
clothing.

Pensé que se proponían exhibirme, hasta que, poco a poco, me fue
subiendo un sollozo, el primero, indignado y rebelde. No quería
llorar. Me parecía absurdo llorar vestida de hombre y lancé un grito.—
¡No quiero ser varón! ¡No quiero ser varón! (Lange 1979: 43)

I thought they wanted to make a spectacle of me until, little by little,
I felt the first sob rising in my throat, indignant and rebellious. I
didn't want to cry. Dressed up as a man it seemed ridiculous to cry.
I shouted—I don't want to be boy! I don't want to be a boy!

The whole family corrects what might have been an almost
intolerable deviation. Femininity has to be achieved through
a process of apprenticeship which begins in early childhood.

---

[11] Sylvia Molloy offers another interpretation of the roof scene. Although we
both share the view that it prefigures Norah Lange's speeches at literary banquets,
our readings differ in places because the objects of our investigations are different.
Molloy is concerned with Hispano-American autobiography, and her chapter on
Cuadernos de infancia should be read in this light. She sees this scene as the cul-
mination of Lange's autobiographical project, contrasting it with other texts which
represent childhood as a family treasure to be kept and cherished: 'Lange in her
own way, had inscribed scandal and not conformity, combative performance and
not passivity, at the very core of the eccentric self-portraiture; if that avant-garde
perspective had allowed her to see the by now conventional childhood plot with
different eyes, her gender had allowed her in turn to contrive, within the fragmentary texture of her story, the figure of her own difference as a woman' (Molloy
1991: 135). In the roof scene Molloy sees the girl-narrator, carried away by her
public discourse. I, on the other hand, see the disguise itself which, in the simultaneous appearance of two genders, permits the inscription of gender dissonance.

Cross-dressing allows both genders to become visible, and their horrifying dissonance to be displayed.

The family constitutes the gender narrative as a norm which is enacted only with difficulty. The power of gender thus features as a practice which regulates identities in accordance with a coercive binary scheme. In *Cuadernos de infancia* the circus woman's deformity allows her to act as the mother's other face; representations of maternity as repeated performance expose all private activity as public, while the cross-dressing scenes raise the possibility of conceiving of sex itself as construction. All these inscriptions unsettle and displace the novel's hegemonic gender narrative, which is also destabilized when the girl questions or rejects marriage, preferring to think of herself as a future writer.[12]

Los dos retratos works on the family model itself, which it posits as representation, as text. The modern family is sustained by the multiplication and reproduction of the same positions. The novel posits a first text (the first photograph) around which the interpretive chain is assembled. A whole series of disagreements is subsequently generated around this image of the family. They focus on issues of representation, interpretation, and position—that is, on the power of private relations. The voice of a young woman dismantles the family's workings, penetrates its core, and reduces it to a question of language. But if that woman is to become a narrator her literary authority must be legitimated, and this is achieved through the apprenticeship process. *Los dos retratos* is the text which best exemplifies the novel of initiation. This double initiation (into life and into literature) is contingent on knowing precisely how to look at the family, how to interpret it, and how to read the relations it generates between women.

The family history is summarized in accounts of a scene which takes place every Sunday in the dining-room—site of the family's social life, of meaning and enigma. In this room there is a long table, and a large mirror in which the table and its occupants are reflected. There are also two almost identical portraits, which are in fact enlargements of family photographs. The photographs are themselves reflected in the mirror, filling

---

[12] According to Molloy, it is by constructing herself as a girl who privileges the visual and experiments with language that Lange the writer is produced (Molloy 1991: 133).

the dining-room with multiplying faces: 'Nunca vi un comedor con tantas caras. Y como si esto no bastara, un espejo precisamente enfrente' (I have never seen a dining room with so many faces in it. And as if that weren't enough, with a mirror directly in front of them) (Lange 1956: 150).[13] The grandmother presides over this table, deciding who can enter the mirror and thus the family. She is herself the object of a powerful gaze. She also determines that the reflection of this powerful gaze and its object will endure through time, revealed and reproduced in the mirror. The grandmother simultaneously establishes the system of inclusions and exclusions, exercises the power of interpretation, and trains the disciple in whom this power and its continuity will be vested.

The position from which the family is narrated is an ambiguous one, involving both distance and engagement, spying and interpretation, participation and detachment. It is from this mobile and uncertain position that the novel emerges: 'A excepción de Teresa, soy la única que no está en los retratos: la única que puede mirarlos desde afuera' (Apart from Teresa, I am the only one who is not in the pictures; the only one who can look at them from outside) (1956: 70). This phrase generates the whole novel, since the starting-point of the narration is its narrator's externality. The 'I' is a 'necessary witness' to the events which are to be seen and interpreted, but one which remains absent from the picture. Starting from this shared absence and exteriority, picture and narration merge. The grandmother and the narrator transform these pictures into literary material, making them the beginnings of a framework for interpreting the family. They give form to this material in conversations and secret phrases, and reflect on the type of gaze which should be directed at it. These pictures attain literary weight only after they have been converted to discourse:

a no ser por esa frase (se refiere a la primera), habría convivido con ellos, con los retratos y el espejo, sin percibir la atmósfera que variaba de intensidad, las maneras con que unas palabras tanteaban un reproche, la insistencia de una voz que ya no podía más. (Lange 1956: 29)

if it hadn't been for this phrase (that is, the first one), I would have coexisted with them, with the pictures and the mirror, without noticing

---

[13] All quotations are from this edition.

how the atmosphere varied in intensity, how words fumbled towards
a reproach, the insistence of a voice that had reached its limit.

Lange underscores her conception of literature: the literary
referent is always another text, and in this case a photograph which functions as text. But what exactly does this photo-
referent do?

Photographs provide information about a past to which not
everyone has equal access. As John Berger indicates, photogra-
phy is replacing family memory (Berger 1987: 51–63). On the
one hand it registers an image of the past which, as image, per-
sists in the present. On the other, it supplies comparative information, in this case enabling an autobiography to be constructed
for those who were in the photograph and are now in the
dining-room. In *Los dos retratos* the photo-texts allow the representation of family memory, enabling current relationships to
be interpreted and the past to be assessed. Although the text
relates the disagreement between the grandmother and her
sister-in-law Elena to the photograph, the interpretation of their
disagreement depends on the context constructed for the
photograph. This context includes the other photograph,
the mirror, the dining-room, and the narration itself. Where
the family narrative is concerned, the photograph is a relic
of the past, a trace of what has taken place. The narration produces the context which situates this photo in time and space
and gives it meaning. The family memory is not a peaceful
landscape of joy and harmony but a site beset with bickering
and disputes. The photo-text sets off a chain of interpretations
and raises the very question of how to interpret. *Los dos retratos*
offers something like a reply: interpretation is from a specific
position and perspective. This reply emerges from the photographs themselves—the difference between the first photo and
the second lies in a glance—and from all the other systems of
representation that relate to this first one. All representation
implies a glance, and the direction of that glance determines the
representation. All representation is the staging of a glance or
perspective, both of which imply forms of interpretation and the
assignment of meaning. Various glances figure in the text: the
one that first captured the representation, the representation
of the glance in the photo, and the glances which subsequently
determine the different interpretations. These interpretations

are themselves constructed by different contexts: another photo, a mirror, a dining room, a story. The interpenetration of these diverse and specific systems of coherence determines different groups of meanings.

A common feature of these systems is *privacy*: private photos and mirror, private family dining room, the narration of privacy. Rather than reinforcing it, the exaggerated importance given to this sphere throws it into question. Danger lurks in the disputes over interpretation, for the private world contains suppressed bitterness. The story gives this bitterness substance, linking its muteness and deafness to an old law suit, a misunderstanding which is resolved by the exercise of power. The grandmother replaces the photograph at the centre of the quarrel with a picture of her own. The model breaks down. The private, self-generated, and self-sufficient world promotes hierarchical relations between women, rather than resolving them.

While the glance links the different systems, a voice is needed to articulate and realize what the surfaces and mirrors reveal. The voice which interprets the image in the mirror and the history of the pictures functions rather like the inscription on the back of a photograph or painting. It is a voice in writing, neither image nor history but both, converted to story. It is a voice constructed from a specific enunciating site, and which unifies the whole network of representations. In order for this world/these worlds to be interpreted, an inheritance, some form of interpretive legacy, must be established and must pass from woman to woman. The grandmother has the terms of comparison and the representational contexts at her disposal, and she bestows on her granddaughter the possibility of finding a voice with which to adopt them and adapt them to the present.

What emerges from *Los dos retratos* is that there are no fixed representations, that all representation bears the marks of its process and reveals itself as effect. The possibility of different representations—photos, mirror, dining room, text—which vary in space and time according to changing interpretations exposes representation as construction. At the same time it points to a further possibility: that meaning emerges from relations between these constructions. The original vanishes, and the text is able to posit an original site only by repudiating and fragmenting it. The gaze pushes back its boundaries and confers new meanings—meanings which are not fixed but constructed and reconstructed by changing contexts.

Narration and family are inseparable for Norah Lange. Her interrogation of literature and its referent is at the same time a meditation on relations between the model of the modern family and disrespectful or imperfect repetitions of that model.

While elaborating a subjectivity in process, the *Bildungsroman* demonstrates how this subjectivity represents itself. The 'I' of the narrator in *Cuadernos de infancia* rehearses a range of gender roles, fascinated by some and horrified by others. She cuts out words and plays with their sounds, disguising herself, adopting others' faces. At the beginning of *Antes que mueran* she writes: 'No sabes—me dijo—las posibilidades que se mueven detrás de las palabras' (You don't know the possibilities which move behind words, she told me) (Lange 1944: 7–9), using her own name—Norah—to demonstrate these transformations.[14] In 1950 *Personas en la sala* was published. In it a nameless female narrator watches three women in the house opposite and constructs a narrative around them (Lange 1981).[15] The privilege granted to the visual as the activator of imagination, the problematizing of the gaze, and the process of character construction all become crucial elements in the writer's progress towards self-representation. For the novel's narrator this is played out in a constant tension between a desire to emulate these women, their voices and manners, and the need to distance herself from them. This is how Lange fictionalizes the endless struggle between a woman author and the voices with which she decides to disguise herself. In the final chapter this struggle unfolds in all its drama as the female narrator reaches the last, unhappy, moment of textual construction: the point at which writing stops and the world of fiction vanishes.

Yet *Personas en la sala* announces a shift in the narrative voice towards a different picture-story, and one which progressively corrects modes of self-representation. In *Los dos retratos* the narrator continues to imprison a face in a mirror. She finds the face of the person she wants to resemble—her grandmother—and assumes that person's voice and place in both dining-room and mirror. She uses another visual reproduction to relate the

---

[14] All quotations are from this edition.
[15] All quotations are from the 1981 edition.

family history and fulfils her apprenticeship (de Nóbile 1968).[16] She rejects the sad women's story with the words: 'Yo siempre seré feliz' (I will always be happy), suggesting that narrative happiness is achieved by a narrator who manages to say precisely what the author dictates. The relation between grandmother and granddaughter, mistress and pupil, synthesizes the necessary splitting of author and narrator. The phrase 'Yo pienso lo que Ud. me diga' (I think what you tell me) (159) marks the end of an imaginary writing pact (Masiello 1992; 1985).[17]

This group of texts by Norah Lange stages the development of an experience of gender and writing. It demonstrates the play of their internal relations and conceives of gender as performance, an event which is never repeated in quite the same way, an act to be interpreted in accordance with the contexts available and the direction of the gaze focused on them. It presents writing as an exercise in tentative interpretation, an act of literary will which reveals its own processes. Gender and writing are exposed in the process of their construction. Their interconnections point to an emphatically textual (that is, not natural) family mechanism, exposing the artificiality of gender and positing it as a cultural construct. They also reveal a literature which displays its working parts and stages the key questions of literary production. This is an intimate world, where intimacy's fleeting and slippery space is translated into the intimist literature of that most private act—the act of writing.

It may be inappropriate to ask how consciously and deliberately Lange's literature resisted or obeyed the demands of aesthetics and family. No reading, however historical, can rush into such futile and exorbitant questions. Consciously or otherwise, women writers had to exercise reading and writing strategies which would permit them to be 'worthy' of their social spheres. This was the trap and the handicap they faced. Though socially and culturally privileged Lange was not a conventional woman, and she and Oliverio were the model of a fun-loving

[16] See *Palabras con Norah Lange* (de Nóbile 1968: 22 and 24) for her observations on the source of visual material in her last two novels.

[17] See Francine Masiello (Masiello 1985; and 1992, Part III) on how Lange's novel of apprenticeship confronts similar projects by men, while separating itself from them in ideological terms. Personally, I would add that where Lange's project ends Beatriz Guido's begins. Guido, also Argentinian, used the family as a literary resource but supplemented it with historical and political material and linguistic violence.

and irreverent literary couple. She was the muse and inspira-
tion of the vanguardist *Martín Fierro* group, a skinny, red-haired
Valkyrie. In the social and public domain she appeared as a
witty, talkative, and rowdy aesthetic object, always in disguise.
In this context the nurse's uniform or a mermaid's tail were no
more than the attractive and amusing repetition of a gender. It
was as a woman highlighting her gender that Norah Lange won
approval, while her literature focused on gender dissonance.

Translated by Anny Brooksbank Jones
and Catherine Davies

LIST OF WORKS CITED

ARMSTRONG, NANCY (1987), *Desire and Domestic Fiction* (New York and
Oxford).
BERGER, JOHN (1987), 'Usos de la fotografía', in *Mirar* (Madrid), 31–
63.
BUTLER, JUDITH (1990*a*), *Gender Trouble* (New York and London).
—— (1990*b*), 'Gender Trouble, Feminist Theory, and Psychoanalytic
Discourse', in Linda Nicholson (ed.), *Feminism/Postmodernism* (New
York and London, 1990), 324–40.
DOLL, RAMÓN (1928), 'Literatura femenina', in *Nosotros*, 22/230
(July), 88–90.
GARBER, MARJORIE (1992), *Vested Interests* (New York).
LANGE, NORAH (1925), *La calle de la tarde*, prologue by Jorge L. Borges
(Buenos Aires).
—— (1927), *Voz de la vida* (Buenos Aires).
—— (1933), *45 días y treinta marineros* (Buenos Aires).
—— (1944), *Antes que mueran* (Buenos Aires).
—— (1956), *Los dos retratos* (Buenos Aires).
—— (1968), *Estimados congéneres* (Buenos Aires).
—— (1979), *Cuadernos de infancia*, 7 edn. (Buenos Aires).
—— (1981), *Personas en la sala* (Buenos Aires).
LAURETIS, TERESA DE (1984), *Alice Doesn't: Feminism, Semiotics, Cinema*
(London).
—— (1987), *Technologies of Gender* (Bloomington, Ind.).
MASIELLO, FRANCINE (1985), 'Texto, ley, transgresión: especulación
sobre la novela (feminista) de vanguardia', '*Revista Iberoamericana*,
132–3, (July–Dec.), 807–22.
—— (1992), *Between Civilization & Barbarism: Women, Nation & Literary Criticism* (Lincoln, Neb., and London).

MIGUEL, MARÍA ESTHER DE (1991), *Norah Lange* (Buenos Aires).

MOLLOY, SYLVIA (1991), *At Face Value: Autobiographical Writing in Spanish America* (Cambridge).

NÓBILE, BEATRIZ DE (1968), *Palabras con Norah Lange* (Buenos Aires).

3

The Dialogics of Testimony
Autobiography as Shared Experience in Nellie Campobello's *Cartucho*

DORIS MEYER

AMONG the early 'novels' of the Mexican Revolution, the only one written by a woman was *Cartucho*, published in 1931. From that date to the present, Nellie Campobello's contribution to this genre has not received the attention it deserves nor has she been adequately recognized as the precursor of more well-known writers like Elena Garro, Rosario Castellanos, and Elena Poniatowska. This neglect may well be related to the impact *Cartucho* had when it was published and the nature of its idiosyncratic narrative style which few studies have examined in depth.[1]

Among scholars of the literature of the Mexican Revolution, the issue of genre has occasioned some debate. There is no doubt that *Cartucho*, like many so-called novels of the Revolution, is based closely on the author's personal experience. Nellie Campobello was born and raised in the region near Chihuahua where combat between *villistas* and federal troops regularly invaded the life of families like hers; as a young girl she saw fighting in the streets and knew many of the combatants personally. Her storehouse of memories included tales told to

---

[1] For a resumé of earlier critical literature dealing with Campobello as well as the most recent studies of her work, see Nickel 1990. Dennis J. Parle, in his article 'Narrative Style and Technique in Nellie Campobello's *Cartucho* (Parle 1985), studies Campobello's narrative strategies but does not take gender into consideration. The general lack of attention to Campobello's work extends to recent feminist critical studies where she might well have figured. For example, in her seminal book on autobiographical writing in Spanish America (Molloy 1991), Sylvia Molloy does not mention Campobello's works in her text or bibliography; likewise, Jean Franco does not include Campobello in her insightful work, *Plotting Women* (Franco 1989).

her by others who witnessed, as she did, events that were both horrific and heart-breaking. In *An Annotated Bibliography of the Novels of the Mexican Revolution,* John Rutherford classifies *Cartucho* as an 'autobiography' noting that 'nearly all these works have even more documentary content than is usual in novels, and a smaller proportion of imagination, invention and artistic reorganization' (1972: 3–4). In Campobello's case, this classification may not be as clear-cut as Rutherford suggests.

According to Richard O. Woods, Mexican life-writing has been widely practised but historically undervalued and ignored by critics and publishers: 'the itinerary of autobiography throughout Mexican literature evidences mislabelling, cursory treatment and general confusion of "experts" on the disposition of this genre'. *Cartucho* is a prime example of what Woods refers to as autobiography's 'perilous history in Mexico' (Woods 1991: 11–12).[2] Campobello herself gave *Cartucho* the subtitle 'relatos de la lucha en el norte de México' (tales of the struggle in the north of Mexico). Others have referred to it as autobiography, first-person historical narrative, testimonial chronicle, and episodic novel. Clearly Mexican authors themselves have contributed to the genre debate by their avoidance of the term autobiography and, in Campobello's case, by creating a work that has a 'borderlands quality' of resistance to definition by the dominant culture.[3] The purpose of this essay is to examine how and why *Cartucho* crosses the boundaries between autobiography and testimony, and to discuss the implications this holds for understanding the autobiographical imperative from a female perspective. I will also address the connection between narrative and history as modes of discourse whose boundaries are blurred by the act of bearing witness from the transgressive, subaltern perspective.[4] My critical approach will

[2] Also of interest on this subject is the 'Mexican Autobiography Issue' of *a/b: Autobiography Studies* (1988), which includes a bibliographic essay by Woods.

[3] My use of the term 'borderlands' intentionally evokes the recently acclaimed essay/verse/autobiography by chicana author Gloria Anzaldúa, entitled *Borderlands/ La Frontera: The New Mestiza* (1987). Campobello's work contains much of the spirit of female autonomy and pride in mestiza roots along the US–Mexican border that characterizes Anzaldúa's approach to life-writing.

[4] A useful text in this regard is Felman and Laub's *Testimony: Crises of Witnessing in Literature, Psychoanalysis, and History* (1992). Felman's chapters on the post-war narrative writings of Albert Camus offer intriguing parallels to Campobello's situation, although not from the subaltern position. To cite Felman: 'Camus, I would maintain, exemplifies the way in which traditional relationships of narrative to

draw heavily on the theories of Russian linguist Mikhail Bakhtin and subsequent feminist adaptations of his concept of dialogism.

Cartucho can legitimately claim a place in the long genealogy of Spanish American testimonial literature whose roots go back to the era of the 'New World' explorations. In terms of voice and perspective, however, Campobello's narrative has more in common with the testimony of the Nahuatl survivors of the Conquest, those 'voices of the vanquished' left out of accounts written by Hernán Cortés and the Eurocentric chroniclers who followed him. Lesser-known sixteenth-century documents record the eyewitness testimony of the Aztec people who preserved a rich oral culture despite defeat; their spirit of resistance identifies them as contestatory narratives that, once heard, call into question the mythology of Amerindian submission and acquiescence.[5] Similarly, in the terminology of today's revisionist critics, Campobello's *Cartucho* is testimonial literature that reads 'from within but against the grain' of official history to record subaltern consciousness (Spivak 1988: 13). In its oppositional challenge to the historiography controlled by Mexico's ruling classes, it was bound to raise hackles among the traditional reading public in the 1930s, just as Nellie anticipated. She could not have known, however, how much its difference as a woman's testimony of the Revolution would also inhibit its acceptance among literary critics unaccustomed to such inversions of normative discourse.[6]

Campobello has documented the genesis of *Cartucho* in a brief prologue she wrote for its first edition and also in a longer autobiographical essay included in a 1960 collection of her complete works.[7] In 1930 she and her younger sister Gloria were

history *have changed* through the historical necessity of involving literature in action, of creating a new form of *narrative as testimony* not merely to record, but to rethink and, in the act of rethinking, in effect *transform history* by bearing literary witness to the Holocaust' (1992: 95).

[5] e.g. León-Portilla (1992). For a discussion of the evolution and general characteristics of testimonial discourse in Latin America, see Prada Oropeza (1986).

[6] Lillian Manzor-Coats (1990) identifies Alicia Partnoy's *The Little School: Tales of Disappearance and Survival in Argentina* (1986) as a testimonial discourse of collective female resistance to oppression. This is but one of several testimonial narratives by Latin American women (Domitila Barrios, Rigoberta Menchú, Elena Poniatowska) which could be compared to Campobello's work. It should be noted, however, that *Cartucho* predates most of the well-known examples of this genre by women.

[7] See Nellie Campobello, *Cartucho: relatos de la lucha en el norte de México* (1931) and *Mis libros* (1960). By explaining her approach to writing in these confessional

visiting Havana, Cuba, where they were welcomed into the literary circle of the Fernández de Castro family, hosts at that same time to Langston Hughes and Federico García Lorca. The journalist and critic, José Antonio Fernández de Castro, was very taken with the Campobello sisters and would refer to them affectionately as 'mis muñecas mexicanitas, serias y formales' (my serious and proper little Mexican dolls)—a typical example of the way women's intelligence was trivialized while also being celebrated, and a cultural paradox that did not escape Campobello's notice. The Mexican Revolution was the topic of many conversations in Havana, and Nellie was distressed to hear the distortions of truth that had become common currency at home and abroad. When José Antonio was unexpectedly hospitalized, the sisters visited him every afternoon and, at his urging, Nellie began to write down her memories of the Revolution to share with him,

Así fue como cada tarde le llevaba al Hospital del Cerro mis fusilados escritos en una libreta verde. Los leía yo, sintiendo mi cara hecha perfiles salvajes. Vivía, vivía, vivía. . . . Acostaba a mis fusilados en su libreta verde. Parecían cuentos. No son cuentos. Allá en el Norte, donde nosotras nacimos, está la realidad florecida.[8]

So that's how each afternoon I would take my dead ones to the Cerro Hospital written down in a green notebook. I would read them to him, feeling my face becoming those wild profiles. I lived, lived, lived. . . . And I put my dead ones to sleep in their green notebook. They seemed liked stories, but they aren't stories. Up there in the North, where we girls were born, reality is in full bloom.

---

essays, Campobello focuses reader attention on the *process* of producing testimonial discourse, thus underscoring its literary nature. See ch. 6 of Roberto González Echevarría, *The Voice of the Masters* (1985) and Lucille Kerr, 'Gestures of Authorship' (1991), for their insights on the literary relationship between the author and the narrator-witness. Much more could be said about Campobello's consciousness of technique and her selection of a narrative voice than I am able to broach in the space of this essay. The symbiotic relationship this entails has class and gender implications that can be see in her other works as well. See Meyer, 'Nellie Campobello's *Las manos de mamá*: A Rereading' (1985).

[8] I quote from the special introductory remarks to the original 1931 edition; the translation is mine. All subsequent quotes and references will be from the 1960 revised edition of *Cartucho* included in *Mis libros*. All translations are mine unless otherwise stated. For a detailed explanation of the textual evolution of *Cartucho*— from the shorter 1930 to a longer 1940 edition, and to the final edition of 1960— see Nájera (1980). Most notably, the main changes involved a heightening of the collective aspect of the text by reduction of references to the first person, and an addition of 23 more sketches (to make 56 in total) in the second edition.

The sketches that became *Cartucho* allowed Campobello to bring to life—to dramatize with stark verbal images—truths that official history had suppressed. As she brought her memories to words, writing became a transformative and redemptive act akin to the ritual dances of Mexico that Nellie and her sister knew so well.[9]

For Campobello, to write about the Revolution was essentially an act of justice. In the small town of Hidalgo del Parral where she grew up, Pancho Villa was the hero of both peasants and landowners such as her family who knew him personally. But after his assassination in 1923, those in power in the capital had relentlessly tried to discredit him and write him out of history. As Campobello recalled,

A Francisco Villa lo consideraban peor que al propio Atila. A todos sus hombres los clasificaban de horribles bandidos y asesinos. Yo leía esto día a día, escuchaba las odiosas calumnias y comprendía la injusticia, la barbarie de estos nuevos ricos mexicanos hartos de dinero, del dinero que robaban a este pueblo al cual tanto defendió aquel glorioso señor general don Francisco Villa. (1960: 14)[10]

Francisco Villa was considered to be worse than Attila the Hun. His men were all classified as bandits and murderers. I would read this day after day, listen to the hateful lies, and get to know the injustice, the barbarism of those newly-rich Mexicans, stuffed with the money they stole from the people so staunchly defended by that glorious man, Don Francisco Villa.

Lest there be any doubt about who was responsible for the miscarriage of justice for political benefit, Campobello stated her position unequivocally,

Los enemigos del general Villa eran los envidiosos de su triunfo, los señores presidentes que se autonombraban en nuestra admirable y sufrida República. . . . La verdad debe decirse. Nosotros, los hijos de

---

[9] Nellie and Gloria Campobello were experts in the indigenous dances of Mexico. In the late 1920s and 1930s, as part of the enlightened educational programme of the Ministry of Public Education, they travelled all over the country performing national dances in schools and towns. This close contact with the realities of Mexican life, and the self-interested attitudes of many people she met, apparently reinforced Nellie's distaste for the hypocrisy and greed she saw around her (1960: 23). In 1937 Nellie was named Director of the National School of Dance in which Gloria was a principal ballerina.

[10] All translations from this autobiographical essay are from Irene Matthews's translation published in Meyer (1995). I would like to thank Irene Matthews and Doris Sommer for their helpful comments on an earlier version of this paper.

los verdaderos revolucionarios, tenemos la obligación de hablar y
pedir que se descorra la cortina. La historia lo pide así, pues nuestra
patria no es propiedad de unos cuantos, carrancistas, obregonistas o
callistas. (1960: 44)[11]

General Villa's enemies were the ones who envied his triumph, the
presidential gentlemen who elected themselves in our admirable and
suffering Republic. ... We, the children of the true revolutionaries,
have the obligation to speak and demand that the veil be drawn back.
History demands it, since our fatherland is not the property of a few
followers of Carranza, of Obregón, of Calles.

Campobello intended *Cartucho* as a personal literary undertaking for the collective benefit of her compatriots, and in this
regard her autobiographical writing finds common ground with
earlier Spanish American examples of this genre. According
to Sylvia Molloy, early autobiography in Spanish America is
'basically a public story' because it serves the public more than
the individual interest (1991: 82). However, unlike the typical
nineteenth-century author-statesman whose self-writing was
conceived as part of the larger story of nationhood in the
making, Campobello's autobiographical narrative was counter-
hegemonic and thus transgressive. Intentionally written from
outside, rather than inside the nationalistic ideology of post-
revolutionary Mexico, *Cartucho* more closely resembles the self-
figuration of Cuban-born Mercedes de Merlín (1798–1852)
than Argentina's Sarmiento, for example. As both a political
dissident and an atypical woman in the upper levels of Mexican society, Campobello was doubly unauthorized to voice her
opinion,

Comprendí que decir verdades me ponía en situación de gran
desventaja frente a los calumniadores organizados. Me ponía en el
peligro de que me aplastaran aquellas voces enemigas, siempre
incrustadas en lugares estratégicos de la más alta autoridad. Caería
estruendosamente del buen lugar que tenía—ambiente amable para

---

[11] It is interesting to note that Jesusa Palancares, the narrator of *Hasta no verte
Jesús mío* by Elena Poniatowska (1969; 1990), has exactly the opposite opinion of
Pancho Villa and his men, given the fact that her father was a *carrancista* soldier
(95–6). Not only does this bring up the polyphony of the subaltern consciousness
but it also highlights the relativity of testimonial discourse as, in Kerr's words,
'truth ... proposed as the negation of a lie, and not only as an assertion of a truth'
(Kerr 1991: 384). Testimonial literature thus takes its place with all literary discourse as verisimilar at best, with no special claim to representing historical 'truth'
any more than fiction itself.

mí, pero no para los héroes de mi infancia, ni para los ideales de mis padres y mis parientes, todos ellos engullidos por la Revolución. Podía yo seguir cómodamente donde estaba. . . . Pero no era correcto el hecho de que, sabiendo yo las cosas, no las dijera. (1960: 14)

I understood that to tell the truth placed me in a situation of real disadvantage in confrontation with organized liars. I was facing the risk of being demolished by those enemy voices that were always cemented into strategic positions of the highest authority. I could come crashing down from the nice place I occupied, the environment so pleasant for me but not for the heroes of my childhood, nor for the ideals of my parents and my relatives, all of them swallowed up by the Revolution. I could continue comfortably where I was. . . . But it wasn't right that, if I knew things, I shouldn't say them out loud.

Anticipating the resistance and prejudice with which her writing would be received, Nellie knew she would have to find a way to make her readers more receptive to her message and her testimony more credible. She needed a technique, or what she referred to as a 'discipline' in which historical facts could be told without sentimentalizing or trivializing them (1960: 16). The solution she found—the rhetorical strategy she developed—shows a clever, transformative approach to the 'autobiographical situation'.[12] As Sidonie Smith has pointed out, the female autobiographer is extremely sensitive to reader expectations *vis-à-vis* her own expressive needs and thus 'responds in a complex double-voicedness' which demands unusual narrative strategies (1987: 50). In Campobello's case, she managed to turn a testimonial position of authorial weakness into one of strength through a technique that has much in common with 'focalization', according to the narrative theory of Mieke Bal,

Focalization is the relationship between the 'vision,' the agent that sees, and that which is seen. . . . The reader watches with the character's

---

[12] For a full discussion of this concept which is particularly applicable to my approach to *Cartucho*, see ch. 1 of Janet Varner Gunn, *Autobiography: Towards a Poetics of Experience* (1982). Gunn rejects the classical theory of autobiography (exemplified by Georges Gusdorf) in favour of a three-part concept that stresses the impulse, perspective, and response of the autobiographical activity—all situated in a world of contingent historical experience (1982: 12). This concept does not take women's experience into particular consideration but it lends itself to a feminist approach to autobiography by virtue of its recognition of the 'worldliness' of self-writing (ch. 5) which makes autobiography 'an act of plural, not singular, reflexivity' (140).

eyes and will, in principle, be inclined to accept the vision presented by that character. (1985: 104)

In *Cartucho*, which takes place between 1914 and 1918, the primary focalizer is the child, Nellie, portrayed between the ages of 6 and 10. Actually, this is a partially fictive identity in view of the fact that Campobello was really in her teens at the time of the Revolution, having been born in 1900 according to baptismal records which she preferred not to acknowledge. This semi-disguise enables her to use the young child's 'I' (eye) as the filter for a more direct testimony, one that draws the reader into her response to the Revolution. According to Bal's theory, the difference between how the child sees the events and how the adult reader interprets them determines the work's special effect (1985: 105).

In terms of autobiographical writing, focalization allows the female author to shift the focus from the 'auto' (or unauthorized self) to the 'bio' (or familiar world she and others inhabit). This self-narrative process ironically involves detachment from self in order to achieve a larger credibility, a strategy often found in women's autobiography (Jelinek 1980: 15–16). To quote Susan Stanford Friedman,

This impulse for disguise . . . reflects the anomalous position of women in a patriarchal tradition that has constituted femininity as selfless and the artist as inherently masculine. The alternate self created in a woman's autobiographical text is an act of rebellion, born of alienation and moving toward affirmation. . . . Precisely because the cultural construction of the self has been different for men and women, feminist theories of autobiography frequently redefine the self of women's texts as collective or communal, not purely individual. (1983)

Essentially, Campobello turns the classical notion of autobiography—the writing of a timeless, private self—into the shared experience of a public, grounded self. The child's testimony acquires meaning and depth through ratification by other witnesses in the shifting optics of the text. Through this multifocused approach, Campobello collectivizes her testimony and shares the narrative function with others. The true protagonist thus becomes the *pueblo*. Although individual voices speak through her memory, they all represent one group—the common people of the north who collectively witnessed the Revolution. By having them share the authorizing gesture with the child-narrator, Campobello accomplishes what Cuban author Miguel Barnet has identified as the primary objective of the artist-originator of the testimonial novel: to articulate the collective memory of the we (*nosotros*) and not the I (*yo*) (1986: 294).

Cartucho resembles other narratives of the Revolution in its episodic structure, its autobiographical format, and its epic vision of the national upheaval. Yet it has been called 'the most unusual' work of this genre because it is 'paradoxically both the most poetic and the most violent novel of the Revolution' (Parle 1985: 201). Its fifty-six brief sketches are divided into three sections: the first offers individual portraits of soldiers well known to Nellie and her family in Parral; the second and longest section chronicles the death of many who touched their lives in one way or another; and the third describes scenes of life on the margins of battle, emphasizing the vagaries of war and the price of survival. Nellie's child-voice narrates many of the early episodes in a matter-of-fact way, as if the horror around her were commonplace. She records details of the war that captured her childlike fancy: like the time that the soldier nicknamed Cartucho took her baby sister Gloria for a walk and was suddenly ambushed by *carrancistas* and had to fire back with his 30–30 still holding the baby in his arms; or when she learned of the death of Babis, a soldier-friend who owned the local candy store and dreamed of wearing a uniform with silver buckles; or when she and her mother witnessed from a train window the summary hanging of a man who had sat next to them moments before; or when she and her sister watched with delighted anticipation as bullets whizzed by their house and a horseman they knew rode towards his death. These brief scenes evoke through metonymic impression the dramatic psychological effect of war's intrusion into, and disruption of, normal life; they also create a cinematic effect through the use of montage-like images. This fragmentary and shifting optical approach to writing gives Campobello's narrative technique a modernist quality unlike conventional models of autobiography.

In the second and third sections, Nellie's voice frequently assumes the role of a background narrator without first-person commentary; then she gradually introduces the voices of others whose stories she has heard, directly or indirectly. The most frequent secondary narrator is her mother, Rafaela Luna, whose heroism on a domestic level is comparable to Villa's in the

child-Nellie's eyes. For example, one sketch begins: 'Le contaron
a Mamá todo lo que había pasado. Ella no lo olvidaba. Aquellos
hombres habían sido sus paisanos' (They told Mama everything that had happened. She never forgot it. Those men had
been her *paisanos* [countrymen]).[13] The story of the execution
of Tomás Urbina is then told through the mother's memory.
Later in the sketch, Nellie interjects,

me gustaba oír aquellas narraciones de tragedia, me parecía verlo y
oírlo todo. Necesitaba tener en mi alma de niña aquellos cuadros
llenos de terror, lo único que sentía era que hacían que los ojos de
Mamá, al contarlo, lloraran. (1931: 105–6)

I liked hearing those tragic stories. It seemed to me I could hear and
see everything. I needed to have those terrifying pictures in my child's
soul. I only regretted that it made Mama's eyes fill with tears to tell
them. (1988: 38)

The child's detachment in the face of daily tragedy, her enjoy-
ment of the spectacle of battle and its recounting, has the
effect of jolting the reader into a heightened awareness of
war's brutal toll on the innocent. The literary understatement
achieved by her fascination with the surface of events is coun-
teracted by the mother's emotional involvement in them. From
either angle, there is no idealization, no glossing over the violence. The mother's valiant efforts to protect her family provoke the reader's sympathy, but not because she is the epitome
of female self-sacrifice. Rafaela Luna is a gutsy, independent
woman whose ethics are clearly partisan: she's capable of bald-
faced lies and rash acts of defiance to rescue a loved one in
harm's way. When we see how much she admires Villa and his
men, we want to accept her point of view.

General Villa comes to life most vividly in the third section
of *Cartucho*, which is also the most polyphonic part of the book
and the one in which the testimony of ordinary Mexicans is
most clearly heard. Until recently, according to William Beezley,
historians and social scientists documenting the Revolution have
overlooked the rich oral tradition of the Mexican *pueblo* as a
source of information and have thus relegated these voices to
historical silence (Beezley 1983: 376–7). Campobello perceives
the potential for authorizing the 'truth' of those traditionally

[13] *Cartucho* (Compobello 1931: 105; 1988: 38).

considered marginal to history even if it requires a measure of literary manipulation to compile and convey their testimony. As Lucille Kerr has observed in regard to Elena Poniatowska's novel, *Hasta no verte Jesús mío,*

the authority of the subject in such a text derives precisely (though paradoxically) from the denial of his or her authority elsewhere. This figure of marginality, then, becomes a figure of textual as well as testimonial authority, much like the authorial figure that also authorizes Jesusa's performance in the novel. (1991: 386–7)

By multiplying the voices in *Cartucho*, Nellie dialogizes the discourse of testimony and shares the authorizing gesture.

The sketches in this third section are framed by the child-narrator who introduces the story and then lets others speak:] 'Allá en la calle Segunda, Severo me relata, entre risas, su tragedia: "Pues verás, Nellie, cómo por causa del general Villa me convertí en panadero"' (1931: 153) (Right there on Segunda Street, Severo told me, between laughs, his tragedy: 'Well, Nellie, now you'll hear how, on account of General Villa, I learned how to bake bread') (1988: 70). Or another example, 'Pepita Chacón, entre risas amables, recordó que en su casa cayó una vez nada menos que el general Villa' (1931: 159) (Pepita Chacón, laughing amiably, recounted the time General Villa himself turned up at her house) (1988: 73). Or, 'Era febrero, llegaron las fuerzas del general Villa. Dice Chonita, contenta de recordarlo: "Hacía mucho aire, los sombreros nomás se les pandeaban en la cabeza"' (1931: 177) (It was February, and General Villa's troops had arrived. Chonita happily remembers it this way: 'The wind was blowing and the brims of their hats were bent against their heads') (1988: 86). Many times the witness is a woman, and invariably we hear the colloquial language of northern Mexico. Time and again, Villa appears as a man of the people; he can be cunning and intimidating but also gentle and considerate, as could his soldiers. By portraying Villa and his men through the voices of the common folk who knew them best, *Cartucho* debunks the anti-Villa black legend. In its place emerges a counter-legend created by communal devotion. As expressed by one of Nellie's informants,

'Los villistas eran un solo hombre. La voz de Villa sabía unir a los pueblos. Un solo grito era bastante para formar su caballería'. Así dijo Severo, reteniendo en sus oídos la voz del general. (1931: 155)[14]

'The Villistas were one single man. Villa's voice could unite them all. One shout from him was enough to mount his cavalry'. That's what Severo said, with the echo of the General's voice still ringing in his ears. (1988: 71)

A recent collection of essays entitled *Feminism, Bakhtin and the Dialogic* focuses on the intersection of Bakhtinian theory and female literary expression, which in turn sheds light on Campobello's approach to writing *Cartucho*. According to Bakhtin, the multivoiced nature of novelistic discourse reflects the organic interrelatedness of all communication. His theory of self and 'otherness' in language, which did not take gender directly into account, nonetheless lends itself to describing the ex-centric, intersubjective experience of female identity. Feminist scholars working with Bakhtin's theories often observe that the resistance to authority characteristic of women's narrative written from outside official ideology is both parodic and subversive. According to Diane Price Herndl, 'A feminine language lives on the boundary. . . . Like the voices Bakhtin hears in the novel's carnival, the female voice laughs in the face of authority' (1991: 11). In the same collection Josephine Donovan points out how early women's novels often have a paratactic, patchwork structure that is 'closer to the real world' and 're-flects the associative, random connections of consciousness in immediate response to its environment'; such narratives evince a 'blurring of the boundaries between the literary and the nonliterary' (1991: 88, 90). These stylistic elements are in consonance with the female relationship to the 'authoritative word', a discourse which Bakhtin characterizes as 'located in a distanced zone, organically connected with a past that is felt to be hierarchically higher . . . it is, so to speak, the word of the

---

[14] Among other positive testimonies written by those who knew Villa was that of the respected author and friend of Campobello, Martín Luis Guzmán, in *El águila y la serpiente* (1928). According to a recent study by Manuel A. Machado, Jr., 'Villa's deeds elevated him to secular saint. In the popular culture he was the Mexican *Ubermensch*, Superman, who took the cause of his people and against overwhelming odds successfuly led his armies against the oppressors of the Mexian *peones*' (1988: 178).

fathers' (1981: 342). Authoritative, official discourse, according
to Bakhtin, avoids the 'zone of contact' where ideologies inter-
mingle and everyday life intrudes (1981: 345).

By dialogizing *Cartucho*'s testimonial discourse in paratactic
fashion, Campobello rejects the monologic appropriation of
Mexican history by the post-revolutionary power structure. Her
insistence on orality and polyphony challenges the official
pronouncement of Pancho Villa's role as barbaric and inhu-
man. Indeed, *Cartucho* calls into question the entire nationalistic mythology of civilization vs. barbarism in which the
revolutionary struggle in Latin America had been cast.[15] From
the perspective of everyday life in the villages of northern
Mexico, Villa was a father figure to thousands who responded
to his battle cry against the *carranzistas*. In Bakhtinian terms,
he was the folkloric hero, the anti-feudal, Rabelaisian 'great
man' whose qualities were merely those of ordinary men, writ
large (1981: 241).

Campobello also challenges the master discourse in her
portrayal of childhood in *Cartucho*. Autobiographical narratives
in the patriarchal tradition commonly represented childhood
as an idyllic prelude to the narrator's heroic destiny of preserving an established way of life. Ironically, Nellie's compatriot
and friend, José Vasconcelos, was writing his autobiography,
Ulises criollo, at the same time Nellie was writing *Cartucho*; in his
first volume, as Sylvia Molloy has pointed out, Vasconcelos's
protective and adoring mother is the dominant figure who
'beholds him as a hero . . . destined to lead a nation, to set
down its law' (Molloy 1991: 199). Compare this to the mother's
role in *Cartucho*: Rafaela Luna is nurturing but not indulgent,
self-possessed rather than self-denying. Her gaze rarely focuses
on her daughter who must fend for herself as her mother
copes with the perilous realities of a life under siege. *Cartucho*
clearly contests the androcentric notion of the doting, servile
mother by foregrounding the mother as an independent agent,

---

[15] For an in-depth interpretation of how patriarchal discourse has manipulated
this mythology in the formulation of Argentine nationhood, see Francine Masiello,
Between Civilization & Barbarism (1992). Masiello argues that over the past two
centuries Argentine women authors have responded to manipulated notions of
gender and otherness with counter-discourses: 'In collapsing these false dichotomies, women writers alter the discursive space to redefine the nature of literature
and knowledge and to form alternative prestige systems that test the dominant
expressions of power through speech'(10).

directly involved in the dynamics of history. The 'foundational fictions' of Latin American male self-narratives are thus subverted by *Cartucho*'s insistence on reformulated notions of heroism and historical agency.[16]

In 'Discourse in the Novel' (1934–5) Bakhtin points out the socio-historical interaction of all utterances but stresses that 'primacy belongs to the response, as the activating principle: it creates the ground for understanding' (1981: 282). The rhetorical strategies of *Cartucho* appear to reflect this Marxist-oriented principle of dialectics.[17] In the concluding pages of *Cartucho* we see how crucial the concept of response was to Campobello's moral imperative to deconstruct the exclusionary official discourse and authorize a place in history for the marginalized. In the fiftieth sketch, after multiple voices have shared their recollections of Villa and the men who fought and died by his side, Nellie concludes the story of Pablo Mares with these personal words,

Pablo Mares era de nuestra tierra (jamás imaginó que yo le hiciera este verso sin ritmo); conozco su retrato y sé su cara de memoria. Me tuvo en sus brazos—yo era chiquita—, dijo Mamá que me durmío y me cantó. 'Fue como un hermano mío, a todos mis hijos los quería como si fueran suyos', afirmó Mamá guardando el retrato de Pablo Mares. Yo creo que sus brazos se durmieron junto con el rifle después de un canto de balas. (1931: 163–4)

Pablo Mares was one of ours, from our land. (He never dreamed I'd write these rhythmless verses to him.) I've seen his picture and I know his face by heart. He held me in his arms when I was very little. Mama said he sang me to sleep. 'He was like a brother to me. He loved all my children as if they were his own', she said, holding the picture of

[16] I borrow this term from Doris Sommer's book, *Foundational Fictions: The National Romances of Latin America* (1991), dealing with romantic novels in Latin America. In their link to patriotic history based on a male-formulated 'erotics of politics' (1991: 6), which subordinates the female to a domestic role in nation-building projects, the early Latin American novel and autobiography were similarly motivated.

[17] It is unlikely that Campobello would have known of Mikhail Bakhtin (1895–1975) or his theories of dialogism when she wrote *Cartucho*. However, she does mention that the Fernández de Castro brothers introduced her to certain poetry of the Russian Revolution in Havana and that her family friend, the Mexican artist and teacher, Dr Atl, had studied in Russia. It was he who arranged for the publication of her first book of poetry *Yo, por Francisca* in 1929 and later helped to bring *Cartucho* into print (1960: 17–18). Nellie's sympathy with the *villistas* and her privileging of the voices of the 'underdogs' indicate a Marxist orientation, although she does not openly espouse any political ideology.

Pablo Mares. I think his arms fell asleep alongside his rifle after a song of bullets. (1988: 76)

Three times in this paragraph Nellie makes a reference to music, as if to emphasize its fundamental connection to the daily life of the *norteños*. Immediately thereafter, in the final half-dozen sketches, she incorporates various examples of ballads and *corridos* that were sung by the *villistas* and passed on from one generation to another: 'Cada uno tenía una canción preferida y las fueron dejando de herencia a los que las quisieron' (1931: 166) (They all had favorite songs, which they left as an inheritance to others who loved them too) (1988: 78). In northern Mexico, especially in the area where Nellie grew up, composing *corridos* to record tragic occasions—the death of a famous person, a catastrophic event, or a miscarriage of justice—was a natural and customary response to life.[18] These anonymous songs embodied the spirit and voice of the Mexican people, the authentic national identity. Campobello herself was a recognized expert in the *corrido* tradition of the regions of Durango and Chihuahua, and she could still sing them heartily when she was in her eighties.[19]

More than any other revolutionary hero, Villa inspired the response of the common folk who composed *corridos* (Machado 1988: 170). In the last section of *Cartucho*, Campobello devotes one *estampa* entirely to a *corrido* commemorating the death of Martín López, Villa's most trusted assistant. In the words of one stanza: 'Pancho Villa lo lloraba, lo lloraban los dorados, lo lloró toda la gente, hasta los más encuerados' (1931: 175) (Pancho Villa and his *dorados* have cried for the departed. And

---

[18] For an overview of the history of the *corrido* in Mexico, see Merle E. Simmons, *The Mexican Corrido as a Source for Interpretive Study of Modern Mexico* (1957). Parle makes this significant statement, 'the narration of *Cartucho* approximates the form and vision of the *corrido*, the popular ballad of the Revolution. Besides its parallel rhythmic effect, the style and thematic content of the narration also recall the *corrido*. As in the *corrido*, the basic narrative language is simple, colloquial, and spontaneous, creating the sensation that the speaker (narrator) and listener (reader) share in an intimate community of common interests and experiences' (1985: 209).

[19] I met Campobello in Mexico City in 1983, visited her in her home, and, during a long conversation, heard her sing fragments of ballads of the Revolution with a gusto that belied her age. Vicente T. Mendoza in *El romance español y el corrido mexicano: un estudio comparativo* (1939) cites Campobello as a source and authority on the regional music of Durango and Chihuahua. See Parle (1985: 211 n. 13).

so have all the people, even the most hard-hearted) (1988: 85). By shifting the narrative voice to the collective *pueblo* in this dramatic way, Nellie makes an unequivocal statement about the legitimacy of orality and the folk tradition in the documentation of history and the formulation of nationhood. She has ceded the final word to the anonymous Mexicans who knew Villa best and whose emotion-laden songs testify as eloquently as the written word.

Ultimately, as Campobello realized, much of the burden of memory fell on mothers, wives, and daughters, 'testigos de las tragedias' (1931: 178) (witnesses to the tragedies) (1988: 87), although she also recognized the importance of *soldaderas* (women soldiers) who inspired many *corridos* in their own right.[20] The next-to-last sketch of *Cartucho* is entitled 'Las mujeres del norte' (Women of the north), and here she evokes the common situation of women all over the north of Mexico who were witnesses to the exploits of the *villista* soldiers and keepers of the collective memory. One of them was Chonita whom the soldiers called 'madrecita' (little mother) when they stopped at her kitchen for a rare hot meal for which she never charged as she always feared it might be their last. Women like Chonita and Nellie's mother were the 'madrecitas de ocasión' (sometime mothers) who nurtured, mourned, and remembered the *villistas*—and passed this folk history along to the next generation in stories, pictures, and songs.

In *Cartucho*, then, Campobello's response to those who maligned Villa's role in history was to testify to the shared experience of the people of the north—and particularly the women —who kept alive the oral tradition of how the Revolution was fought. Since official history in Mexico remained hostile to the truths of the *pueblo*, her efforts were met with scorn and derision,

[20] Interestingly, in the only sketch in *Cartucho* entirely devoted to a *soldadera*, Nacha Ceniceros, Campobello points out that there are two versions of her story; one, a false legend of Nacha's shooting of her lover for which Villa had her executed, and another, the true story of her exploits involving no conflict with Villa. The sketch concludes with the adult Nellie saying that this is yet another part of the 'red de mentiras' (network of lies) surrounding the real Revolutionary heroes (79–80). By drawing this parallel, she seems to suggest that women's role in the fighting has also not been recorded properly, a point made by various recent revisionary histories. For a discussion of *corridos* and *soldaderas* of the Revolution, see Elizabeth Salas, *Soldaderas in the Mexican Military: Myth and History* (1990: 89–94).

Me negaron el saludo gentes que se habían dicho amigas, pues no
querían nada con la defensora, según ellos y sus mentiras, de bandidos.
Así los calificó la calumnia organizada. (1960: 26–7)

People who called themselves my friends no longer greeted me on
the street, since they wanted nothing to do with the defender, according to them and their lies, of bandits. That's what the organized
slander called them.

Despite this, she published another book about Villa and a
study of indigenous music and dance of which she later said,

Cuando terminé estos dos libros, yo estaba envuelta en el amor más
apasionado que se puede y debe sentir por obras que vienen a deshacer
mitos; obras que llegan a desbaratar falsos decorados y dejan ver la
forma en su más digna y elevada expresión histórica. (1960: 43–4)

When I finished these two books, I was caught up in the most passionate love one can and must feel for works that dismantle myths; works
that manage to debunk false embellishments and allow the true shape
to be seen in its most worthy and noble historical expression.

The courage to do this, she claims, was inherited from her
mother to whom she dedicated *Cartucho*: 'A Mamá, que me
regaló cuentos verdaderos en un país donde se fabrican leyendas
y donde la gente vive adormecida de dolor oyéndolas' (1931:
49) (To Mama, who gave me the gift of true stories in a country where legends are invented and where people lull their
pain listening to them) (1988: 4).

Campobello's words have renewed resonance in the context
of the 1990s as pressure from subaltern classes in Mexico tries
to unmask government injustices. Sixty years earlier, Nellie
Campobello dared to contest official versions of Mexican history. She joins a fertile tradition of women writers in Latin
America who have been inspired to speak out through identification with the folk culture of their foremothers. Her testimony and theirs is part of a resistance literature that has
changed our perception of the relationship between politics
and gender in Latin America as well as our way of reading
history.

LIST OF WORKS CITED

ANZALDÚA, GLORIA (1987), *Borderlands/La Frontera: The New Mestiza* (San Francisco).

BAKHTIN, M. M. (1981), *The Dialogic Imagination: Four Essays*, ed. Michael Holquist, trans. Caryl Emerson and Michael Holquist (Austin, Tex.).

BAL, MIEKE (1985), *Narratology: Introduction to the Theory of Narrative*, trans. Christine van Boheemen (Toronto).

BARNET, MIGUEL (1986), 'La novela testimonio: socio-literatura', in René Jara and Hernán Vidal (eds.), *Testimonio y literatura* (Minneapolis, 1986), 280–302.

BEEZLEY, WILLIAM H. (1983), 'In Search of Everyday Mexicans in the Revolution', *Revista Interamericana de Bibliografía/ Inter-American Review of Bibliography*, 33/3: 366–82.

CAMPOBELLO, NELLIE (1931), *Cartucho: relatos de la lucha en el norte de México* (Mexico, DF).

—— (1960), *Mis libros* (Mexico, DF).

—— (1988), *Cartucho and My Mother's Hands*, trans. Doris Meyer and Irene Matthews (Austin, Tex.).

DONOVAN, JOSEPHINE (1991), 'Style and Power', in Dale M. Bauer and S. Jaret McKinstry (eds.), *Feminism, Bakhtin, and the Dialogic* (Albany, NY, 1991), 85–94.

FELMAN, SHOSHANA, and LAUB, DORI (1992), *Testimony: Crises of Witnessing in Literature, Psychoanalysis, and History* (New York and London).

FRANCO, JEAN (1989), *Plotting Women: Gender and Representation in Mexico* (New York).

FRIEDMAN, SUSAN STANFORD (1983), 'Theories of Autobiography and Modernist Self-Creations in H.D.'s Canon'. Typescript of a paper delivered at the Modern Language Association Convention; quoted by permission of the author.

GONZÁLEZ ECHEVARRÍA, ROBERTO (1985), *The Voice of the Masters: Writing and Authority in Modern Latin American Literature* (Austin, Tex.).

GUNN, JANET VARNER (1982), *Autobiography: Towards a Poetics of Experience* (Philadelphia).

GUZMÁN, MARTÍN LUIS (1928), *El águila y la serpiente* (Mexico, DF).

HERNDL, DIANE PRICE (1991), 'The Dilemmas of a Feminine Dialogic', in Dale M. Bauer and S. Jaret McKinstry (eds.), *Feminism, Bakhtin, and the Dialogic* (Albany, NY, 1991), 7–24.

JELINEK, ESTELLE C. (1980) (ed.), *Women's Autobiography: Essays in Criticism* (Bloomington, Ind.).

KERR, LUCILLE (1991), 'Gestures of Authorship: Lying to Tell the Truth in Elena Poniatowska's *Hasta no verte Jesús mío*', *Modern Language Notes*, 106/2 (Mar.), 370–94.

LEÓN PORTILLO, MIGUEL (1992) (ed.), *The Broken Spears: The Aztec Account of the Conquest of Mexico*, 2nd edn. (Boston).

MACHADO, MANUEL A., Jr. (1988), *Centaur of the North: Francisco Villa, the Mexican Revolution, and Northern Mexico* (Austin, Tex.).

MANZOR-COATS, LILLIAN (1990), 'The Reconstructed Subject: Women's Testimonials as Voices of Resistance', in Lucia Guerra Cunningham (ed.), *Splintering Darkness: Latin American Women Writers in Search of Themselves* (Pittsburgh, 1990), 151–71.

MASIELLO, FRANCINE (1992), *Between Civilization & Barbarism: Women, Nation, & Literary Culture in Modern Argentina* (Lincoln, Neb., and London).

MENDOZA, VICENTE (1939), *El romancero español y el corrido mexicano: un estudio comparativo* (Mexico, DF).

'MEXICAN AUTOBIOGRAPHY ISSUE' (1988), *a/b: Autobiography Studies*, 3/4 (Summer).

MEYER, DORIS (1985), 'Nellie Campobello's *Las manos de mamá*: A Rereading', *Hispania*, 68 (Dec.), 747–52.

—— (1995) (ed.), *Rereading the Spanish American Essay: Women Writers of the 19th and 20th Centuries in Translation* (Austin, Tex.).

MOLLOY, SYLVIA (1991), *At Face Value: Autobiographical Writing in Spanish America* (Cambridge).

NAJERA, VALESKA STRICKLAND (1980), 'La obra de Nellie Campobello' (Ph.D. diss., Northwestern University).

NICKEL, CATHERINE (1990), 'Nellie Campobello', in Diane E. Marting (ed.), *Spanish American Women Writers: A Bio-Bibliographical Source Book* (Westport, Conn., 1990), 116–27.

PARLE, DENNIS J. (1985), 'Narrative Style and Technique in Nellie Campobello's *Cartucho*', *Kentucky Romance Quarterly*, 32: 201–11.

PONIATOWSKA, ELENA (1969; 1990), *Hasta no verte Jesús mío* (Mexico, DF).

PRADA OROPEZA, RENATO (1986), 'De lo testimonial al testimonio: notas para un deslinde del discurso-testimonio', in René Jara and Hernán Vidal (eds.), *Testimonio y literatura* (Minneapolis, 1986), 7–21.

RUTHERFORD, J. D. (1972), *An Annotated Bibliography of the Novels of the Mexican Revolution* (Troy, NY).

SALAS, ELIZABETH (1990), *Soldaderas in the Mexican Military: Myth and History* (Austin, Tex.).

SIMMONS, MERLE E. (1957), *The Mexican Corrido as a Source for Interpretive Study of Modern Mexico* (Bloomington, Ind.).

SMITH, SIDONIE (1987), *A Poetics of Women's Autobiography: Marginality and the Fictions of Self-Representation* (Bloomington, Ind.).

SOMMER, DORIS (1991), *Foundational Fictions: The National Romances of Latin America* (Berkeley).

SPIVAK, GAYATRI (1988), 'Subaltern Studies: Deconstructing Historiography', in Ranajit Guha and Gayatri Spivak (eds.), *Selected Subaltern Studies* (New York and Oxford, 1988), 3–32.

WOODS, RICHARD O. (1991), 'Mexican Autobiography within Mexican Literature', *Revista Interamericana de Bibliografía/Inter-American Review of Bibliography*, 41/1: 3–14.

4
The Wandering Text
Situating the Narratives of Isabel Allende

SUSAN FRENK

NEGOTIATING a path through the critical geographies which have mapped the academic reception of the narratives and public personae of Isabel Allende is a disorienting experience indeed. For all their differences, however, most of these geographies participate in a general deterritorialization as they steer her texts down unmarked roads. This essay offers a reading of the faded signposts and diversion signs along the way, with a tentative sketch for an alternative journey.

Texts are produced and exchanged in a global market-place. In the process a woman, some women, come to represent 'women's writing'—as Jean Franco notes, a commodity that currently sells well in pluralist regimes (Franco 1992). Allende's texts, which engage from exile with Chilean society, are marketed additionally through a dehistoricized 'magical realism' (Martin 1989) and through an academic 'teaching machine' which markets cultures to students while simultaneously feeding the media profiles of trends and superstars (Spivak 1993). It is from within this machine that I write, an outsider to Chile trying not to fall into too many of the potholes excavated by critics working on post-colonial terrain. As they wander from Chile to North American and UK academe and through different fields of discursive struggle Allende's texts generate many readings. The readings produced here are motivated in part by a need to celebrate the achievements of a woman writer in institutions and societies where (despite recent market successes) writing by women and the work of women who teach and research it remain devalued. This essay starts, however, from the assumption that we risk compounding these women's difficulties if we fail to contextualize the voices we gather, or to tease out the threads of 'woman' into the women who speak through these texts, those who do not, and those who are spoken by them inadequately.

What follows is a first stage in this process. It starts with the women's movements which, in different ways, have challenged the linguistic regime of *lo no dicho* (the unsaid) and the attempted abolition of the interlocutor, risking gendered, 'private' bodies in order to assert a broader integrity of the body. Allende's first novel, *La casa de los espíritus*, appeared only in 1982 and cannot be read as part of the literature of immediate resistance (Boyle 1992) nor assimilated to the different forms of *testimonio* (testimonial) generated by women inside Chile.[1] Nor is *La casa de los espíritus* as radically disjunctive in formal terms or as wide-ranging in its representation of subaltern relations as the writing of, for example, Diamela Eltit. Instead, I would argue, it is precisely the familiarity of Allende's narrative modes which empowers women readers, enabling them to respond through different forms of resistance and rebellion. This involves the reappropriation of their bodies, not as the liberation of a natural body, but through the reinscription of bodies in new discourses, including the expansion of political rights to a similarly de- and reconstructed pleasure. What is at stake here is not pleasure as a libidinal escape route from the social but an investigation of the politics of romance. Unlike Wolfgang Karrer—who has claimed that in *Eva Luna* 'Mimí and Eva submit gender structure to change, but ultimately preserve it' (Karrer 1991: 161)—I would argue that the politics of romance in Allende's narratives preserve the specificity of different bodies while troubling the dominant sex-gender naturalizations of them.

A reading of the integrity of sexually differentiated bodies, and of the discursive empowerment of gendered subjects as a strategic response to the situation of Chilean women, can take us beyond the theoretical impasse of 'feminist misogyny'. In her recent exploration of this phenomenon Susan Gubar notes that, since both feminists and misogynists must exploit and

[1] All references will be to the following editions of Allende's novels: *La casa de los espíritus*, 18th edn. (Barcelona, 1985), *De amor y de sombra*, 3rd edn. (Barcelona, 1984), *Eva Luna*, 3rd edn. (Mexico, DF). Unless otherwise indicated, all translations are my own.

expropriate words from a common linguistic store, 'their discourses necessarily intersect in numerous ways, undercutting or supplementing each other over time [in] a cultural "heteroglossia" of gender ideologies and power asymmetries' (Gubar 1994: 465). This is helpful in reassessing the articulation of two pivotal elements in the seemingly polarized critical reception of Allende's writing, and in writing on Latin American women generally: femininity and motherhood. Anxious to escape the straitjacket of motherhood as naturalized self-abnegation, critical writings as diverse as Jean Franco's illuminating but ultimately negative analysis of motherhood in Rosario Castellanos (Franco 1992) and Debra Castillo's lament at the prominent role of marriage in Allende's narratives (Castillo 1992) seem to want to abolish positive representations of motherhood. However, such writing can be revised in a matrix which recognizes the systemic positioning/construction of women while at the same time enabling their agency—in negotiating, resisting, and transforming systemic relations and generating new identities—to be appraised.

If we relate *La casa de los espíritus* to the power of motherhood in the mobilization of Chilean women's groups, and to the rearticulation in the novel of this power in opposition to the discourse of the Pinochet regime, motherhood emerges as historically variable. Mother–daughter relations in particular do not replicate a natural femininity but accommodate new versions: they do not reinforce the patriarchal power of the father but instead provide a mode of empowerment of women's bodies and psyches which the patriarch cannot control. The later novel, *Eva Luna* (1988), expands this type of intergenerational relation between women beyond the biologically grounded narrative of motherhood. It also removes female–male relations almost completely from marriage. This, I would suggest, is related both to a more developed concern with subaltern experience and to the growing autonomy of women's movements (in Chile and elsewhere) through the 1980s, as a consciousness took shape of the need to negotiate political alliances with and within mixed, but still masculinist, opposition groups from a separate sphere of female identification and empowerment.

Allende's narratives can also be read as confronting the oppressive regime through a discursive experience of pleasure and desire which can seem scandalously inappropriate to the scale of suffering under Pinochet. Yet if we read Allende in the light of Patricia Chuchryk's study of women's organizations in the Chilean transition to Democracy (Chuchryk 1989) we can trace a process in which survival and resistance lead to a questioning of patriarchal relations, and in which pleasure and desire are no longer perceived as luxuries but identified as the very substance of those relations. These pleasures are produced in relations of denial and internalized self-denial, prohibited by external and self-imposed surveillance, and mobilized in the service of powerful others. They are harnessed within a specific phallic order which must be reappropriated and redirected according to a different imaginary economy, as a vital part of political projects to alter other relations. These relations include the socio-economic, which was until relatively recently the only sphere recognized as political by the Left.

In this analysis, the question of the integrity of the body expands from the bodies of the disappeared to include the discursive relations in which the bodies of the protesting women are imprisoned. It links domestic violence and state violence through the deconstruction of relations of gender and sexuality. There is a growing corpus of critical work which argues convincingly that Allende does more than 'put "quality" writing . . . at the service of the formulas that have always acted as female pacifiers—heterosexual romance combined with seigneurial goodwill toward the subaltern classes' (Franco 1992: 73). Franco goes on in the same piece to include Allende among a number of women writers who unsettle 'the stance that supports gender power/knowledge as masculine . . . displacing the male-centred national allegory and exposes the dubious stereotyping that was always inherent in the epics of nationhood that constitute the Latin American canon' (Franco 1992: 75). Yet her earlier comment implicitly excludes Allende from the confrontation of the middle-class woman's specific social positioning and the 'ambiguous overlapping of privilege and the aesthetic' (1992: 75) in women writers, a confrontation which she analyses in the writing of Clarice Lispector, Carmen Ollé, and Tununa Mercado. The analysis of post-colonial gender politics here must therefore integrate the representation of subaltern relations.

In *Eva Luna* and *La casa de los espíritus* these relations are associated with appropriations of bodily and discursive pleasure,

[Consuelo] sacó la cuenta de que en sus treinta y tantos años no había conocido el placer y no lo buscó, convencida de que era un asunto reservado a los protagonistas del cine. Resolvió darse este gusto y de paso ofrecérselo también al enfermo a ver si partía más contento al otro mundo. (Allende 1988: 22)

[Consuelo] looked back over her thirty-odd years and realized that she had not experienced pleasure, nor sought it, convinced that that sort of thing only happened in films. She resolved to have a taste of it herself and to offer some in passing to the sick man, to see if he would depart this world in a happier state.

In *Eva Luna*, Consuelo's appropriation of the pleasure which has been unavailable to her as marginalized *sirvienta* (maid) comes about through a process of rebellion. This process is linked to the issue of discursive power, which initiates a series of actions that affirm her as an agent, gradually transforming her from the mirror image of her master's desires. When she decides to try to save the life of the indian gardener (who has been bitten by a poisonous snake) we are told that 'por primera vez en su silenciosa existencia, Consuelo desobedeció una orden y tomó una iniciativa' (for the first time in her silent existence Consuelo disobeyed an order and took the initiative) (Allende 1988: 21).[2]

Consuelo reappropriates her body in a ritual undressing which culminates in loosening her hair: 'deshizo el rodete que llevaba enrollado en la nuca como exigía su patrón' (she unfastened the hair which, at her master's insistence, she wore coiled at the nape of neck) (Allende 1988: 22). Then, as she begins to make love for the first time, she initiates a dialogue with the stricken indian/subaltern/male other in a language produced by her own desire: 'Susurrándole palabras recién inventadas' (murmuring newly invented words) (1988: 23). The love she offers the indian is accepted, he is restored to agency, and in the mutual pleasure and exchange of their lovemaking Eva is conceived.

A second ritual of reappropriation and inscription marks Eva's birth, celebrating it as 'el momento más importante' (the most important moment) of Consuelo's life and deromanticizing the birth process by foregrounding the 'labour' involved (1988:

---

[2] Consuelo's employer, Professor Jones, has no interest in trying to save the indian's life and, indeed, is eager to add an indian mummy to his 'museo de estatuas humanas' (museum of human statues), in true colonialist fashion.

23–4). Consuelo's apparent self-sufficiency becomes mutual dependency with the woman who helps her to cut the cord and to whom she eventually entrusts her daughter before dying. This relation is the first of a series of encounters between women which challenge their internalization of patriarchal discourses of the feminine body. It is the godmother who says 'Mala cosa, es hembra' (What bad luck, it's a girl) (1988: 24) and insists on baptizing Eva and giving her a surname, the traditional marker of women as the property of men. Consuelo counters with positive reinscriptions and compromises based on respecting the beliefs of the other. By choosing the tribal name of the father as the child's surname Consuelo simultaneously endows it with a different collective meaning. She identifies Eva with the marginalized indians rather than the *criollista* patriarchal order and reinscribes her in a feminine lineage, since the tribe's name means 'children of the moon' (1988: 24).

Eva's birth brings further release from Consuelo's long education in self-silencing. Consuelo is represented as generating a rich store of counter-stories about herself and the dominant order. Because that order refuses a dialogical relation with her, however, these stories can only be told when Eva becomes first a listener and then their mediator/narrator: 'Aprendió a permanecer quieta y guardó su desmesurado caudal de fábulas como un tesoro discreto hasta que yo le di la oportunidad de desatar ese torrente de palabras que llevaba consigo' (She learned to remain silent, treasuring her boundless stock of stories discreetly until I gave her the opportunity to unleash the torrent of words within her) (1988: 13). Consuelo's discursive transformations are confined to *la intimidad*, the private sphere: in public she maintains a silence that renders her invisible to the powerful, 'como si no existiera' (as if she didn't exist) (1988: 5).

Consuelo's empowerment and double legacy of *rebelión* (rebelliousness) and storytelling are central to her daughter's eventual transformation,

De mi padre heredé la sangre firme, porque ese indio debió ser muy fuerte para resistir tantos días el veneno de la serpiente y en pleno estado de agonía darle gusto a una mujer. A mi madre le debo todo lo demás ... Las palabras son gratis, decía y se las apropiaba, todas eran suyas. (1988: 25–6)

I inherited my strong blood from my father, because that indian must
have been pretty tough to hold out against the snake venom all those
days and make love to a woman when he was on the point of death.
Everything else I owe to my mother... words are free, she would say,
and she appropriated them, they were all hers.

As *Eva Luna* progresses, Eva saves her own life by appropriating language and storytelling, sometimes adapting to the
desires and discourses of others, eventually constructing alternative her/ histories. Despite economic and social disempowerment, her belief in the integrity of her healthy woman's body
and the possibilities of discursive exchange as a counter to capitalist relations enables Eva both to survive and to participate
in the process of social transformation and public discourse.

Eva is the sole, albeit extraordinarily complex, narrator of
Eva Luna. In *La casa de los espíritus*, bodily integrity and discursive power are explored through counterposed female and
male narrative voices. Trueba embodies the monologic regime
of authoritarian patriarchy, which encompasses censorship,
disempowerment through discourses which demean the other
(*campesinos*, women, or communists), and physical violence
(raping *campesina* women or hitting Clara). His granddaughter
Alba is eventually revealed as the female narrator who restores
the interlocutor, both by directly contradicting Trueba and by
writing down a counter-herstory of the forms of resistance
offered by other women and *campesino* men, socialist politics,
and protest songs. Gabriela Mora's concern about what she
sees as Alba's 'passivity', too-ready desire to forgive past injustice, and her 'limiting' of political activity to writing can thus
be rethought through a new understanding of politics in the
novel (Mora 1987: 58–9). The centrality of discursive relations
to regimes of power, the establishment of a solidarity between
women which is not contained within a single party politics,
and the dimensions of sexual politics in Alba's relationship
with Manuel are all part of this rearticulated politics. Furthermore, as Ronie-Richele García Johnson has shown, Alba's situation at the end of the novel represents the apex of a gradual
'conquest of space' in the house (García Johnson 1994). We
can read this as the democratization of the private which the
Chilean women's movements came to see as indivisible in
the struggle to democratize the public sphere in the 1980s.
The difficult issue of Alba's discourse of forgiveness needs to

be reread in the light of Susan de Carvalho's interesting study of male narrative voice in *La casa de los espíritus* and *El plan infinito* (Carvalho 1993–4). Carvalho argues that,

Allende's male narrators in the novels both reach a nadir at which they are forced to admit their impotence; but the narrative perspective allows also a portrait of the 'post-masculine' male, the man emerging from that nadir, who then reviews his past in segments intercalated throughout the novels. Thus the narrative structure involves various externalized images of the male character, each followed immediately by the repentant male narrator's enlightened commentary on the man he had once been, his recognition of lost opportunities—in most cases opportunities to express love (1993–4: 271)

It is in this context of self-analysis, repentance, and reconstruction by authoritarian figures that Alba's projection of a future forgiveness is situated.

The integrity of the (gendered) body is restored, then, through the dismantling of an authoritarian regime which exchanges bodies as commodities, the property of the patriarch, in the different but interrelated economies of desire, discourse, and money. Women and other subaltern groups reappropriate their bodies through acts of resistance that simultaneously rewrite the political discourse of the Chilean Left. The strategic foundationalism of bodies can play a multiplicity of roles in this process. First it celebrates—without idealizing—the female body which has traditionally been discursively deployed to sublimate the male body, while male bodies are *desublimated*, brought under scrutiny in a deconstruction of their phantom identification with the phallus of power (Gimbernat de González 1991). It also reasserts the integrity of the body against physical and discursive violations, while separating the body into bodies which have historically been gendered differently. Finally, it provides a point of identification across the specific struggles of different women which acts as a mooring post in a journey of collective transformation.

By representing desires that cannot be reduced to the specularisms of desire for the phallus—whose rejection in *Eva Luna* is linked to Eva's reassertion of an autonomous gender difference—Allende undermines the monologic system of patriarchal difference. Instead of Lacan's descriptive/prescriptive family romance, *Eva Luna*, for example, starts from a refigured family in which the maternal and feminine are privileged. Eva first reaches out to the male other not in psychic rejection of her dead mother, nor even in substitution of that mother('s lack). She reaches out in desire and, in part, in response to the economic positioning of women and to the problematic models of femininity internalized by her other 'mothers' (Madrina and Elvira).

Eva undergoes a learning process which begins with love for the father, Riad Halabi. As she later realizes, his paternalist form of patriarchy permits her to appropriate the positive aspects of his discourse of femininity, to survive through his protection, and to be encouraged by him to depart on a journey towards an equal subject status which transcends paternalism. Nostalgia for the 'protection' afforded by a paternalist patriarchy was a common feature of the early years of the Pinochet regime, not only in the regime's own refiguration of the ideal family but amongst many women obliged to take on sole responsibility for family income in harsh economic conditions (Chuchryk 1989; Boyle 1992). In the novel, Eva's nostalgia is dissipated in a double movement. On the one hand, there is her realization that a paternalist regime infantilizes women. On the other, there is Riad Halabi's failure to recognize her as an independent woman who seeks equal subject status. She is thus outside the specularisms of paternalism, desirable neither as daughter nor as daughter/lover.

This experience is related to the reader in the critical self-commentary which characterizes key moments in the complex time shifts of the narrative voice (Aguirre Rehbein 1991). Another mode of critical appraisal is dialogue between characters of equal status united by bonds of affect and shared experience, as in Eva and Melecio-Mimí's discussions of bodies, genders, and relationships. Contested positions are set out in terms of both feelings and possible outcomes. Although, when Melecio-Mimí chooses not to have the operation, the narrative ultimately reinforces Eva's position, the different discourses have nonetheless illuminated their relationship and brought into play a range of evaluation systems. The final selection of one rather than another refers once again to the possibility of rejecting the violation of the body required to normalize Mimí in patriarchal gender terms. Having found a male lover who is not rigidly bound to the patriarchal order, Mimí goes on to make his/her gender troublingly public in Eva's *telenovela*.

Eva's journey takes her through a series of relationships with seductive patriarchal masculinities. However she finally chooses not the Romantic hero Huberto—whose performance of machismo continues in the gendered politics of the guerrilla group—but the contrasting male character Rolf Carlé. Despite their different histories Eva and Rolf are able to construct a common, hybrid, narrative together. Or rather Eva constructs one for them both. It is significant that, despite their equal socio-economic status, shared politics, companionship, and erotic compatibility, as in the basic pattern of romance literature there is still a difference to address—in this case Rolf's emotional difficulties: 'Ese hombre tan veloz cuando se trata de captar una imagen con la cámara, resulta bastante torpe ante sus propias emociones' (That man is quick to catch an image on film but pretty sluggish when it comes to his own emotions) (1988: 279).

Their relationship rejects configurations of unequal complementarity, absolute incommunication, or domination/submission. Instead it proposes an equality that works not through the abolition of difference (which would mean the death of the subject) or through the subsuming of one difference into the realm of the other (the logic of specularity) but through respect for what Jacques Derrida terms 'the trace of the other'. Here the reassertion of gender difference functions to preserve the integrity of ethnic and other differences in a rearticulation of hybrid micro and macro identities. So, where Karrer reads the metaphors of fusion in Allende's writing as part of a homogeneous post-war *mestizaje*, I would argue a need to differentiate between specific ideologies of *mestizaje* in the context of emergent articulations of hybridity and transculturation.[3]

Yet we do need to look at the effects of the heterosexual focus in Allende's work, both locally and more broadly: in relation to the regime of *lo no dicho* (the unsaid) and the growing audibility of lesbian voices in Chilean women's groups, but also in relation to to the global reception of Allende's work in contexts where the politics of sexuality have played a more

[3] *Mestizaje* is affirmed uncritically in Karrer's article as it has been in much academic writing on Latin America. For a more critical discussion of recent Latin American theorizations of hybridity, see *Travesía*, 1/2 (1992), and Rowe and Schelling (1991).

crucial role in the 1980s. These other reterritorializations of her texts need to consider whether their magic realism resists or risks reinforcing the exoticism and hierarchical otherness of Latin America, and the tendency to represent machismo as a 'Latin' problem. I will argue that the discourse of magical realism in *La casa de los espíritus* challenges the capitalist destruction of nature and people not merely with a picture of suffering victims but with alternative knowledges and economic relations, forcing the Western reader to engage with them. Through the family of Rolf Carlé, *Eva Luna* can in some ways be seen to take this process further, placing authoritarian regimes and patriarchal relations in Latin America in juxtaposition with Fascist European regimes of the 1930s. This pre-empts the discourse of Latin America as a continent predisposed to authoritarian politics. At the same time it explores the colonial and post-colonial relationships between the two continents through Rolf's wanderings (including his period in the determinedly isolationist enclave of his aunt and uncle) and through the figure of Professor Jones, while problematizing masculinities in Europe as well as Latin America.

The question remains whether, given the situation of a double censorship—that of the regime's compulsory heterosexuality, and the women's movement's initial inability to move beyond the association of lesbianism with an imperialist, man-hating version of Western feminism—we can nonetheless mobilize lesbian and/or homoerotic desire in Allende's texts. And whether, even in this highly coded form, it can still disrupt the compulsory heterosexuality that may be pivotal to authoritarian masculinity and social relations. If we accept Adrienne Rich's theorization of a lesbian continuum, rivalry for any kind of male attention can be resituated along this continuum as forms of appreciation, affect, and solidarity. In this way, the self-love of women can resist patriarchy without recourse to representations of physical lovemaking. The view that the containment of women's erotic desire and pleasure within heterosexual relations requires a form of self-rejection, even self-hatred, would be displaced by a concept of self-love which can include a fully erotic lesbianism but does not depend on it. In this picture erotic desire is displaced from the central position it commanded—at least in Western politics—in the 1970s and 1980s and placed on a continuum, or field, of positively valued relations between women and between women and men. Relations between men are not reconstructed to the same extent in Allende's work. The sole instance of an openly homoerotic relation—Melecio-Mimí and Aravena—is caught up in Melecio's hatred of his own male body, although this becomes a partial self-acceptance as transvestite when he turns down the opportunity to have his body surgically remodelled as female. This seems to suggest that the patriarchal regime is less amenable to micro resistance and modification by men than by women.

If, as Mario Rojas has suggested, the relationship between Férula and Clara in *La casa de los espíritus* may be read as one-way lesbian desire it is hardly a positive representation (Rojas 1986). In its possessiveness it is a specularism of her brother's authoritarian, controlling desire, in which woman is once again object or private property. Yet, as Rojas goes on to argue, Férula is part of the textual opposition between the 'amor/cadena' (chained love) of the Trueba dynasty and the 'amor libre' (free love) of the Del Valle women (1986: 73). Nonetheless, as the clearest coded representation of lesbian desire it remains problematic.

The concept of a 'lesbian continuum' still allows us to read the all-female households, the friendships, sisterhood, and even the political consciousness-raising and alliance between the women in the concentration camp and between Ana Díaz and Alba at the end of the novel as instances of the self-love that empowers women and makes it possible to resist the system of misogyny. Like Férula and Clara in *La casa de los espíritus* or Eva and Rolf's cousins in *Eva Luna*, all transform their rivalry for male attention into friendship. However, it remains the case that the fulfilment of erotic pleasure in mutual love between equals is exclusively located in the (future) heterosexual relationship between Alba and Manuel in the former novel and between Rolf and Eva in the latter. Similarly, Melecio-Mimí's homosexual relationship with Aravena is represented as an attenuated version of dominant-submissive relations between a purely performative femininity and a powerful masculinity. Although set in political opposition to the authoritarian regime this masculinity still represents the name of the father for Rolf, whom Aravena addresses as *hijo* (son). Literally and metaphorically miles from Rolf's tyrannical biological father, he is none the less in power.

Here too, however, the text projects a dynamic of potential change. The possibility of the guerrillas entering the sphere of democratic political power and Rolf's defiance of his 'father's' injunction not to do anything too risky both point to the emergence of new relationships between men. Within such a relationship Melecio-Mimí, for example, would no longer need to deny the male body as the embodiment of the phallic order. In the novel, this need is positioned in terms of Melecio's brutal experiences and therefore figures as a historically produced desire, rather than the genetically imprinted imperative of the discourse first mobilized to explain his/her sense of self. However, there is nothing comparable for male readers to the spectrum of female to female relationships in Allende's writing: the mother–daughter relationships which permit change without requiring absolute separation or alienation; the sisterhood which moves from a biological representation, which acquires political and historical dimensions in *La casa de los espíritus*, to the metaphorical mother and sister relationships in *Eva Luna*. Even the male guerrillas—that potential site of homoeroticism and non-biological brotherhood and, perhaps, misogynist homosociality—remain locked in the mode of charismatic leadership.

This returns us to the issue of the mobilizing potential of texts which represent problems as well as solutions. Eva adopts a fraternal, friendly relationship with Huberto that is imbued with its own erotic history and posited as a temporary political alliance. However, it is rejected as a model for ideal relations between women and men within a narrative that ends in transition —political transition in the state, transitional relations between women and men—as the Utopian discourse of a reworked romance is both relativized and reiterated.

The representation of bodies in Allende's work is inseparable from the issue of her magical realism. Critics have broadly tended either to focus on Allende's debt to García Márquez or to read it as technique. Philip Swanson (1994) gives both of these tendencies a political twist in his analysis of *La casa de los espíritus*, and concludes that the magical eventually retreats as the women become more politically active. However, his assimilation of the magical to happy times now departed and his reduction of magical discourses to the status of anachronisms seem rather schematic. The early part of the novel has its share of horror after all, and the loss of the house identified with Clara is part of 'la época del estropicio' (the destructive era) in which the Pinochet coup takes place (Swanson 1994: 232). Moreover, the novel does not seem to support the parallel between Clara's magic and Trueba's fantasies asserted by Swanson. Rather, Clara's magic is recuperated by Alba in her (collective) narrative while Trueba finally comes to view his own law as part of a ninety-year history of lies.

A more productive line of enquiry is opened up by William Rowe's rearticulation of magical-realism, which he equates broadly with 'the suspension of Enlightenment rationalism with its emotion of superstition' (Rowe and Schelling 1991: 214). He traces its development to 'the imposition of the label "idolatry" upon native cultures [which] both foregrounded magic and denied it any cognitive dimension' (1991: 214). Magic thus became a marginal, syncretic,

alternative knowledge . . . shared by different social classes [and] primarily the province of women . . . In a second sense, insofar as the term has been used say of Arguedas' work, it involves native ritual practices which include not only the idea of magic as action produced by 'irrational' agencies but also a network of shared meanings which the practitioner engages with and reproduces. (Rowe and Schelling 1991: 214)

In neither case is it reducible to the fantasy projections of individual desire.

Rowe goes on to note that magical belief is not treated exclusively as positive, but that its legitimation 'can be a vindication of pre-capitalist culture, against the logic of capitalist accumulation and positivist social engineering' (Rowe and Schelling 1991: 214). To this extent Allende's refashioning of the national allegory in *La casa de los espíritus* can be seen as a representation of a hybrid culture which differs from both the authoritarian capitalist modernization discourse of the regime and from the proletarianized vision of the Unidad Popular. Rather than an uncritical romanticization of *campesino* and female magical discourses, it is an evaluation of their power/ knowledge relationships from the perspective of an outsider discourse—a discourse which proposes an ethics and politics of equality which does not threaten the integrity of equal embodied subjects. Where either the magical or the scientific are analysed as constructing subjects unequally, perpetuating inequality and/or violating the integrity of bodies, they are critiqued or abandoned. This is a postmodern relativization of discourses which confronts the politico-ethical dilemma of addressing conflict *between* discursive regimes. It also effects the troubling of the discursive boundaries between magical and non-magical to which Rowe refers.

In *La casa de los espíritus*, for example, *campesino* knowledge is represented as more efficacious than Western scientific knowledge in dealing with the plague of ants. This is a particularly richly layered scene in which the son who is modernizing distances himself from the discourse of his father yet has to recognize its validity. At the same time, the Western capitalist system is savaged for its 'black magic', for its reduction of people, the land, and knowledge to commodities, and for the large-scale destruction of peoples and territories set in train by these economic and discursive relations. Furthermore, the *campesino* resists this system with a narrative which symbolizes an alternative discursive relation to Nature, that of a conversation which places humans on an equal, not superior, level with the other inhabitants of the earth in relations of ecological negotiation. At first the son and the capitalist can only read this narrative literally, from the perspective of discourses which are constructed in the devaluation of the other. However, in the alliances between the different generations of *campesino* men and the Del Valle women the narrative proposes a place for both groups in an alternative narrative of the nation, presenting *campesino* patriarchy as different from the landowner's yet still in need of transformation.

The scene which ties these issues most closely to the integrity of bodies in *La casa de los espíritus* is the much commented-upon autopsy/rape of Rosa which leads to the symbolic silencing of Clara. Debra Castillo has written persuasively of the productive potential of analysing silence in writing by women. In this case it is a form of internal resistance to the regime which continues in Clara's spiritualist activities. As Swanson has noted, her second silence is part of an outward-looking rebellion which takes various public forms (Swanson 1994: 228).

Like silence, the discourse of love has made some critics uncomfortable and needs to be analysed in its specific (re)articulations. This is not the domain of the isolated couple of

heterosexual romance, in which the dominant male and submissive female supplement one another's lack. Instead it offers
a spectrum of affective relations which construct subjects re-
spectful of the trace of the other, a will to relationship, perhaps, which can construct an equality in difference.

Towards the end of *Eva Luna*, Eva's bodily integrity is restored when she realizes that she has started menstruating again.
She inscribes this in a discourse of love as an openness to a
relation of mutual desire with the other, in this case with Rolf.
This begins in companionship, in shared dreams and fears in
the jungle, taking on an erotic dimension. It does not exhaust
their relations, however. Eva is embedded in multiple relationships with others, across a spectrum of affect which sometimes
includes sex but in which non-eroticized relations are highly
valued. The dual ending may reintroduce a particularly valued
gran amor (great love) but it effectively relativizes Romantic
versions of it: unlike Zulema, Eva will not die for or in love.
She seeks not to annihilate Rolf's difference or her own, but
to weave a collective story in which each participates equally, a
conversation in which divergent histories are brought together.
The Utopia inscribed here can thus be read in terms of the
Chile of the transition to democracy. Suspicion of the authoritarian regime's motivation is coupled with hope for the possibilities of a better future. This hope emerges in the privileging
of gender difference in the empowerment of women readers,
the continuing struggle in both authoritarian and pluralist
regimes, the representation of political alliances with Left men.[4]

The deconstruction of the Liberal Enlightenment subject
has tended to rearticulate an ideal postmodern subject as infinitely mobile, while the deconstruction of oppressive sex/
gender configurations in Western societies has tended to reduce
the body to pure libidinality. As Spivak (1993) has reiterated,
if the subject 'effect' is 'useful'—and in the case of the disappearances it is fundamental—then it can be deployed strategically
(1993: 5). In *La casa de los espíritus*, economically privileged

---

[4] These alliances assume a clear consciousness of the machismo that has to be
resisted, not least as a construction of desire in some forms of romance. Carlos
Monsiváis is one of the few contemporary male cultural critics in Latin America
to analyse machismo in both its historical and contemporary modes. For an introduction to his work which includes articles by a range of male critics, see *Fem*'s
special issue, 'Hombres', 18 (Apr.–May 1981).

subjects are transformed through respect for the other, while Eva Luna's self at the end of her narration is indelibly marked with the traces of the others who have peopled her life in different kinds of relationships. The vision of subjectivity which emerges is kaleidoscopic, and memory mobilizes history not in the real time of events but in the simultaneity of each successive present,

Yo escribía cada día un nuevo episodio, inmersa por completo en el mundo que creaba con el poder omnímodo de las palabras, transformada en un ser disperso, producida hasta el infinito, viendo mi propio reflejo en múltiples espejos, viviendo innumerables vidas, hablando con muchas voces. (Allende 1988: 273)

Every day I would write a new episode, completely immersed in the world I was creating with the all-encompassing power of words, transformed into a scattered self, repeated to infinity, glimpsing my own image in multiple mirrors, living innumerable lives, talking with many voices.

In this narrative various subaltern figures undergo fables of transformation, yet Allende's texts do not explore 'the heterogeneity of the subaltern' (Spivak 1993: 5) to the same degree in all cases. Broadly speaking *La casa de los espíritus* recognizes the subaltern *nana* but situates her entirely in the borrowed discourses of the dominant order. In *Eva Luna*, by contrast, Consuelo is the author of counter-discourses and Eva becomes an author of publicly circulated (televized) stories. Kavita Panjabi has argued persuasively that the figure of Tránsito Soto moves from the margins of Trueba's world to a central role which illustrates the interdependency of prostitute and wife in patriarchy and the need for the struggle of the women's movements to encompass *all* women (Panjabi 1991). She is nonetheless a sketchy figure in comparison with the narrative space occupied by the privileged female characters, and to this extent contributes to the long history of writing in Latin America which effectively silences subaltern women.

So while the integrity of bodies in Allende's work represents a powerful counter-discourse to both authoritarian and pluralist regimes, these texts cannot be said to harness the empirical 'thickness of description' (Geertz 1983) which testimonial pursues with varying degrees of success. They do, however, reposition different subaltern groups and legitimate subaltern discourses, while, in *Eva Luna*, subaltern women move from the textual margins of Allende's writing to the foreground.

Both locally and globally, then, Allende's writing constructs readings which are intimately bound to the political struggles of women. In the seminar room, absences and problematic issues can be productively mobilized to discuss the sex/gender/sexuality systems of different cultural contexts. The readability of these texts and their critical engagement with familiar narratives—family romance, the *telenovela*—enables political, ethical, and discursive dilemmas to be worked through in relation to theory which is otherwise often intractable in its performativity, universalism, and abstraction. This is a space where it is also possible to bring together other texts whose availability is often limited. The question remains, however, as to how work carried out in the 'teaching machine' can play a wider role in the transformation of postcolonial relations, in different discursive spaces and political movements.

LIST OF WORKS CITED

AGUIRRE REHBEIN, EDNA (1991), 'Isabel Allende's *Eva Luna* and the Act/Art of Narrating', in Riquelme Rojas and Aguirre Rehbein (1991), 179–88.

ALLENDE, ISABEL (1984), *De amor y de sombra*, 3rd edn. (Barcelona).

—— (1985), *La casa de los espíritus*, 18th edn. (Barcelona).

—— (1988), *Eva Luna*, 3rd edn. (Mexico, DF).

BOYLE, CATHERINE (1992), *Chilean Theatre 1973–1985* (Rutherford, NJ).

CARVALHO, SUSAN DE (1993–4), 'The Male Narrative Perspective in the Fiction of Isabel Allende', *Journal of Hispanic Research*, 2.

CASTILLO, DEBRA (1992), *Talking Back: Toward a Latin American Feminist Literary Criticism* (Ithaca, NY).

CHUCHRYK, PATRICIA (1989), in Jane S. Jaquette (ed.), *The Women's Movement in Latin America: Feminism and the Transition to Democracy* (Boston, 1989), 149–84.

FRANCO, JEAN (1992), 'Going Public: Reinhabiting the Private', in George Yudice, Jean Franco, and Juan Flores (eds.), *On Edge: The Crisis of Contemporary Latin American Culture* (Minneapolis, 1992).

—— (1990), *Plotting Women: Gender and Representation in Mexico* (London).

GARCÍA JOHNSON, RONIE-RICHELE (1994), 'The Struggle for Space: Feminism and Freedom in *The House of the Spirits*', *Revista Hispánica Moderna*, 47/1 (June).

GEERTZ, CLIFFORD (1983), *Local Knowledge: Further Essays in Interpretive Anthropology* (New York).

GIMBERNAT DE GONZÁLEZ, ESTER (1991), 'Entre principio y final: la madre/materia de la escritura en *Eva Luna*', in Riquelme Rojas and Aguirre Rehbein (1991).

GUBAR, SUSAN (1994), 'Feminist Misogyny: Mary Wollstonecraft and the Paradox of "It Takes One To Know One"', *Feminist Studies*, 20/3 (Fall), 453-73.

KARRER, WOLFGANG (1991), 'Transformation and Transvestism in *Eva Luna*,' in Riquelme Rojas and Aguirre Rehbein (1991), 151-63.

MARTIN, GERALD (1989), *Journeys Through the Labyrinth* (London).

MORA, GABRIELA (1987), 'Las novelas de Isabel Allende y el papel de la mujer como ciudadana', *Ideologies and Literature* (Spring).

PANJABI, KAVITA (1991), 'Tránsito Soto: From Periphery to Power', in Riquelme Rojas and Aguirre Rehbein (1991), 11-19.

RIQUELME ROJAS, SONIA, and AGUIRRE REHBEIN, EDNA (1991) (eds.), *Critical Approaches to Isabel Allende's Novels* (New York).

ROJAS, MARIO (1986), 'Aproximación socio-lingüística a la narrativa de Isabel Allende', in Marcello Coddou, *Los libros tienen sus propios espíritus* (Xalapa).

ROWE, WILLIAM, and SCHELLING, VIVIENNE (1991), *Memory and Modernity: Popular Culture in Latin America* (London).

SPIVAK, GAYATRI CHAKRAVORTY (1993), *Outside in the Teaching Machine* (London).

SWANSON, PHILIP (1994), 'Tyrants and Trash: Sex, Class and Culture in *La casa de los espíritos*', *Bulletin of Hispanic Studies*, 71: 217-37.

ZURITA, RAÚL (1993), 'Chile: Literature, Language and Society (1973-1983)', *Travesía*, 2/2.

5

Topologies of Catastrophe
Horror and Abjection in Diamela Eltit's
Vaca sagrada

JO LABANYI

IN an interview given in 1991, just before the publication of her novel *Vaca sagrada*, Chilean writer Diamela Eltit described how her experience of reading *For Whom the Bell Tolls* at the age of 10, while ill, set up a lasting association in her mind between writing, the body, illness, and death (Piña 1991: 227).[1] The central image of *Vaca sagrada* is menstruation, which traditionally associates the female body with defilement. What interested Eltit here was the female body not as biology but as cultural map:

Como metáfora, como hecho simbólico, parto de la menstruación; pero más que referirme a este tema desde la perspectiva biológica, me interesa . . . ver ahí qué miedos detona, qué imágenes, qué fantasías. . . . Me parece que el cuerpo es uno de los territorios más ideologizados por la cultura, y se ha transformado especialmente en un territorio moral del cual no se libra nadie. (Piña 1991: 249)

My starting-point is the metaphor, the symbolic fact of menstruation; but rather than deal with the subject from a biological point of view, I want . . . to see what fears it triggers, what images, what fantasies. . . . I think the body is one of the most densely ideologized cultural sites, above all it's been turned into a moral territory none of us can escape.[2]

---

[1] Diamela Eltit was born in Santiago de Chile in 1949. Outside of Latin America she is probably known chiefly for her novels—*Lumpérica* (1983), *Por la patria* (1986), *El cuarto mundo* (1988), and *Vaca sagrada* (1991)—and for her sociological study, *El padre mío* (1989). However, she is also and increasingly involved in scriptwriting and performance and video art.

[2] All translations from the Spanish, including those from *Vaca sagrada*, are my own.

Menstruation is seen as a way of exploring horror: 'miedos' (fears). In this essay I want to look at the uncomfortable relationship established in *Vaca sagrada* between the female body and political terror: specifically that of the military dictatorship in Chile, through which Eltit lived. The novel shows how political terror inscribes itself on the female body because the latter constitutes an economy of horror: what Julia Kristeva, in her essay *Powers of Horror: An Essay on Abjection*, calls a 'topology of catastrophe'. The relationship is an uncomfortable one because it raises the question of whether the female body is a zone of resistance to political terror, or an accomplice to it. The equation between horror and the feminine allows it—requires it?—to be both.

In *Powers of Horror*, Kristeva develops the anthropologist Mary Douglas's suggestion that, if on the one hand 'The social body constrains the way the physical body is perceived', so too 'The physical experience of the body, always modified by the social categories through which it is known, sustains a particular view of society' (Douglas 1973: 93). Douglas's insight allows a political reading of the concept of 'writing the body' that is central to French feminist theory, rescuing it from the tendency to slip into biological essentialism for which it has been criticized. In particular, Douglas notes that societies concerned with the protection of boundaries and fear of contamination are likely to be obsessed with the control of bodily boundaries: bodily orifices and everything that penetrates or issues from the body will be seen as a source of pollution (Douglas 1973: 16–17; 1984: 115, 121). Persons in a marginal state, even if they are not doing anything morally wrong, will similarly be seen as a threat to the body politic because they are neither firmly inside it nor firmly outside it (Douglas 1984: 95–6). But, as Douglas notes, those societies that regard the marginal—meaning everything that subverts boundaries—as a threat also implicitly recognize its agency: the policing of boundaries curbs the power of the marginal while contributing to it (Douglas 1984: 94).

This emphasis on the agency of the marginal is clearly attractive to Kristeva, who notes that many of the examples of pollution discussed by Douglas relate to the female body. Following Douglas's argument, she concludes that the female body is likely to be associated with pollution in societies where women are powerful (Kristeva 1982: 64–5, 77). In fact, Douglas had proposed a number of different models of the body which can operate as cultural ciphers, according to the priorities of the society concerned, not all of which are concerned with the policing of boundaries (Douglas 1973: 16–17). Kristeva, how-ever, argues that all societies constitute themselves through an exclusion process: what in psychoanalytical terms is called 'abjection' (Kristeva 1982: 2). Culture requires the demarca-tion of the limits of the 'clean and proper body' (in French 'le corps propre'), achieved by expelling (abjecting) that which is labelled 'improper' or 'abominable'. Just as Douglas notes that the marginal is both inside and outside, so Kristeva argues that the abject (the source of abomination) is at some level recog-nized as part of the body from which it has been expelled; in accordance with the double logic of the disavowal process, the 'abject' is both that which is expelled and that part of the self which inspires horror. One 'abjects' and 'is abject'. The move from the former position to the latter, such that the results of one's actions come to be experienced as suffered, is what Kristeva calls 'passivization'; she cites the example of Freud's patient, little Hans, whose fear of blinding expressed itself through a fear of being blinded, a motif central to *Vaca sagrada* (1982: 39–40). This passivization process, whereby the self which has constituted itself through abjection comes to expe-rience itself as abject, is for Kristeva the basis of masochism (1982: 5). The latter, consequently, involves a splitting process: the separating of the self which abjects (active) from that part of the self experienced as abject (passive) (1982: 6–7). The 'fallen' self constituted by the abject—the 'deject' in Kristeva's terminolgy—is a spatial construction for whom the question 'Who am I?' is recast as the question 'Where am I?' (1982: 8). The deject can never escape 'his' constitutional state of dejec-tion for 'he' can never know where 'he' stands. The deject is 'a deviser of territories' who 'never stops demarcating his uni-verse whose fluid confines . . . constantly question his solidity and impel him to start afresh. . . . He is on a journey, during the night, the end of which keeps receding' (1982: 8). We shall come back to the use of the male subject pronoun and possessive adjective shortly.

Kristeva also notes that abjection, in offering release from the constraints of boundaries, is experienced both as horror and as *jouissance*: a 'sublime alienation' (1982: 8–9, 59). Douglas had concluded that holiness is wholeness: a state of perfection in which things conform to the class to which they belong (1984: 53). Kristeva, however, sees the ecstatic release from boundaries, which allows the subject to experience the 'power of horror', as the mark of the sacred. Or rather, the abject is a 'sacred configuration' (1982: 6) because it allows the self to experience formlessness while distancing it from that formlessness by equating the latter with horror (1982: 9, 54). The experience of horror is also a defence against horror. As Kristeva comments: 'One thus understands why so many victims of the abject are its fascinated victims—if not its submissive and willing ones' (1982: 9). The title of *Vaca sagrada* (*Sacred Cow*) similarly links defilement with the sacred: just as the body and products of the sacred cow defile because they are holy, so woman is degraded (cow) and revered (sacred).

A major problem raised by Kristeva's brilliant analysis is the lack of any explicit discussion of whether women experience the abject differently from men. This question seems paramount since Kristeva's concept of abjection is a clearly gendered one: her major addition to Douglas's discussion is her observation that the female body, with its flows and 'holes', stands as an image of the leaking boundaries that threaten the solidity of the self. This observation would seem to provide a basic insight into why masochism should be a predominantly female drive. Here, Kristeva's argument could usefully be related to the work of Jessica Benjamin, who has analysed female masochism as a product of the post-Enlightenment Western notion that the individual self is constituted through separation from the pre-Oedipal union with the mother, producing a consequent devaluation of the feminine which requires women to base their identity on self-denial. Kristeva similarly relates the abject to the pre-Oedipal mother–child bond. Noting that the 'abomination' listed in Leviticus, discussed by Douglas, stresses the polluting nature of milk and menstrual blood, she suggests that it is above all the maternal body that is feared (1982: 56–9, 64–5, 69–71, 77–85, 91, 96, 99–100, 106). As Elizabeth Gross comments, Kristeva's association of the abject with the feminine places it in opposition to 'the paternal, rule-governed symbolic order' (Gross 1990: 93).

Kristeva's opening section uses the first-person 'I' (which may or may not refer to herself as a woman writer) to talk of the subject who creates/suffers abjection, but this quickly slips into the masculine third-person 'he' used almost exclusively for the rest of the text. The reason for this masculine usage is no doubt that, for part of the self to be abjected, there has to be a self in the first place, and the predominantly Lacanian framework used—not uncritically—by Kristeva implies that, since the female is defined by lack, a female self is an impossibility. Thus, on the one occasion when Kristeva uses the formula 'she as well as he', she qualifies this with the observation that, when a woman enters the realm of horror, 'it is usually to gratify, in a very maternal fashion, the desire for the abject that insures the life . . . of the man whose symbolic authority she accepts' (1982: 54). Although she goes on to suggest that, on rare occasions, a woman may 'tie her desire' to the abject through writing (presumably because language is the mark of the phallic symbolic order which woman must inevitably internalize), in practice the writers whose work she analyses as examples of modern 'abject' literature are all male: Céline's *Journey to the End of the Night* above all, and more briefly Dostoyevsky, Proust, Joyce, Borges, and Artaud.[3]

This essay offers *Vaca sagrada* as a case of the female abject writing missing from Kristeva's discussion. Eltit's novel suggests that woman's exploration of the abject is not an expression of a 'maternal' desire to shore up male authority—the abject female body it depicts is not a maternal one, and it is associated with images of male castration—but that it is a way of dealing with her own precarious sense of self: a self constructed through a bodily relationship not only to men but also to the *polis* (the city). The most significant difference between Kristeva's and Eltit's exploration of abjection is the latter's insistence that horror is not just the projection of inner drives but a material, political reality. Kristeva leaves in abeyance the question 'is the social determined by the subjective, or is it the other way round?' (1982: 67), but in practice concentrates on abjection as a psychological projection: hence its association in her work with the male subject constituted by the construction of boundaries. When, as in *Vaca sagrada*, the chief source of horror lies without,

---

[3] In discussing the 'jouissance' afforded by the abject she mentions mystical discourse, but her only example is again a man: St Francis of Assisi (1992: 127). This is particularly surprising since mysticism is often seen as a specifically feminine form of self-expression; see, for example, Irigaray 1985.

it is woman—with her permeable boundaries—who is likely to be the more seriously affected. What particularly interests Eltit is the question of the consequences for women of the equation of horror with the feminine.

Eltit has insisted that, for her, the feminine stands for everything that is marginal:

si lo femenino es aquello oprimido por los poderes centrales . . . podemos, por ejemplo, pensar lo étnico, las minorías sexuales e incluso a países completos, como lo femenino. (Piña 1991: 244)

if the feminine is that which is oppressed by the central system of domination . . . we can, say, think of ethnic groups, sexual minorities and even whole countries as the feminine.

This bracketing together of different kinds of marginality may be questionable, but the point Eltit is making is that, for her, to write as a woman is to be political. As she has noted, the theme of margins runs through all her work (Piña 1991: 238–9, 242).[4] By 'marginality' she means 'exclusion', but she also insists that the marginalized are not just passive victims but construct a way of life out of their marginality (Piña 1991: 240). As we shall see, *Vaca sagrada* depicts abjection, which requires and problematizes margins, as a dual active–passive process.

Eltit's focus on margins poses the problem of identity as one of positioning. In *Vaca sagrada*—as in *Powers of Horror*—the self is a spatial construct dependent on the demarcation of an external zone of horror: 'Convulsa, mis dudas se remitían, en esos días, al peligro de afuera' (In a state of turmoil, I transferred my anxieties at that time to the danger outside) (Eltit 1991*b*: 31). But the horror outside constantly threatens to install itself within: 'La ciudad entera tenía un virus helado que deambulaba por dentro de los habitantes' (The whole city was chilled by a virus worming its way through its inhabitants) (1991*b*: 155). This spatial instability is depicted in the novel through repeated images of falling (literal and metaphorical),

---

[4] In the late 1970s, Eltit embarked with Lotty Rosenfeld on an experimental video project documenting Santiago's *lumpen* elements; this later gave rise to the book *El padre mío* (1989), reproducing the discourse of a male tramp. Her first novel *Lumpérica* focuses on a female down-and-out. Her third novel *El cuarto mundo* (1988) deals with incest as a form of marginality at the centre. I have not been able to obtain a copy of her second novel *Por la patria* (1989), which she describes as connected with the decision in 1983 to send common delinquents to the former concentration camp of Pisagua (see Piña 1991: 242).

reminiscent of Kristeva's concept of the self as 'deject'. The self is thus a 'deviser of territories' that have always to be reconstructed: 'Desarmada, confundida, dejé atrás toda mi historia para reiniciar el aprendizaje del mapa de la ciudad' (Disarmed, confused, I left my whole history behind me to relearn the map of the city) (1991*b*: 31). Although the city functions here as a projection of the self, it nonetheless represents a very real horror: that of the 'disappeared':

En ese momento la sensación de muerte se acababa de instalar en la ciudad. Manuel no dio ninguna señal de acercamiento hasta que me enteré de que había sido detenido en el Sur junto a toda su familia. (1991*b*: 31)

At that moment a sense of death had installed itself in the city. I heard nothing from Manuel till I learnt he'd been arrested in the South with the rest of his family.

The novel's other spatial image, 'el Sur' (the South), similarly functions both as a psychological projection—an exclusion zone idealized by the narrator and Manuel to make its horror palatable, 'transfigurando todo aquello que nos horrorizaba' (transfiguring everything we found loathsome) (1991*b*: 19)—and as a real zone of horror, since it is there that Manuel is arrested.[5] The psychological process of ab-jection is placed in the context of political ab-jection: the 'disappeared'. Despite her emphasis on the abject as psychological projection, Kristeva also notes that the ultimate form of abjection is the Nazi concentration camp (1982: 3–4).

The novel relates the positioning of the self with regard to the city to the psychological process of narcissism. Kristeva notes that abjection is a 'narcissistic crisis' (1982: 14) because the fascination with a self that is other involves a recognition of the instability of boundaries; she also notes that the phobic self is narcissistic because it is obsessed with the double process of looking at the abject and being looked at as abject. Here too, Eltit's narrator is reacting to political repression: her narcissistic conversion of her self into 'la espectadora de su propio espectáculo' (the spectator of her own spectacle) (1991*b*: 68)

---

[5] This dual figuring of the South corresponds to its contradictory role in Chilean culture as the image, promoted by Neruda, of an idyllic, unspoilt nature (shown in the novel to be a lie), and as the location after the 1973 military coup of several notorious concentration camps.

is a response to surveillance by the city: 'el centro de la ciudad era uno de los lugares en donde me sentía más vigilada' (the city centre was one of the places where I was most aware of being watched) (1991*b*: 52).[6] She deals with this surveillance by constructing herself as abject object for display, rather than simply allowing herself to be abjected by the city. If for Kristeva the splitting process involved in the narcissistic contemplation of the self as other is a form of passivization, Eltit suggests rather that narcissism permits a self reduced to object status to recuperate its subjectivity. But this is achieved at the cost of internalizing abjection.

This dual active–passive mode is reflected in the splitting of the narrative voice into a 'yo' (subject) and an 'ella' (object): 'Resiste Francisca, agarrada al cabezal de la cama con todas mis fuerzas' (Francisca resists, gripping the bedstead with all my strength) (1991*b*: 94).[7] As Kristeva puts it: 'when the boundary between subject and object is shaken, when even the limit between inside and outside becomes uncertain, the narrative is what is challenged first' (1982: 141). This narrative splitting makes the self simultaneously active (looking) and passive (looked at):

Armó la figura de la desdicha y cuando levantó la mirada ya no era ella la que miraba. Era otra. . . . Sintió la necesidad de un espejo y se levantó silenciosamente a buscar su imagen.(1991*b*: 160–1)

She constructed a figure of wretchedness and when she raised her gaze it was no longer she that was looking. It was someone else. . . . She felt the need for a mirror and silently got up to find her image.

Although in this example the female narrator is being looked at by her male lover, it is she who constructs herself as object.

[6] Eltit has talked of how the experimental video group, Colectivo de Acción de Arte (CADA), with which she worked in the late 1970s, focused on the city since public spaces were the main target of military repression (Piña 1991: 233). Her first novel *Lumpérica*, set in a public square, explicitly takes the city under surveillance as its theme: a female down-and-out exposes herself narcissistically to the spotlights trained on her. In watching herself be watched, she makes herself abject in the double sense of externalizing the self while marking it as abominable (metaphorically expressed through her self-mutilations; Eltit performed excerpts from the novel in a Santiago brothel with her wrists slashed). This emphasis on representation places Eltit's writing within a postmodernist tradition; for discussion of this aspect of her work, see Williams 1994.
[7] In Eltit's words: 'se me complicó el narrador, se me amplió, se extravió' (my narrator grew and got complicated, out of control) (Piña 1991: 249–50).

Throughout the novel, mirrors reflect the self back as other, and others function as mirrors reflecting back an abject/ abjected self. This splitting, which is both a defence against the precariousness of ego boundaries and a reminder of it, produces an uncertainty as to the identity of the female narrator, who at times is Francisca, and at others may be Ana or an unnamed third party (the relationship between the unnamed narrator and Ana is based on a typically abject mutual attraction-loathing, such that they merge and split alternately). Kristeva refers to this splitting process as 'a forfeited existence' (1982: 9), a phrase echoed when the unnamed narrator, her desires 'usurped' by those of Ana and Sergio, describes herself as condemned to 'una existencia despojada' (1991*b*: 176).

This narrative splitting is always between female selves (there is a possible exception on page 151, where the normally female narrator is addressed with a masculine adjective). Gender identity is thus not disturbed. The male lovers shared by the various incarnations of this shifting narrator (Manuel, Sergio) are also driven by abjection, realized through their bodily relationship to woman perceived as abject. Manuel begs the narrator to 'pollute' him with her menstrual blood (1991*b*: 25). Sergio is attracted to Francisca because he senses she is on the verge of an abyss: 'Francisca lo salvaba. Para Sergio el amor a esa caída era la única posibilidad de evitar su propio vértigo' (Francisca was his salvation. For Sergio loving that fall was the only way of avoiding his own vertigo) (1991*b*: 66).

The female selves in the novel, however, experience abjection through their own bodies. They are not simply reacting to their male lovers' perception of them as abject; they need to make themselves abject in order to have a sense of self. They invite male violence to satisfy not their lover's needs but their own; it is this that makes the novel's treatment of female masochism disturbing. When Francisca achieves orgasm through violence, she is constituting herself as conventional passive object: 'la golpeó con el puño cerrado en uno de sus ojos, y sólo entonces ella se aferró a él para lograr la unión más perfecta que tuvieron (he punched her in the eye with his clenched fist, and only then did she cling to him achieving their most perfect union) (1991*b*: 73). But the unnamed narrator (also Francisca at this point?) actively instigates her repeated pursuit by a man waiting in the street to blind her:

'Ofrecí mi visión para que él no me siguiera más, para no necesitar que siempre anduviera detrás de mí' (I offered up my sight so he wouldn't follow me any more, so I wouldn't need him to keep pursuing me) (1991*b*: 114). Blindness and the active pursuit of horror are also associated in Manuel's abandoned wife Marta, whose eye is clouded by a mote, and who invites the narrator's false story of her passionate romance with Manuel to confirm her worst fears:

me pregunté por lo que buscaba esa muchacha sureña con un ojo nublado. No encontré más respuesta que el miedo. El miedo . . . estaba traspasándonos de manera silenciosa e irreversible. (1991*b*: 20–1)

I asked myself what that girl from the south with a mote in her eye was seeking. The only answer I could think of was fear. Fear. . . was seeping into us silently and irrevocably.

Here, the seeking out of fear is depicted as an antidote to the climate of political fear in the city (represented in the novel by the repeated motif of night). By blinding oneself physically and psychologically, one stops the 'seepage' of political terror into the self. But one also installs the night (darkness) within. In *Powers of Horror*, Kristeva produces a political reading of the Oedipus story, whereby his self-blinding ('exclusion from sight') mirrors his self-exile ('a spatial exclusion') as a 'symbolic substitute intended for building the wall, reinforcing the boundary that wards off opprobrium' (1982: 84). By keeping horror at bay (out of the city, out of sight), Oedipus saves (purifies) both city and self. But this expulsion (abjection) is achieved at the expense of recognizing the existence of the abject within the city (incest), and of inscribing it on one's own body in the form of a wound:

Blinding is thus an image of splitting; it marks, on the very body, the alteration of the self and clean into the defiled—the scar taking the place of a revealed and yet invisible abjection . . . In return for which city-state and knowledge can endure. (1982: 84)

This raises the question of the individual's collusion with the State. In showing how women—and men—internalize political horror by constructing the female body as abject, Eltit raises similar questions, even—particularly?—though she suggests that women can be agents in this process.

As a bleeding wound, blinding is related to the novel's central motif of menstruation. The narrator becomes narcissistically fixated on the emission of menstrual blood from her 'hermosa herida constante entre las piernas' (beautiful constant wound between my legs) (1991*b*: 103) as a defence against Manuel's arrest and the general climate of terror in the city:

> La sangre que expulsaba era la única respuesta. . . . Debía presentar la sangre para evitar mi propio ajusticiamiento . . . Terminaba empapada en mi propia sangre para no olvidar lo que era la sangre. . . . Manuel estaba detenido en el Sur y mi sangre conseguía suspender su muerte por una noche. . . . Sufría una especie de desintegración, sentía que la ciudad podía explotar por todas partes. . . . No intenté frenarlo porque necesitaba permanecer atada a la violencia para equiparar la otra violencia. (1991*b*: 50–1)

> The blood I was emitting was my only reply. . . . I had to go on producing blood to avoid my own execution . . . I ended up soaked in my own blood so as not to forget what blood was. . . . Manuel was under arrest in the South and my blood could stave off his death for a night. . . . I was suffering a kind of disintegration, I felt the whole city could explode. . . . I made no attempt to halt the process because I needed to stay bound to violence to match that other violence.

Kristeva suggests that the 'erotization of abjection' is a demand for more flow and discharge, and at the same time 'an attempt at stopping the hemorrhage' (1982: 55), since it permits the ecstatic release from boundaries while labelling the self as loathsome and therefore safely other. In *Vaca sagrada* the flow of menstrual blood, traversing bodily boundaries, gives rise to a savage form of *jouissance*: 'Era ahí, entre la sangre, cuando tocábamos el punto más preciso de la turbulencia genital' (It was there, in that blood, that we reached the keenest point of genital turbulence) (1991*b*: 25). But the bleeding female body is also associated with dissolution of the self in the form of death: 'la sangre había perdido en mí cualquier rango que no fuera su irreversible conexión con la muerte' (blood had for me lost any status other than its irrevocable connection with death) (1991*b*: 51). The invisible sense of death which infiltrates the boundaries of the self—'Estaba adentro de mi cabeza y estaba sólo en el espacio exterior' (It was inside my head and it was solely in the world outside) (1991*b*: 41)—triggers a sequence of childhood memories of bleeding female bodies (1991*b*: 43–5): the narrator (Francisca?) cutting her leg on broken glass, and her pregnant dog haemorrhaging to death,

linked to her grandmother whose bleeding, dying body is recalled throughout the novel as a horrific image of the collapse of
boundaries: 'Brotaba sangre por todos los orificios del cuerpo'
(Blood was spouting from all her bodily orifices) (1991*b*: 161).

The narrator's abject autoeroticism is also illustrated through
her ingestion and expulsion of food. Following Douglas, Kristeva
notes that food is regarded as one of the chief sources of pollution because, like menstrual flow, it traverses bodily boundaries. The novel insists on images of vomit, caused by excessive
drinking (1991*b*: 16) or by the bulimic gorging of rotten food:
'Sobras, materias putrefactas, gusanos empezaron a atraer mi
fantasía' (I started to crave leftovers, decaying matter, maggots)
(1991*b*: 89). At another point the narrator goes through an
anorexic phase which produces a disgusted fascination with
her own body, 'expandida, fracturada, con la piel marcada
por una inusitada transparencia' (distended, ruptured, its skin
tinged with a rare transparency) (1991*b*: 126). Kristeva describes the internalization of the abject as a fascination with
the body's workings:

The body's inside shows up in order to compensate for the collapse
of the border between inside and outside. It is as if the skin, a fragile
container, no longer guaranteed the integrity of one's 'own and clean
self' but, scraped or transparent . . . , gave way before the dejection of
its contents. Urine, blood, sperm, excrement then show up in order
to reassure a subject that is lacking its 'own and clean self' (1982: 53)

This is also a fascination with waste, which Douglas and Kristeva
rank alongside food as a major category of the abject. Indeed,
polluted food is waste since it may not be eaten and, if it is,
causes vomiting. Kristeva associates menstrual blood with the
maternal body; Eltit has linked her use of menstruation in *Vaca
sagrada* to the concept of waste, for it is blood expelled precisely because reproduction is not taking place: 'una sangre
que desde la inutilidad . . . marca una relación corporal' (a
blood whose uselessness . . . determines a bodily relationship)
(Piña 1991: 249). The novel insists on the bleeding female
body as an image, not of fertility, but of disintegration and
death. Kristeva has noted that the ultimate sign of waste is the
corpse, and that it is because it converts living bodies into
waste that the concentration camp is the most horrific form of
abjection (1982: 3–4, 108–10, 149–50).

Vaca sagrada relates the unproductive female body–which bleeds and vomits—to the economic repression of Chile under military dictatorship, which marginalizes workers from the production process. Eltit has said that, in this novel, she wanted for the first time to tackle the concrete issue of systems of production (Piña 1991: 249). Throughout the novel, the narrator refers to herself, and to her hand which writes, as 'asalariada' (waged). At several points, she talks of wage cuts and mass lay-offs of workers (1991*b*: 94, 99–100, 109–10, 112–13, 128). While Sergio gives up looking for a job and transfers his sense of abjection (expulsion) on to the narrator's body, she continues the search because, for her, abjection is survival: 'Yo, en cambio, me sumaba a todas la iniciativas internándome en una zona de fracasos. . . . Quería sobrevivir' (Whereas I took up every chance, plunging into a zone of failures. . . . I wanted to survive) (1991*b*: 128). The relationship between economic redundancy and a female bodily economy based on abjection is an ambivalent one. On the one hand, her menstrual bleeding is 'priceless': 'no tiene precio, no es asunto de asalariadas, no lo hacen las trabajadoras' (it doesn't have a price, it's nothing to do with wage-earners, it's not what women workers do) (1991*b*: 104). The lack of solidity of her body prevents her from taking a clear-cut political stand: 'Tengo algo interiormente resbaladizo, que me impide alinearme con las trabajadoras' (Something inside me that keeps shifting stops me siding with the women workers) (1991*b*: 105). But at the same time her sexuality places her in another kind of 'contract': 'Soy solamente una asalariada, una trabajadora entre muchas, curvada, abierta de piernas' (I'm just a wage-earner, another woman worker, bowed, legs parted) (1991*b*: 105).

Towards the end of the novel, the narrator takes part in a female workers' demonstration: a literal 'body politics' whose slogan, demanding the right to 'body room', is tattooed on the demonstrators' thighs in another wounding which becomes infected and abject (1991*b*: 131–2). The demonstration takes the form of a *fiesta* which becomes a carnivalesque parody of political in-fighting. The narrator concludes:

Las trabajadoras estaban infiltradas desde sus propios cerebros. No habría entendimiento. Habría sólo una abortada danza, el maquillaje, la parodia verbal. (1991*b*: 170)

The women workers' heads were infiltrated. There would be no agreement. Just an abortive dance, make-up, verbal parody.

Earlier, the narrator had had an anticipatory vision of the women workers' failure, expressed through the image of bleeding:

Las trabajadoras caminan en línea recta y sangran por las narices. Quiero sangrar, desfilando con el puño en alto, gritando por la restitución de nuestros derechos. . . . Sangrando, con el puño en alto, alcanzo a entender que aún sobro en todas partes. (1991*b*: 115–16)

The women workers march in a straight line and blood streams from their noses. I want to bleed, marching with fist raised, demanding the restitution of our rights. . . . Bleeding, fist raised, I come to realize that everywhere I'm still redundant.

The implication is that the attempt at 'body politics' is 'abortive' because the permeability of the women's bleeding, wounded bodies makes the adoption of a firm position impossible. The feminine self stands in opposition to the paternal symbolic order, but this does not make it revolutionary in any straightforward sense; it cannot represent political opposition because it is subversive in the sense of undermining all oppositions. Towards the end of the novel, the narrator finds herself trapped in a passive, unproductive routine in which bleeding no longer affords *jouissance*:

Ya no sangraba. Supe que ya no sangraba cuando dejé de esperar la llegada de la sangre. . . . Sangraba sí, seguía sangrando, pero únicamente como el deber físico que me imponía una repetición biológica desprovista de toda utilidad. Por inercia y desde un signo monótono me había uniformizado con los otros cuerpos que estaban obligados a acusar los signos de una herida, el costo de un nacimiento inmemorial. (1991*b*: 178)

I'd stopped bleeding. I knew I'd stopped bleeding when I stopped looking forward to starting to bleed. . . . I was bleeding, of course, I went on bleeding, but purely as a physical duty required by a senseless biological routine. Through inertia and repetition, I'd become like all the other bodies obliged to bear witness to a wounding, the price of an ancestral birth.

This bodily economy whose 'price' is a bleeding wound is 'un territorio infértil' (an infertile territory) that is also 'un espacio sin historia' (a place without history) (1991*b*: 179).

It is at this point that the narrator decides to journey to the South, to discover 'cuál era la realidad posible de una historia, cómo se llegaba a construir la farsa de una historia' (what the reality of a history might be, how to construct the farce of a history) (1991*b*: 179). This journey to the zone of horror that is the South—the image of night used here, as with the city, brings to mind Céline's *Journey to the End of the Night*, Kristeva's major example of abject literature—is a journey to a verbal space, created initially by the narrator's and Manuel's 'mentiras' (lies), and at the end of the novel through the narrator's decision to start writing in order to 'inventar para mí una historia con un final que se hiciera legible' (invent for myself a history/ story with a readable ending) (1991*b*: 184). Writing creates a history which is a 'lie' and a 'farce' because it is a story, but which nevertheless is real because it gives reality meaning: makes it 'legible'.

The narrator's other reason for writing is to 'combatir el vuelo de los pájaros' (combat the birds' flight) (1991*b*: 184). Throughout the novel birds, and the related words 'bandada' (flock) and 'desbandada' (dispersal, as when a flock of birds breaks up), function as a complex network of images of the phallic symbolic order. Apart from the traditional association of flying with the sexual act (the French *bander*—to have an erection—is perhaps also relevant),[8] in Chilean Spanish, as Eltit notes (Piña 1991: 250), *pájaro* (bird) is a term for 'penis'. The opening of the novel describes the sense of horror in the city as a 'forma pajaril' (birdlike form) (1991*b*: 11). It also links the bird imagery to the phallic symbolic order that is writing: 'se han desbandado todas mis historias' (all my stories have dispersed like a flock of birds) (1991*b*: 11). The narrator's 'body writing'—like the tattooed 'grafía popular en el musol' (workers' thigh writing) (1991*b*: 131) of the women demonstrators— prevents her from adopting a firm political position because the 'wounded' female body refuses clear-cut definition; but it is this which allows it to resist the phallic order—the 'forma pajaril'—governing both the city and language. As a wound, menstruation is an alternative form of writing: 'Debía presentar la sangre . . . tenía que inventarlo todo en esas noches ágrafas' (I had to go on producing blood . . . I had to invent everything

---

[8] My thanks to Anny Brooksbank Jones for pointing this out.

during those nights without writing) (1991*b*: 50). Kristeva sees defilement rituals as a form of writing:

Finally, the frequency of defilement rituals in societies *without writing* leads me to think that such cathartic rites function like a 'writing of the real.' They parcel out, delineate an order, a framework, a sociality. . . . One might ask, proceding in reverse, if all writing is not a second level rite, at the level of language, that is, which causes one to be reminded, through the linguistic signs themselves, of the demarcations that precondition them and go beyond them. Indeed, writing causes the subject who ventures in it to confront an archaic authority, on the nether side of the proper Name. The maternal connotations of this authority never escaped great writers, no more than the coming face to face with what we have called abjection. (Kristeva's italics, 1982: 74–5)

Writing is a 'sublimation of abjection' (Kristeva 1982: 26) because the act of demarcation involves a cathartic confrontation with what one is trying to exclude.

Kristeva suggests that, for the male subject, abjection, in its obsession with the inner workings of the body, is an immersion in the 'horrors of maternal bowels' which, because they are imagined inside the self, 'enables him to avoid coming face to face with an other', thus sparing him 'the risk of castration' (1982: 53). This implies that abjection is not the 'collapse of paternal law' as Kristeva claims (1982: 20), but rather a way of experiencing what paternal law forbids while allowing the latter to remain intact. Writing as a woman, Eltit links abjection with the castration of the male symbolic order. The female narrator's childhood experiences of sexuality are associated with bleeding male bodies: that of the first penis she saw when a man, his diseased legs covered in blood, exposed himself to her (1991*b*: 46); that of Juan, interrupting her 'games' with her cousin in the bathroom, with his eye gouged out by the spoke of a bicycle wheel (1991*b*: 106). Men's bodies too are abject and vulnerable: 'un pájaro en agonía' (a dying bird) (1991*b*: 46), 'un pájaro degollado' (a beheaded bird) (1991*b*: 102). Birds in the novel function both as the image of a repressive order, and as an image of ecstatic release. Manuel in prison, Francisca's dying grandmother, and the female demonstrators are all pursued by a 'bandada' (flock of birds) (1991*b*: 49, 65, 69, 74, 171). Birds are constantly linked with the horrors of night: 'Hubo una noche extremadamente hostil, una bandada de pájaros enloqueciendo' (There was one excessively hostile night, a flock of birds in a fury) (1991*b*: 102). Their association with wounding and blinking recalls Hitchcock's film *The Birds*:

Hay tres enormes pájaros, pájaros negros, parados en la cumbre de un acantilado. . . . Uno de esos pájaros . . . viene a mí a una velocidad electrónica. . . . En el sueño ya estoy muerta debajo del agua y el pájaro se sumerge para picotearme. . . . Caí desde lo alto de un acantilado, fracturándome la cabeza después de que el pájaro negro me voló un ojo. (1991*b*: 117)

There are three huge birds, black birds, perched on a clifftop. . . . One of those birds . . . comes at me electronically propelled. . . . In my dream I'm already dead underwater and the bird dives down to peck at me. . . . I fell from a clifftop, fracturing my skull after the black bird pecked out my eye.

The female narrator's journey to the South ends with the apocalyptic vision of a vast flock of birds migrating north, 'dividiendo mi retina' (splitting my retina) (1991*b*: 183) and themselves becoming a 'gran ojo ciego' (huge blind eye) blocking the horizon (1991*b*: 184).[9] Their blind aggression and determination makes them an image of horror: 'un único cuerpo desplegado en monstruosos movimientos dibujando en el cielo la imagen de una pesadilla' (a single body unfurled in monstrous movements, sketching a nightmare image in the sky) (1991*b*: 181). As an image of horror, they are also an image of the sublime, producing in the narrator a kind of catharsis:

Pero lanzaban, especialmente, graznidos de placer . . . un graznido público tan lícito que transformara ese vuelo cobarde de los pájaros en una epopeya redentora. (1991*b*: 183)

But above all their cawing was an expression of pleasure . . . a cawing so public and legitimate it transformed the birds' cowardly flight into a redemptive epic.

The image of 'la bandada' is, in the end, indistinguishable from its opposite 'la desbandada', for both involve movement

[9] Eltit has said that this final image was based on the endless flocks of migrating birds she saw when flying from Chile to Mexico, where she was until recently Chilean cultural attaché (Piña 1991: 250).

and flight. In a similar way, the city is an image both of repression and of chaos, where 'se empiezan a desbandar los signos' (signs are thrown into flight) (1991*b*: 41). The narrator's final confrontation with horror in the form of the migrating birds sends her back to the city to write, because she has realized 'que sólo tenían realidad los espacios y las bandadas' (that places and flocks of birds are the only reality) (1991*b*: 184). She will thus opt for writing 'una historia cuya forma era, en extremo, peligrosa' (a story whose form was especially dangerous) from a marginal position where sensations 'que pertenecían a lugares diversos' (belonging to different places) meet (1991*b*: 187). It is in the middle of the night that she starts to classify her papers, tapes, and photos ready to write, for she has learned that writing, as an attempt to order experience, is an encounter with horror.

In his classic study *Male Fantasies* (1987), which Kristeva seems not to know despite considerable similarity between their work, Klaus Theweleit suggests that Fascism is the result of a male horror of the unboundedness of women's—and particularly mothers'—bodies. This appears to leave women in a position of political innocence. Eltit is not arguing that women's bodies have been made into an image of horror by men afraid of being engulfed by the maternal body, but that both men and women turn the female body, with its bleeding wound, into an image of horror that helps stave off political terror. This allows men to abject horror successfully, by associating it with an alien body, albeit one that is internalized. But for women the abjection process involves self-identification with horror. This makes the female body a replication of the horror outside; it is for this reason above all that the female narrator and her fellow women demonstrators are unable to take a firm opposition line. But the unboundedness of the female body also makes it a threat to all forms of control; the more it becomes identified with horror, and the more this identification becomes self-conscious, the more it is able to provide a kind of salvation. *Vaca sagrada* is a political novel but it cannot be called a committed novel— Eltit has said she hates 'right-on' feminist fiction (Piña 1991: 244)—for it argues that both women and men must recognize their need for, and complicity with, horror. The equation of horror with the female body makes this an especially uncomfortable message for women readers.

LIST OF WORKS CITED

BENJAMIN, JESSICA (1990), *The Bonds of Love: Psychoanalysis, Feminism and the Problem of Domination* (London; orig. 1988).

DOUGLAS, MARY (1973), *Natural Symbols: Explorations in Cosmology* (Harmondsworth).

—— (1984), *Purity and Danger: An Analysis of the Concepts of Pollution and Taboo* (London; orig. 1969).

ELTIT, DIAMELA (1986), *Por la patria* (Santiago).

—— (1988), *El cuarto mundo* (Santiago).

—— (1989), *El padre mío* (Santiago).

—— (1991*a*), *Lumpérica* (Santiago; orig. 1983).

—— (1991*b*), *Vaca sagrada* (Buenos Aires).

—— (1995), *Sacred Cow*, trans. Amanda Hopkinson (London).

GROSS, ELIZABETH (1990), 'The Body of Signification', in John Fletcher and Andrew Benjamin (eds.), *Abjection, Melancholia and Love: The Work of Julia Kristeva* (London, 1990), 80–103.

IRIGARAY, LUCE (1985), *Speculum of the Other Woman*, trans. Gillian C. Gill, (Ithaca, NY; orig. 1974).

KRISTEVA, JULIA (1982), *Powers of Horror: An Essay on Abjection* (New York; orig. 1980).

PIÑA, JUAN ANDRÉS (1991), 'Diamela Eltit: Escritos sobre un cuerpo', in *Conversaciones con la narrativa chilena* (Santiago), 223–54.

THEWELEIT, KLAUS (1987), *Male Fantasies*, 1 (Cambridge).

WILLIAMS, RAYMOND L. (1994), *The Postmodern Novel in Latin America* (London).

6

Narcissus in Bloom
The Desiring Subject in Modern Latin American Narrative—María Luisa Bombal and Juan Rulfo*

ADRIANA MÉNDEZ RODENAS

Para Doña Victoria y Joseph

ONE of the most subtly disparaging criticisms of Latin American women's writing came from the pen of Jorge Luis Borges in the 1938 issue of *Sur*, where the Argentine recounted his initial negative reaction to the projected plot of *La amortajada* (Borges 1938: 80–1).[1] María Luisa Bombal had conveyed to Borges that her tale was to centre on a sole woman character who anticipates her own burial by looking back over the events of her life in a lucid moment of agonizing self-reflection. Borges was sceptical, however, as to the very possibility of narrating the story, which, for him, was 'de ejecución imposible' (impossible to carry out) (1938: 80).

According to Borges, Bombal's attempt to re-create in fiction the deceased woman's soliloquy would suffer from two inevitable consequences: either the supernatural fact of a dead but demonstrably conscious character would eclipse the events narrated in the novel, or else those same events would overshadow the surprising speech act beyond the grave (1938: 80). In his words, 'la zona mágica de la obra invalidaría la psicológica, o viceversa' (the work's magical dimension would invalidate

---

* This essay was finished at the University of Iowa Obermann Center for Advanced Studies in the Fall of 1994. I am grateful to Jay Semel and to Lorna Olson for their kind assistance, and to Maria Fitch, who helped to edit the manuscript.

[1] María Luisa Bombal, *La amortajada*, 1st edn. (Buenos Aires, 1938).

the psychological one, or vice versa) given the insurmountable conflict between the otherwordly sphere of death and the psychological dimension of the protagonist's love life (1938: 80). For Borges such a fiction was not only an impossible but also an extremely risky enterprise as, in his judgement, it veered dangerously towards one of two extremes: fantastic literature, on the one hand, and high realism, on the other. In a gesture typical of the bias against women's writing prevalent in Latin American letters, Borges's review practically dismissed the tale of the shrouded woman, despite his apparent praise of Bombal's literary talents (Bombal 1988: p. i).[2]

In contrast to Bombal, who was chastised for her effort to name the unimaginable, the Mexican Juan Rulfo was praised for daring to write another 'impossible' novel, his highly acclaimed *Pedro Páramo* (1955). In fact, many critics have pointed out Rulfo's extraordinary ability to conjure in his fiction an uneasy balance between life and death, portrayed as a sustained narrative ambivalence between the real and the fantastic. Both Carlos Blanco Aguinaga and Joseph Sommers have described *Pedro Páramo*'s two-part narrative structure, which consists of an initial sequence in which Juan Preciado comes to Comala to seek his father, and a second half in which all the characters of the town appear as ghosts (Sommers 1974: 48–9; Blanco Aguinaga 1955: 78–9). The climactic turning-point is the scene in which Juan Preciado encounters the incestuous earth woman who seduced him one hot summer night (Rulfo 1969: 61). Neither critic points out an inherent contradiction between the real and supernatural realms, as did Borges in the case of *La amortajada*; rather, they both reconcile this apparent tension by acknowledging Rulfo's ability to situate the reader within the tenuous border zone between life and death (Sommers 1974: 47–8, 50). Sommers, for example, categorically claims that: 'En la primera mitad, la presencia de la muerte contamina la existencia; la vida es un infierno viviente. En la segunda mitad, la vida contamina la muerte, haciendo de esa condición también un infierno' (In the first half of the novel, the presence of death contaminates existence; life is a living

---

[2] 'Today, in Santiago, Chile, or Buenos Aires, in Caracas or Lima, when they name the best names, María Luisa Bombal is never missing from the list' (Jorge Luis Borges, preface to Bombal 1988: p. i). *La amortajada* was first published by Editorial 'Sur.'

hell. In the second half, life contaminates death, making of it also a hell-like condition) (1974: 49).

Since the authors' gender has clearly determined, at least in part, the reception of their novels, I would like to reverse this tendency by redirecting Borges's charge against *La amortajada* to Rulfo's masterpiece. Seen from the point of view of Jacques Lacan's register of the Real, both works spring from the same linguistic impossibility—the fact that only a dead silence emanates from the tomb (Gutiérrez Mouat 1987: 112).[3] However, in the Symbolic dimension occupied by literature this speech act becomes not only possible but yearned for as locus of desire or trace of the desiring subject.[4] As Julia Kristeva observes, 'the signifying voice . . . shape(s) the visible, hence fantasy' (Kristeva 1987: 37). Through the voice runs the ebb and flow of desire, the conjunction of the two pulsional realms of Eros and Thanatos, life and death.[5] Hence, both drives—Eros and Thanatos—transverse (criss-cross) the voice as 'an echo chamber' or resounding box of infinitely repeating phrases or sentence fragments (Sarduy 1978: 57, 59). The voices of the dead in *Pedro Páramo* and *La amortajada* emanate from a deep instinctual yearning—the wish to love and to be loved which constitutes the very core of subjectivity and which translates into the 'phantasmatic' quality of both tales.

Hence, Rulfo and Bombal's narratives originate from the same psychological root: the conjuction/disjunction between

[3] Ricardo Gutiérrez Mouat argues, however, that 'decir (o escribir) "yo muero" es anular el acto real de la muerte (lingüísticamente, el performativo)' (to say (or write) 'I'm dying' is to cancel the real act of death (in linguistic terms, a performative)) (1987: 112).

[4] Gutiérrez Mouat adds, 'En *La amortajada* la muerte se difiere para que pueda ser narrada por el deseo: morir también equivale a no narrar (y a no desear)' (In *La amortajada* death is deferred so that it may be narrated by desire: to die means, in effect, not to narrate (and not to desire)) (1987: 112). Here I hold a slightly different point of view: that the experience of dying *in itself* constitutes an act of desire, or, more precisely, a displacement of repressed desire that had no other outlet during Ana María's lifetime.

[5] The voice as libidinal marker is effectively dramatized in Severo Sarduy's *Para la voz* (1978). The English version, *For Voice*, trans. Philip Barnard (1985), only captures one of the two meanings of the title, 'towards the voice', thus missing the more significant semantic charge implied by the secondary meaning of the phrase, the command to 'stop the voice'. In Sarduy's work, the juxtaposed meanings of the Spanish original also suggest the voice as an instinctual repository beyond death. It is this notion which frames my discussion of voice.

life and death, marked by the constant tension between Eros as preserving life force, and Thanatos, the death drive that ultimately returns the living organism to an earlier, inanimate state, the state of primeval matter (Freud 1970: 30–1).[6] According to Freud, these two forces coexist in a paradoxical yet complementary relation with each other (Freud 1970: 55). In *Pedro Páramo*, this conjunction of opposites is marked by the dual function fulfilled by the character of Eduviges Dyada: at the same time that she leads Juan Preciado to the mystery of his origin, she also prepares the way for Miguel Páramo's crossing into death (Rulfo 1959: 25–6). Eduviges's name symbolically ciphers the pulsional dyad life/death, the complementary nature between the erotic drive and the opposite 'Nirvana principle' that yearns to rest in the state of non-arousal caused by death (Freud 1970: 49–50). In a parallel manner, Ana María in *La amortajada* is able to manifest her love-hate only after death (Bombal 1984: 145–7), showing the reversibility or exchange between the two instinctive forces, for, as Kristeva claims, echoing Freud, 'love is no more than a chancy statis [*sic*] of hatred' (Kristeva 1987: 124; Freud 1970: 48).[7]

Classical psychoanalysis has taught us that recurring sounds and echoes demonstrate the effect of the death drive, which operates by means of the repetition compulsion (Freud 1970: 15–17, 50). In the Rulfian universe, what remains after death as supplement or libidinal residue is sheer *voice*, the sighs and sorrows emitted from the grave, the 'murmullos de ultratumba' (murmurs beyond the grave) of Juan Preciado and Dorotea, followed by the tormented cries of an eternally restless Susana San Juan (Sommers 1974: 50). When Juan Preciado begins to decipher the enigma of Comala as a town inhabited by ghosts, his poignant question to Damiana Cisneros, '—¿Está usted viva,

---

[6] For a brilliant reading of *La amortajada* from the point of view of Freud's theory of the drives, see Barbara F. Ichiishi, 'Death and Desire in *The Shrouded Woman*' (1989). Latin American literature has long been obsessed with this desire for the origin or fusion with the eternal mother earth, an impulse best demonstrated in Alejo Carpentier's short story 'Journey Back to the Source' (1970).

[7] Julia Kristeva's *Histoires d'amour* better conveys this idea, 'l'amour n'est qu'une stase hasardeuse de la haine' (love is just a chancy statis [*sic*] of hate (1983: 121)). Kristeva develops Freud's idea that 'hate is ... older than love' by stating that 'if love takes over from narcissism in ulterior sexual drives, it is underlain, borne, and determined by hatred' (1987: 124–5, 125).

Damiana? ¡Dígame, Damiana!' (Rulfo 1969: 47) (Are you alive, Damiana? Tell me, Damiana!) (Rulfo 1959: 41) is answered only by an eerie echo: 'i . . . ana . . . neros! i . . . ana . . . neros!'.

If the voice, echo, and soft murmuring indicate the crossing between the two instinctual poles of life and death, the phantasmatic enunciation common to both *Pedro Páramo* and *La amortajada* originates in the Freudian postulate that the death drive ultimately predominates in psychic life (Freud 1970: 32).[8] This idea is best represented in the Narcissus myth, for Narcissus represents a kind of love that harbours within it its own extinction. Like Echo pining for Narcissus, the dead characters of *Pedro Páramo* and *La amortajada* can vocalize their desire only after death. Both narratives show how the body (and its 'pulsions'), now safely ensconced under the earth and lying at the core and at the ground of matter, can feel the flow of the semiotic *chora*, its previously inarticulate instinctual longings, the repressed waves of desire.

Reshuffling for her own purposes the classic Lacanian categories, Kristeva affirms that 'the experience of love indissolubly ties together the *symbolic* (what is forbidden . . .), the *imaginary* (what the Self imagines in order to sustain and expand itself), and the *real*' (Kristeva 1987: 7). The 'impossible' narration of *Pedro Páramo* and *La amortajada* emerges from the register of the imaginary, that dual relation with the other that constitutes the 'I' as speaking subject (Gutiérrez Mouat 1987: 112). For Kristeva, the speaking 'subject exists only inasmuch as it identifies with an ideal other who is the speaking other', an other that appears as 'a ghost' (Kristeva 1987: 35).[9]

In the Western psychoanalytic tradition, the figure that comes closest to realizing this dual relation is Narcissus. As foundational myth for both a desiring and a speculative subject, Narcissus has been appropriated by psychoanalysis to explain the constitution

---

[8] For Freud, 'the purpose of life is death' (1970: 32). That this is a markedly patriarchal assumption is proven by the fact that women's fiction, such as Bombal's, postulates a radically different order. In the manner of primitive societies, which purportedly conceive of life and death as a recurrent cycle, ultimately returning to the life-bearing principle, Bombal's fiction, particularly 'Las islas nuevas', attests to the pre-Oedipal, maternal element as preserver of life and eternal mystery of regeneration (Bombal 1988: 85–112).

[9] This is the thrust, too, of Gutiérrez Mouat's reading of *La amortajada*, where 'se busca al fantasma del amante en su cuerpo y al fantasma de la muerte en la muerte' (the phantasmatic lover is sought in the body and the phantasm of death in death itself) (1987: 112).

of the self. According to Freud, primary narcissism entails the first choice of love object, the self and the mother, which determines, in turn, the direction of the libido after the onset of sexual maturation, termed secondary narcissism. In this second stage, Freud defines narcissism as a perversion of the libidinal drive in which the subject takes himself as love-object instead of assuming an-other as beloved (Freud 1959: 45).[10]

In *Tales of Love*, Kristeva draws on classical psychoanalysis as well as on Platonism to trace the evolution of the Narcissus myth in Western thought. According to Kristeva, Narcissus is the very pillar of Western subjectivity, for on him hinges the Platonic theory of ideal beauty as well as the later Plotinian version of *Narcissan* love, which blends the Platonic adoration of beauty with the notion of 'internality' or inner psychic space, a notion which is erotically charged as the subject's loving contemplation of himself (Kristeva 1987: 108–9).

It is my contention that the key to the 'impossible' narration of *Pedro Páramo* and *La amortajada* lies in their mythic subtext. In the pages that follow I read this subtext through Kristeva's account of the Narcissus myth, contrasting Rulfo's representation of the 'manic eros, sublime eros' of male sexuality with Bombal's tragic account of woman's experience of sublimated desire, a stunted narcissistic eros unable to fulfil her object choice (Kristeva 1987: 59). From this perspective *Pedro Páramo* and *La amortajada* can be seen as offering variations on the original myth, 'demyths' that repeat the pressing, almost 'impossible' search for the other, and the failure of non-alterity that the Narcissus myth inaugurates in the Western tradition (Kristeva 1987: 105, 108).

Despite their different narrative registers, both *La amortajada* and *Pedro Páramo* trace the emergence of a desiring subject, a subject who, once beyond the frontier of death, *assumes* voice as distillation of desire, as pure relation to a speaking other, or, more precisely, as uninhibited *reply* to the desire of or for the other (Sarduy 1978: 13–56). Both Rulfo and Bombal reveal narcissistic love as a 'new insanity' (Kristeva 1987: 117): the *cacique* Pedro Páramo's delirium for Susana San Juan, on the one hand, and, on the other, Ana María's mad passion for her

---

[10] I thank my colleague Herman Rapaport for bringing Freud's essay to my attention.

cousin Ricardo, a burning, adolescent love whose imprint never left her soul (Gutiérrez Mouat 1987: 106).[11] These two loves, absolutely narcissistic and consequently infinitely tragic, reveal the intimate connection between Eros and Thanatos—the shrouded woman, who never found a love object to correspond to her own 'vehemente amor' (vehement love) (Bombal 1938: 143), and Pedro Páramo, who perpetually lived 'este desesperado intento de sobrepasar su soledad, de poseer en cuerpo y alma a esa mujer que ama desde la niñez' (this desperate attempt to transcend his solitude, to possess in body and soul the woman whom he had loved since childhood) (de la Colina 1965: 20).[12]

There are many resonances to the classical myth of Narcissus in Rulfo's narrative. According to Kristeva in *Tales of Love*, Echo, the beautiful nymph in love with Narcissus, is rejected by the youth and condemned to repeat incessantly the words of others as a punishment for having protected her father's adulterous affairs. Lacking a body, lacking even the materiality of flesh, Echo is reduced to sheer voice: 'she is voice only' (Kristeva 1987: 103).[13] Transformed into the emblem of desire, Echo becomes the phantasmatic enunciation of her frustrated love for Narcissus. Hence, the bits and pieces of words which are Echo's sole pronouncements are intense traces of her desire; like Pedro Páramo, Echo is also 'un rencor vivo' (Rulfo 1969: 10) (just pure hate) (Rulfo 1959: 4), the epitome of nonrequited love. This is why Comala, where Pedro Páramo reigns as supreme *cacique*, is full of circulating murmurs and echoes (Rulfo 1969: 45).

As a foundational myth of Western culture, the figure of Narcissus has been appropriated by psychoanalysis to represent the libidinal energy of the ego which is never totally consumed

[11] 'Las relaciones entre los personajes . . . son uniformemente traumáticas, sobre todo las que involucran a Ana María y los tres hombres de su vida' (The relationships between the characters . . . are equally traumatic, especially those involving Ana María and the three men in her life) (Gutiérrez Mouat 1987: 106).

[12] The Mexican critic adds this insight, 'Su pasión es la pasión terrible, destructora, del amor romántico; es la pasión de Heathcliff por Catalina, en *Cumbres borrascosas*. Una pasión que ha perdido su inocencia y su paraíso en cuanto ha dejado la zona de la infancia' (His passion is the terrible, destructive passion of romantic love; it is Heathcliff's passion for Catherine in *Wuthering Heights*. A passion that has lost its innocence and paradise in so far as it has left behind the zone of infancy) (de la Colina 1965: 20).

[13] Here Kristeva quotes directly from Ovid's *Metamorphoses*.

in its movement towards the object of desire (Freud 1970: 45–6). According to Kristeva, the first complete version of the myth is narrated in Ovid's *Metamorphoses*, and it first tells the tale of Echo's unrequited love, followed by 'the new insanity' of Narcissus's love of self (Kristeva 1987: 103–4). Although Narcissus provokes Echo's mad passion for him, he himself is incapable of surrendering to love, until the day when he peers at the fountain to drink and is captivated by the beautiful face which stares back at him in the water. In love with himself though without knowing it, Narcissus experiences 'the vertigo of a love with no object other than a mirage' (Kristeva 1987: 104). Hence, the fabled Narcissus becomes the symbol of an insane love that inevitably leads the subject to his own destruction. For the tragedy of narcissistic love comes at that poignant 'moment of understanding' when Narcissus 'realized . . . that the loved image is his own' (1987: 104–5). Moreover, when the unfortunate Narcissus senses that his beloved double disappears, he 'dies at the edge of his image' (1987: 104–5). The fading of Narcissus into the ripples of water results in 'a strange resurrection', for the only remaining trace of his body is the mysterious narcissus flower that blooms at night (1987: 105).

Kristeva interprets the Narcissus myth as one of the pillars of 'the history of Western subjectivity' because in Ovid's version the constitution of the subject is based on a double specular movement, what Kristeva calls 'a twin aspect of the lure'. Narcissus becomes the emblem of the Western concept of self because, on the one hand, he experiences 'rapture at the sight of a nonobject', and, on the other, he is fascinated by 'the power of the image' that incited his hopeless passion in the first place (1987: 104–5). In the later, Neoplatonic tradition, the 'sight' and 'reflection' proper to the narcissistic subject become eroticized, a change conjoined to the subject's experience of himself as an interiority (1987: 108–9). Hence, Plotinus transforms Narcissus into the very corner-stone of the 'western consciousness of self' by emphasizing 'the autoeroticism of one's own image' (1987: 108). In Plotinus 'the Platonic quest for ideal beauty' is turned inward, as the subject looks for this ideal beauty not in an external object but inside himself. In this way, Kristeva maintains, the interior gaze constitutes the contemplative space of the soul now occupied by the narcissistic subject (1987: 108–9). Since it is in contemplation that ideal beauty is found, this leads to the experience of 'autoerotic jouissance' as the new-born Narcissus discovers the beauty of form in his own perfect body, rather than in the other's countenance (whether it be a real other or the 'mirage' of Ovid's classical Narcissus).[14] In this way Plotinus arrives at an 'ideal Unity' of the self which gives rise to the speculative subject of the West, who from this point on experiences himself as 'an *internality*' (1987: 109; Kristeva's emphasis).[15] As Kristeva notes, if the interior gaze confers unity to the soul, then 'the soul is established through loving itself in the ideal' (1987: 110).

In *Pedro Páramo*, Rulfo presents us with an emblematic case of a 'Narcissan' in contrast to a narcissistic love because the *cacique*'s subjectivity itself is grounded on his unrequited love for Susana San Juan. As de la Colina aptly put it, 'es por ella que Pedro Páramo ha querido convertirse en el señor de Comala' (it is only for her that Pedro Páramo made himself the lord of Comala) and, furthermore, 'cuando Susana San Juan muere, Pedro Páramo ya no tiene un sólo motivo para sostener el mundo que lo rodea y abdica de su voluntad' (when Susana San Juan dies, Pedro Páramo no longer has a reason to sustain the world around him and so gives up his will) (1965: 20–1). Hence, Pedro's love for Susana is Platonic not only because it is never consummated, but, more significantly, because it is founded upon the Platonic ideal of beauty. If Neoplatonism defines love as 'the luminous radiation, the gleaming reflection of the One, which the soul watches and loves' (Kristeva 1987: 111) there is no better example of such idealized rapture than young Pedro's ecstatic contemplation of his childhood love,

A centenares de metros, encima de todas las nubes, más, mucho más allá de todo, estás escondida tú, Susana. Escondida en la inmensidad de Dios, detrás de su Divina Providencia, donde yo no puedo alcanzarte ni verte y adonde no llegan mis palabras. (Rulfo 1969: 17)[16]

---

[14] In *La última niebla*, Bombal demonstrates this crucial phase in the female's subject constitution of herself.

[15] 'Platonic dialogism is transformed, with Plotinus, into a monologue that must indeed be called speculative: it leads the ideal inside a Self that, only thus, in the concatenation of reflections, establishes itself as an *internality*. To the narcissistic shadow... it substitutes autoerotic reflection, which leads ideal Unity inside a Self that is illuminated by it' (Kristeva 1987: 109; Kristeva's emphasis).

[16] This passage is also quoted in de la Colina (1965: 20).

Susana, you are miles and miles away, above all the clouds, far away above everything, hidden. Hidden in His immensity, behind his Divine Providence, where I can never find you or see you. Where my words will never reach you. (Rulfo 1959: 11; emphasis in original)

The Ideal towards which the youth Pedro aspires is 'the Plotinian One', which 'is simultaneously the *loved one* and *love*; He is *love of himself*, for He is beautiful only by and in Himself' (Kristeva 1987: 111; Kristeva's emphasis).[17] According to Kristeva, this 'autou eros' sublimates narcissistic love by elevating it to the category of the absolute or divine; hence, 'God is Narcissus' (1987: 111).

Kristeva argues that at the creative dawn of the psyche, from this 'Narcissan' ideal emerges a subject that takes himself as his own love object, that loves only its own inverted image, 'a love of self and in itself' (1987: 113).[18] That is why

en Comala, hay una sola presencia vital . . . : Pedro Páramo el cacique. Pedro Páramo es el único personaje porque para crearse a sí mismo, . . . ha aplastado a todos los demás, los ha reducido a rumores, a ecos de su presencia. (Blanco Aguinaga 1955: 80)

in Comala, there is only one vital presence . . . : the *cacique* Pedro Páramo. Pedro Páramo is the only character because, in order to create himself, . . . he has had to crush all the others, reducing them to rumours, to sheer echoes of his presence.

By the same token, Susana San Juan represents the 'love in the feminine' that folds in upon its own interiority, its quiet 'inner solitude' (Kristeva 1987: 112). Susana's active day-dreaming while remembering Florencio evokes mystical rapture or divine love, thus signalling the mysterious earth woman as a direct descendant of St John of the Cross. Susana's lyrical monologue parallels the fulfilment of erotic love in the Song of Songs, as it re-enacts 'the premises of *ecstasy* (of one's going out of oneself) and of *incarnation*, insofar as it is the ideal becoming body' (Kristeva 1987: 94; Kristeva's emphasis). The echo of this biblical model surfaces in Susana's lament for her lost love, whose enunciation takes place fully within the semiotic mode,

[17] Kristeva is quoting directly from *The Enneads*, VI.
[18] Although Kristeva does not mention Sartre explicitly, there is an obvious echo here of the distinction drawn in existential philosophy between being 'in itself' and 'for itself'.

Y yo lo que quiero de él es su cuerpo. Desnudo y caliente de amor; hirviendo de deseos; estrujando el temblor de mis senos y de mis brazos. Mi cuerpo transparente suspendido del suyo. Mi cuerpo liviano sostenido y suelto a sus fuerzas. (Rulfo 1969: 105)

And what I want is his body. Naked . . . hot with love . . . boiling with desire. Pressed against my trembling bosom and arms. My transparent body suspended from his, sustained by his strength. (Rulfo 1959: 99)

Insofar as she bonds in an imaginary and total fusion with the other, Susana San Juan's 'love in the feminine' entails a sublime coupling in which subject and object are made one, and in which she is swayed beyond the ordinary confines of reason (Kristeva 1987: 112–13). This type of sublime union supresses the fissure which guarantees the subject's immersion into the Symbolic order, the barrier of language and thought that makes up the construct we know as reality. In the Narcissus myth, 'insanity comes from the absence of object, which is, in the final analysis, the sexual object' (Kristeva 1987: 116). Hence, Susana's pining for her dead lover Florencio testifies to the fact that the lack of love can only be recompensed by a flight into madness. This is why she moans: '¿Qué haré ahora con mis labios sin su boca para llenarlos? ¿Qué haré de mis adoloridos labios?' (Rulfo 1969: 105) (And what will I do with my lips now, without his mouth to kiss them? What will I do with my poor lips?) (Rulfo 1959: 99). Like the melancholy protagonist of Bombal's *La última niebla*, Susana San Juan keeps alive the flame of her desire by replaying in her mind the imaginary coupling with her phantom lover. In the character's incantatory hallucination, erotic union is metaphorized as a swelling seawave which substitutes for the lack of her beloved's body: 'Entonces me hundo en él, entera. Me entrego a él en su fuerte batir, en su suave poseer, sin dejar pedazo' (Rulfo 1969: 100) (I hid myself in it, in its strength and gentleness) (Rulfo 1959: 94).[19] In such a paradigm, then, the female subject is doomed to inhabit the very border of the Symbolic, enclosed as she is inside the walls of her own erotic imagination. This is represented in Rulfo's novel by Susana San Juan's delirious entrapment in a solitary labyrinth, in which the dream of love constantly resurfaces at the verbal or conscious level.

---

[19] Though I have reproduced the published English translation here, it does not do justice to the full sensuality of the original passage.

The nameless protagonist of Bombal's *La última niebla* also inhabits this other-wordly dimension, for she finds erotic satisfaction only in the embrace of a phantom lover. The famous erotic encounter in *La última niebla* represents the 'exquisite pain of contemplation, daydreaming, or even hallucination' (Kristeva 1987: 112), activities which, for the female subject, compensate for the lack of love object. In the case of Bombal's protagonist, active day-dreaming (*ensoñación*) is her only escape from the dreary reality of a loveless marriage. The nightly seduction scene is then instantly and incessantly replayed in the protagonist's mind, alongside the clouding of the mist which signifies not only the crossing between the erotic and the death drives, but also the blurring and eventual dissolution of the woman's instinctual reserve, her very life force, through lack of love.

Both Susana San Juan and Ana María, the shrouded woman, represent a later development of the Narcissus myth, since they show the 'holy madness' of a love without an object (Kristeva 1987: 83). The feminine version of the myth seems to lead either to the flight into the imaginary, and hence to madness, or else to an overwhelming desire for death. Whereas the first alternative is dramatized in Susana San Juan and the anonymous woman-lover of *La última niebla,* Ana María's story illustrates the wilful choice not to continue to live in a loveless world. True, Ana María 'lives in a state of unfulfilled desire, and it is this hidden longing which slowly consumes her life force, impelling her towards a premature death' (Ichiishi 1989: 18). The whole thrust of the novel shows, however, that this death is actively sought not only as instinctual sublimation of desire but also as an active process of self-affirmation. Ana María's lucid monologue suggests that the death-wish has reached such a level of consciousness that it has become a wilful act, generating the 'impossible narrative' of a dying woman's soliloquy.[20] So, whereas the masculine 'manic eros' represents the soul in flight, reserving for itself the exclusive gaze that looks upward to the divine and toward the ideal of beauty, 'love in the feminine', by contrast, exhibits the soul in descent

---

[20] 'The impossibility of achieving fulfillment within the context of her "real" historical existence motivates on an unconscious level the drive toward death as the only possible means of liberation open to her' (Ichiishi 1989: 18).

toward the mother earth to merge with the elemental matter or matrix.[21]

The male's exclusive right to the contemplation of ideal beauty is dramatized in Bombal's *La amortajada* in young Alberto's manic obsession with his beautiful wife María Griselda, whom he keeps 'aislada en un lejano fundo del sur' (isolated in a country estate in the far south) (Bombal 1984: 117), so that no other man will ever dare look at her.[22] Alberto burns an image of María Griselda in a hopeless effort to eliminate the trace of her alluring beauty,

Ahora pega a la llama de uno de los cirios la imagen de María Griselda y se dedica a quemarla concienzudamente, y sus rasgos se distienden apaciguados a medida que la bella imagen se esfuma, se parte en cenizas. (Bombal 1984: 118)

Now he brings the image of María Griselda close to the flame of one of the candles and wilfully burns it, so that her features relax tranquilly as the beautiful image fades out, breaks up into ashes.

Even though the jealous husband destroys all images of his wife, in a wild effort to eliminate her power, María Griselda's silent presence remains a mystery, a living testimony to the shadowy, pre-Oedipal realm of erotic bliss. In 'La historia de María Griselda', we see the futility of Alberto's 'manic eros' as well as the amorous emotion which the radiance of María Griselda provokes in all the men at the estate. When they stare at her face, these men experience 'the essence of the feminine which man longs to possess but [which] always remains beyond his grasp' (Ichiishi 1989: 24). This is dramatized in Fred's initial encounter with the woman,

¡Maria Griselda! La vio pasar. Y a través de ella, de su pura belleza, tocó de pronto un más allá infinito y dulce . . . algas, aguas, tibias arenas visitadas por la luna, raíces que se pudren sordamente creciendo limo abajo, hasta su propio y acongojado corazón. (Bombal 1984: 179)

María Griselda! He saw her pass by. And through her, through her pure beauty, he suddenly touched a beyond far more infinite and sweet . . . seaweeds, waters, warm sands caressed by the moonlight,

---

[21] In Plato, 'the ascent of the loving soul' is represented by the apt metaphor of 'the flight of a bird' (Kristeva 1987: 63).

[22] I have translated all quoted passages from *La amortajada*.

roots growing mute and rotting deep in the mud, all the way up to his own, anguished heart.

Indeed, in strict accordance with Neoplatonic theory, it is the sight of María Griselda that confers interiority to man's soul, as Fred explains in his amorous reverie: 'Y comprendió lo que era el alma, y la admitió tímida, vacilante y ansiosa, y aceptó la vida tal cual era: efímera, misteriosa e inútil, con su mágica muerte que tal vez no conduce a nada' (And he understood what the soul was, and received her timid, hesitating, and anxious, and accepted life just as it was: fleeting, mysterious and useless, with a magical death that perhaps leads nowhere) (Bombal 1984: 179).[23] Like a new Narcissus who realizes that his love object must remain forever elusive, Fred shoots himself in a tragic gesture of renunciation (Bombal 1984: 180). Whereas María Griselda remains trapped in the perfect enclosure of her body, her iridescent eyes signalling both the prohibition against gazing on the other and the sheer materiality of the universe: '¡Con la punta de un alfiler, pinchar esas pupilas! ¡Habría sido algo así como rajar una estrella' (To prick those pupils with a pin! It would have seemed like slitting a star) (Bombal 1984: 181).

In contrast to the male's upward gaze of longing, 'woman has always been compared to water since, among other things, she is the mirror in which man—Narcissus—sees himself' (Spacks 1975; quoted in Levine 1983: 36). Reversing the dominant paradigm in Western culture according to which, like the unhappy María Griselda, woman can only be a projected image of man's desire, the sensuous protagonist of Bombal's *La última niebla* dives into the pool of water and discovers her body as if for the first time. In this often-quoted scene, the protagonist acknowledges the beauty of her form and the contours of her body, thus liberating herself from the rigid image of 'mujer perfecta' (Bombal 1984: 13) (a perfect woman) (Bombal 1988: 17) imposed upon her by her cold, distant husband,

No me sabía tan blanca y tan hermosa. El agua alarga mis formas, que toman proporciones irreales. Nunca me atreví antes a mirar mis senos; ahora los miro. Pequeños y redondos, parecen diminutas corolas suspendidas sobre el agua. (Bombal 1984: 14)

---

[23] Kristeva remarks, 'It is love that constitutes the inner unity of the soul . . . ; the soul is established through loving itself in the ideal' (Kristeva 1987: 110).

I had no idea that I was so white and beautiful. The water elongates my body so that it takes on unreal proportions. Before now, I never dared look at my breasts. Rounded and small, they seem to me like tiny blossoms suspended above the suface. (Bombal 1988: 10)

Though a vivid example of what Kristeva calls 'autoerotic jouissance', hers is not the empty, objectless eroticism of the classical Narcissus,

Eros, amor confess to having no other object than their own image, a reflection of their own body, an idealized portion that serves for the whole. For eroticism to be autoeroticism, in the watery element of the archaic forest, amounts to a demystification. . . . (Kristeva 1987: 115–16)

Instead, the young woman derives from her immersion in the water a narcissistic substance, a psychic identity previously lost in the neglect and indifference of her past. The image reflected back from the water is not the limpid stare of Narcissus, but the transparent reflection of her own body, which leads to the gratifying recognition of its unique beauty: 'Y así, desnuda y dorada, me sumerjo en el estanque' (Bombal 1984: 14) (And like this, naked and golden, I dive into the water) (Bombal 1988: 10).

This scene thus signals a woman turning a contemplative gaze on herself in order to discover her own 'interiority', her own psychic space. Rather than deriving a sense of self from the outward fascination with ideal beauty, as in the Plotinian variant of the myth, Bombal seems to suggest that woman's 'interiority' can be arrived at only after a sensuous bodily experience involving her entire physical and emotional self (Bombal 1984: 14).[24] Like a new Narcissus, Bombal's protagonist also takes 'the *spring* as [her] partner' (Kristeva 1987: 113). But, whereas, for Narcissus, the water was 'simply a medium', proving that 'the spring merely engulfs and ruins the one who ventures into it' (1987: 113), in *La última niebla*, the water caresses the protagonist in an amorous embrace, helping her to reach a higher level of awareness. This experience eventually shatters the death-driven monotony of the mist and allows

---

[24] The Bombalian protagonist does not merely *see* herself in 'the watery mirror', but rather *knows* herself as she sees, 'No me sabía tan blanca y tan perfecta' (Bombal 1984: 14) (I had no idea that I was so white and beautiful) (Bombal 1988: 10).

the subsequent erotic encounter with the phantom lover (Bombal 1984: 16–18). The scene in the pond in *La última niebla* also reverses the phallic penetration of the water by the classical Narcissus—as Kristeva asks, 'A symbol of the maternal body, is it not after a fashion penetrated by the youth who thrusts his image into it?' (Kristeva 1987: 113)—thus giving way to a non-violent, feminine mode of narcissistic contemplation,

Me voy enterrando hasta la rodilla en una espesa arena de terciopelo. Tibias corrientes me acarician y penetran. Como con brazos de seda, las plantas acuáticas me enlazan el torso con sus largas raíces. Me besa la nuca y sube hasta mi frente el aliento fresco del agua. (Bombal 1984: 14–15)

I sink to my ankles in thick velvety sand. Warm currents caress and penetrate me. Like silky arms, the aquatic plants embrace my body with their long tendrils. The fresh breeze kisses the nape of my neck, cools my feverish forehead. (Bombal 1988: 10)

Hence the protagonist of Bombal's *La última niebla* appears as a 'counter-Narcissus' in the same way that María Griselda shows herself to be a 'counter-archetype' of femininity, 'a prisoner condemned to exist only as the object of man's desire' (Ichiishi 1989: 24).

Woman's problematic subjectivity surfaces again in *La amortajada* as a struggle between conflicting images. After her wedding night Ana María's husband forces her to comb her braids in front of 'un espejo grande' (a large mirror) in order to mould her into the image of a submissive wife (Bombal 1984: 134–5). The nameless protagonist of *La última niebla* had faced a similar predicament, as Daniel, her husband, made her tie up her long, auburn tresses into an austere knot the better to resemble his first wife, the idealized 'perfect woman' (Bombal 1988: 8) required by the male imaginary. As the scene in the pond shows, the husband's coercive gesture was also a means of harnessing the protagonist's excess sexual energy. When Ana María gazes at herself in the mirror, she is yearning, like a female Narcissus, for another face, one that would re-flect back a more authentic self-portrait than the rigid role afforded her by patriarchy: 'Recuerda como si fuera hoy... el estanque de tinta sobre cuya superficie se recortó su propia ima-gen envuelta en el largo peinador blanco' (She remembered as if it were today... the lake of ink whose surface outlined her own image wrapped in the large white dressing-gown) (Bombal 1984: 134). The water in the pond also reflects for Ana María 'the desolate image of her emotional imprisonment' (Ichiishi 1989: 21). Her husband cruelly destroys this image— 'agitó el brazo para lanzar con violencia un guijarro que allá abajo fue a herir a su desposada en plena frente' (he shook his arm in order to throw a pebble violently that hit his wife in the middle of the forehead down below) (Bombal 1984: 135)—a sadistic act that shatters *La amortajada's* budding self-image. The break-up of Ana María's image in the pond signals too 'the fragmentation of her own experience' (Ichishii 1989: 24) and the subsequent loss of self-esteem, which also suggests the woman character's failed narcissism.

Rulfo's *Pedro Páramo* presents us with a far more desolate picture of woman's failure to attain a narcissistic sense of self. Though in her relationship to Pedro Páramo she is portrayed as an object of desire, Susana San Juan suffers from a funda-mental disruption that blocks her status as a subject. Despite the fact that in the novel she is portrayed as a symbol of sub-lime eroticism, Susana San Juan remains entrapped in a child-hood trauma occasioned by her incestuous relationship with her father, Bartolomé. In a flashback to Susana's childhood, Bartolomé orders her to go down a deep well in order to retrieve a hidden object—the lost object postulated by Lacanian psychoanalysis, but also the veritable emblem of the secret, destructive bond they shared. Urging his daughter to descend even deeper into the well, Bartolomé forces her to tell him what she sees: 'Es una calavera de muerto,—dijo' (Rulfo 1969: 95) (It's a skull, she said) (Rulfo 1959: 88). Next to the skull lie scattered pieces of gold that signal the conjunction between the excess and the Lacanian *object a*, the maternal breast or faeces represented metaphorically in the gold (Sarduy 1977: 100). In earlier segments, Fulgor had testified to the fact that Susana San Juan looked more like Bartolomé's wife than his daughter (Rulfo 1969: 85). The experience of father/daughter incest permanently scars Susana's soul and psyche, for it breaks off the source of identity in which she is constituted as subject.[25] Indeed, in contrast to Bartolomé, who knows his name fully, his daughter has no anchor with which to define her own identity,

---

[25] I am grateful to my colleague Herman Rapaport for this insight.

—Sí, Bartolomé.
—¡No me digas Bartolomé. ¡Soy tu padre!

. . .

—¿Y yo quién soy?
—Tú eres mi hija. Mía. Hija de Bartolomé San Juan.

(Rulfo 1969: 88)

'Yes, Bartolomé.'
'Don't call me Bartolomé. I'm your father!'

. . .

'And who am I?'
'You're my daughter. Mine. The daughter of Bartolomé
San Juan.'

(Rulfo 1959: 82)

The father/daughter incest mirrors, in turn, the incest consummated by the mysterious sister and brother whose house
serves as a passageway for Juan Preciado's transit into death,

—Hay multitud de caminos. Hay uno que va para Contla; otro que
viene de allá. Otro más que enfila derecho a la sierra . . . Y otro más,
que atraviesa toda la tierra y es el que va más lejos. (Rulfo 1969: 54)

'There's lots of roads. One of them goes to Contla, and another one
comes in from there. Then there's another that goes straight over the
sierra . . . And there's still another, that goes farther than any of them'.
(Rulfo 1959: 48–9)

This endless road is the 'labyrinth of solitude' in which all of
Rulfo's characters find themselves, lacking as they are as narcissistic subjects.

Besides the universal resonance of their works, Bombal's and
Rulfo's protagonists illustrate the consequences of that patriarchal prohibition which severely curtails the fulfilment of woman's erotic potential. According to Freud, woman experiences
'an intensification of the original narcissism' which compen-
sates for 'the social restrictions upon her object-choice' (1959:
46), her lack of a satisfying love object. At the most intimate
level of her instinctual life, this turning-in upon herself ultimately results in the death of desire, in the waning of any
conscious striving for erotic satisfaction. As the entire tale of
La amortajada so dramatically shows, Ana María has spent her
whole life repressing her most basic and cherished yearning
for love. Her adolescent passion for Ricardo failed when he

cruelly abandoned her, and her husband Antonio likewise rejected her after an earnest attempt at reconciliation (Ichiishi
1989: 23). Thus, Ana María has learned to diminish 'su propio
vehemente amor al amor mediocre y limitado de los otros'
(her own vehement love to the mediocre and limited love of
others) (Bombal 1984: 143) barely surviving on the flicker of
love represented by the symbiotic relationship with the feeble
Fernando, whom she considers, at best, only a pseudo-love
object (Bombal 1984: 130; Gutiérrez Mouat 1987: 108).[26] Because she can never attain true love, the ideal 'love that constitutes the inner unity of the soul' (Kristeva 1987: 110), Ana
María is forced to deny her own existence, joining the company
of the countless, faceless women before her who could find
solace only inside the cemetery walls (Bombal 1984: 153–4).

In the last scenes of the novel, Ana María ultimately finds
satisfaction by surrendering to the embrace of death and melting her body into the warm, primal earth-source, described as
an archetypal womb and matrix (Bombal 1984: 162). But rather
than representing a passive return to the 'inanimate state', an
annihilation and renunciation of the body, as Freud would have
us believe, the death of Ana María celebrates the joyous transformation of the flesh into earth-matter or universal substance,

Pero, nacidas de su cuerpo, sentía una infinidad de raíces hundirse
y esparcirse en la tierra como una pujante telaraña por la que subía
temblando, hasta ella, la constante palpitación del universo (Bombal
1984: 162).

But, sprung from her body, she felt an infinity of roots sink in and
spread out on the earth like a spider's web through which the constant pulsation of the universe trembled up to her.[27]

This exquisite end represents 'the time of the union with the cos-
mos in the total immersion of "the death of the dead"' (Ichiishi
1989: 27).

---

[26] 'El vampirismo de la relación es evidente y se fundamenta en el estatuto de
Fernando como objeto desplazado: quien se inscribe en ese discurso intimista
como objeto de atracción y repulsión es en realidad otro, un ausente (sólo en un
primer momento Ricardo)' (The relationship has an evidently vampirish quality,
based on Fernando's status as displaced love object: he who inserts himself into
this intimate discourse as an object of attraction and repulsion is really an other,
an absent one (only initially Ricardo)) (Gutiérrez Mouat 1987: 108).
[27] I have based this translation on Ichiishi's partial quote from this passage
(1989: 27).

Although, according to Kristeva, every narcissistic subject 'discovers in sorrow and death the alienation that is the constituent of his own image' (Kristeva 1987: 121), *Pedro Páramo* and *La amortajada* present different solutions to the same dilemma. At one level, Ana María embraces death as 'the only possible form of liberation' open to her (Ichiishi 1989: 18). She eventually frees herself from the patriarchal prison, but by a negative route: by consciously identifying with the thousands of 'mujeres enterradas' (buried women) who had been denied 'un espacio libre' (space for freedom) or instinctual satisfaction in life and hence could attain it only after death (Bombal 1984: 153). At another level, Ana María's speculative monologue effectively transforms her into the paradigm of Western subjectivity, defined as 'a Self that ... establishes itself as an *internality*' (Kristeva 1987: 109; Kristeva's emphasis). It is ironic, however, that Ana María can only become a subject at the brink of her grave, because of the heavy weight of patriarchal prohibition curtailing women's speculative activity. Although Bombal's protagonist finally does acquire the 'speculative internality' or interior space of reflexivity with which Plotinus endowed the narcissistic subject (Kristeva 1987: 115), she has to pay for it with her own life: '¿Es preciso morir para saber ciertas cosas? ... ¿Es preciso morir para saber?' (Must one die in order to know certain things? ... Must one die in order to know?) (Bombal 1984: 112). The knowledge attained by Ana María after death is thus the forbidden knowledge which makes woman a subject in her own right. Reversing the Freudian paradigm set out in *Beyond the Pleasure Principle*, which sees death as a return to an inanimate, inert, and consequently unconscious state, in Bombal's fictional world the act of descending to earth—of melting the body down into the earth-womb—is ultimately what confers on woman a sense of her own 'interiority'.

By contrast, Pedro Páramo meets an opposite yet equally tragic fate. Having isolated himself inside his despotic universe as ruler of Comala, Pedro Páramo dies encased within what Kristeva refers to as an 'autarkic' love (1987: 113),[28] where no other is really present: '¿Pero cuál era el mundo de Susana San Juan? Esa fue una de las cosas que Pedro Páramo nunca llegó

---

[28] The original reads, 'Dans cet amour autarcique qui conduit à l'union avec une divinité elle-même autarcique, il n'y a pas d'autre qui ne soit un néant' (Kristeva 1983: 110).

a saber' (Rulfo 1969: 99) (But which world was Susana San Juan living in? That was one of the things that Pedro Páramo never found out) (Rulfo 1959: 93). Unlike Susana San Juan's mystical love for Florencio, Pedro Páramo is incapable of recovering a sense of self due to his failure to merge into another (Kristeva 1987: 120); hence, he dies a victim of his own failed narcissism.

In *La amortajada*, Bombal's protagonist reaches the sublimation of her desire in and through death, in accordance with the Freudian notion that the 'pleasure principle' is always at the service of the death drive (Freud 1970: 57). In the last analysis, the sheer instinctual delight and sensuous autoeroticism with which the shrouded woman experiences her bodily fusion with primeval matter is what converts her into a desiring subject (Bombal 1984: 162). Her loving embrace of earth transforms Ana María into 'la flor ignorada que no vive sino un día de eclipse' (the forsaken flower that lives but a day of eclipse) (Bombal 1984: 162); into Narcissus in bloom (Kristeva 1987: 105). By contrast, Pedro Páramo is alienated from the earth which bore him, first, by the powerful grip he exercised on Comala, and, second, by his boastful usurpation of Dorotea's land, among other injustices. Because his love ultimately had no object, no other beside himself, Pedro, like Narcissus, had to die by his own (tragic) ignorance, and lack of self-speculation and reflection (Kristeva 1987: 116). When Abundio comes to seek him, Pedro Páramo dies 'desmoronándo(se) como si fuera un montón de piedras' (Rulfo 1969: 129) (crumbled to pieces as if he were a heap of stones) (Rulfo 1959: 123), much like the decomposing of Plotinus's Narcissan mirage. As the narcissistic subject, Pedro Páramo 'discovers in sorrow and death the alienation that is the constituent of his own image' (Kristeva 1987: 121). Hence he returns to the inanimate state 'alone with him who is alone', dying as a shattered, fragmented self without a sense of 'internality' (Kristeva 1987: 113; Blanco Aguinaga 1955: 80–2).

Like Narcissus, Pedro Páramo and Ana María, the shrouded woman, both die when they discover that they love 'a fake', a false 'ego ideal' internalized as a projection of the father (Kristeva 1987: 126). The fact that only Ana María is able to attain a consciousness of self suggests a new modality of the Narcissus myth, in which the paternal 'ego ideal' is substituted not by an illusory incarnation of the ideal mother, but by the gap between ideal love and the incommensurability of desire.[29] If, as Kristeva holds, 'narcissistic seeming thus necessarily entails a modification of language' (1987: 126), then both Rulfo and Bombal had to invent 'impossible' narratives in order to sublimate narcissistic love. *La amortajada, La última niebla,* and *Pedro Páramo* inaugurate in modern Latin American fiction the birth of the desiring subject.

[29] Kristeva explains how Narcissus falsely believes that he is his mother's ideal (1987: 126).

LIST OF WORKS CITED

Blanco Aguinaga, Carlos (1955), 'Realidad y estilo de Juan Rulfo', *Revista mexicana de literatura,* 1: 78–9.

Bombal, María Luisa (1984), *La última niebla: la amortajada* (Barcelona).

—— (1988), *New Island and Other Stories,* trans. Richard and Lucia Cunningham (Ithaca, NY).

Borges, Jorge Luis (1938), 'La amortajada', *Sur,* 7: 80–1.

Carpentier, Alejo (1970), 'Journey Back to the Source', *War of Time,* trans. Frances Partridge (New York), 103–31.

Colina, José de la (1965), 'Susana San Juan (El mito femenino en Pedro Páramo)', *Revista de la Universidad de México,* 19/8: 19–21.

Freud, Sigmund (1959), 'On Narcissism: An Introduction', in *Collected Papers,* iv. *Papers on Metapsychology. Papers on Applied Psycho-Analysis* (New York), 30–59.

—— (1970), *Beyond the Pleasure Principle,* trans. James Stachey (New York).

Gutiérrez Mouat, Ricardo (1987), 'Construcción y represión del deseo en las novelas de María Luisa Bombal', in Marjorie Agosín, Elena Gascón-Vera, and Roy Renjilian-Burjy (eds.), *María Luisa Bombal—Apreciaciones críticas* (Tempe, 1987), 99–118.

Ichiishi, Barbara F. (1989), 'Death and Desire in the *Shrouded Woman', Latin American Literary Review,* 17: 17–28.

Kristeva, Julia (1983), *Histoires d'amour* (Paris).

—— (1987), *Tales of Love,* trans. Leon S. Roudiez (New York).

Levine, Suzanne Jill (1983), 'El espejo de agua', *Revista de la Universidad de Mexico,* 26: 36–9.

Rulfo, Juan (1969), *Pedro Páramo,* 10th edn. (Mexico, DF).

—— (1959), *Pedro Páramo,* trans. Lysander Kemp (New York).

SARDUY, SEVERO (1977), *Barroco* (Buenos Aires).
—— (1978), *Para la voz* (Madrid).
—— (1985), *For Voice*, trans. Philip Barnard (Pittsburgh).
SOMMERS, JOSEPH (1974), 'A través de la ventana de la sepultura: Juan Rulfo', in Helmy F. Giacomán (ed.), *Homenaje a Juan Rulfo* (New York, 1974), 39–59.

7

Blood and Mirrors

Imagery of Violence in the Writings of Alejandra Pizarnik

SUSAN BASSNETT

IN his reflections on Foucault's *Madness and Civilisation,* Derrida questions Foucault's premiss that the history of madness is an archaeology of silence and asks whether there can even be such an enterprise as a history of silence.

> Further, is not an archaeology, even of silence, logic, that is, an organized language, a project, an order, a sentence, a syntax, a work? (Derrida 1978: 35)

The conundrum, of course, is whether madness, which both Foucault and Derrida see as an interrupted and forbidden discourse, can be contained within the boundaries of an ordered rational discourse. Derrida proposes that liberation from the totality of the historical language (responsible for, what he terms, the exile of madness), in order to write an archaeology of silence, would only be possible by either not mentioning a certain kind of silence or by following the madman or madwoman into exile. 'A history, that is, an archaeology against reason doubtless cannot be written', Derrida maintains, 'for, despite all appearances to the contrary, the concept of history has always been a rational one' (Derrida 1978: 36). We are left with a dilemma: the way to write the history of madness is either to remain silent, to reproduce those spaces where reason may not enter, or to step into the realm of madness and learn its language, for if we insist on trying to use rational discourse, then immediately we have to confront the history of judical systems that have prohibited and outlawed madness. How can we avoid evaluating, judging, condemning madness since we begin within a framework that has set madness beyond the boundaries of reason?

The problem of the forbidden discourse of madness and its relationship to the rational societal norm is foregrounded in the work of certain women writers, whose lives and writings cannot be slotted neatly into predetermined categories. In *The Madwoman in the Attic* (1979), Gilbert and Gubar argue that the figure of the madwoman is a crucial image of nineteenth- and twentieth-century women's writing, a violent, unstable reflection of contemporary society's idealized image of woman. The madwoman and the angel of the house exist side by side, and the representation of female violence and madness in women's writing can be seen both as a scream of rage and a bid for freedom,

> through the violence of the double the female author enacts her own raging desire to escape male houses and male texts, while at the same time it is through the double's violence that this anxious author articulates for herself the costly destructiveness of anger repressed until it can no longer be contained. (Gilbert and Gubar 1979: 79)

In this view of female creativity, the woman writer creates a dark double, a reflection that refuses to be contained within the bounds of reason and bursts out like a dark secret to commit unspeakable acts against patriarchal society.[1] Although a view that has been seriously challenged on the grounds of its reductionism, it nevertheless offers a radical alternative perspective on women's writing, whereby the rage of the writer is translated into images of madness, delirium, and, frequently, suicide or even murder. Writing is, therefore, a subversive act and reading is equally subversive, if the reader colludes with the woman author's battle for self-liberation.[2]

There are some authors who at particular moments are transformed into cultural icons, figures whose works and life histories become symbols of the struggles of an age. One such writer

---

[1] Irigaray argues that the woman writer can achieve reflecting/reflexive specularization through hysterical writing in which what has been unspoken in her psychic life can be articulated. On this see *Speculum: de l'autre femme* (1974), trans. Gillian C. Gill as *Speculum of the Other Woman* (1985), particularly the chapter entitled (in both the French and English versions) 'La Mystérique'.

[2] This essay exploits both Derrida's notion of the mirror as a marker of reflexiveness and Irigaray's view of it as marking a spurious twoness and, in particular, women's conventional role as men's other.

is Sylvia Plath, another the Russian poet Marina Tsvetayeva. Their sense of rage, outrage, and passion for life as documented in their poetry, combined with their tragic deaths, have led both to be perceived as key precursors, writing in ways that later in the century would be defined as feminist. Other writers, however, remain in relative obscurity, known only to a small group of readers, their writings are quickly out of print and are difficult to obtain. One such is the Argentine writer Alejandra Pizarnik.

Pizarnik killed herself in 1972 at the age of 36 after a prolonged struggle against depression. Like Plath, with whom she has been compared,[3] Pizarnik wrote compulsively about the linked themes of cultural displacement and the unhappiness of loving. Both writers were fascinated by imagery of silence and death, both created what can be described as a continuous poem in multiple fragments, with interconnected patterns of imagery coloured white, red, and black. But here the resemblance ends. Plath was not obsessed with the violence of death in the way that Pizarnik was, and it could be argued that much of Plath's poetry is about struggling to live. Death for Pizarnik was always a presence in her work, death seen as a final solution to the pain of existing in the dangerous, unstable spaces of life. At the same time, the very act of writing was the opposite of life enhancing, and the paradox for her was that language itself was deadly: it fixed and entrapped her remorselessly like an instrument of torture. In a short piece published in 1970, 'Tangible ausencia' (Tangible Absence) she wrote,

Yo muero en poemas muertos que no fluyen, que son de piedra como yo, ruedan y no ruedan, un zozobrar lingüístico, un inscribir a sangre y fuego lo que libremente se va y no volvería. Digo esto porque nunca más sabré destinar a nadie mis poemas. (Pizarnik 1982*a*: 29–30)[4]

I die in dead poems that don't flow, that are made of stone as I am, that roll and don't roll, a linguistic restlessness inscribing in blood and fire that which goes freely and will never return. I say this because I shall never again know how to write poems for anyone.

---

[3] See Susan Bassnett, 'Speaking with Many Voices: The Poems of Alejandra Pizarnik' (1990), 36.

[4] All English translations in this chapter are the author's, unless otherwise indicated. Here and throughout, page references are to the volumes in which poems are collected.

Alejandra Pizarnik is not an easy writer to categorize. She herself sought to be elusive quite explicitly. Her work does not belong to any particular school or tradition, nor does it offer any insights into life and society of contemporary Argentina. One of the games she played during the years she spent in Paris and in Buenos Aires was to claim she despised all politics, whilst moving in leftist circles, and, although she grew up during the years of Peronism and the growing power of the military, she seems to have kept herself apart from any overt political activity, even as a student. Moreover, while Plath and Tsvetayeva can be read as prefiguring issues that feminism was to develop, Pizarnik's writing is more existentialist, her style anarchically surrealist, her subject-matter always herself. An intensely private person, as friends have attested (although her diary entries show that she mingled with fellow Latin Americans in Paris during the early 1960s when she studied painting), she seems to have seen writing neither as an act of communication, nor as a personal statement of any kind.[5] The entry for 8 March 1961 reads,

Si pudiera tomar nota de mí todos los días sería una manera de no perderme, de enlazarme, porque es indudable que me huyo, no me escucho. . . . El más grande misterio de mi vida este: ¿por qué no me suicido? En vano alegar mi pereza, mi miedo, mi distracción. Tal vez por eso siento, cada noche, que me he olvidado de algo.[6]

If I were able to make notes about myself every day it would be a way not to lose myself, to bind myself together, because undoubtedly I flee myself, I don't listen to myself. . . . The greatest mystery of my life is this: why don't I kill myself? It's useless invoking my laziness, my fear, my distraction. Perhaps that's why I feel, every night, that I've forgotten something.

Reflexive self-questioning of this kind recurs throughout her diary and poems (although one of the problems of reading Pizarnik's works is access to the texts, given that so many pirate versions of her fragmented writings exist). In the fragment of a poem 'Para Janis Joplin' (For Janis Joplin) written in 1972, she compares her own situation to that of the dead rock singer,

[5] I feel that the key to Pizarnik lies in something that has not been developed, that is, a feminist surrealism, which also lacks a coherent language.

[6] Pizarnik's diaries have yet to be published. For this essay, I have used extracts published in *Alejandra Pizarnik: Poemas* (1986).

hay que llorar hasta romperse
para crear o decir una pequeña canción
gritar tanto para cubrir los agujeros de la ausencia
eso hiciste vos, eso yo.
me pregunto si eso no aumentó el error

(Pizarnik 1982a: 71)

you have to cry until you break yourself
to make or sing the smallest song,
shout loud enough to hide the gaps of absence
you did all this, I did it.
I ask myself if this increased the error

Writing here is self-destruction. The act of writing cannot change anything, it is part of an inexorable daily torture that is not so much saving her as dragging her towards the edge of the abyss. Her diary entry for 29 December 1962 is explicit,

I change the colour of paper, the colour of ink. I write crying. I write laughing. I write to ward off coldness and fear. I write in vain. Silence has corroded me: some poems remain like a dead person's bones that chisel into my frightened nights. The meaning of the most obvious word has been lost. I still write. I still throw myself urgently to narrate states of astonishment and rage. A very slight pressure, a new recognition of what's stalking you, and you will no longer write. We're just a few steps away from an eternity of silence.[7]

Pizarnik writes constantly about being on the edge, in a place where oblivion is only a hair's breadth away. Significantly, she never writes about salvation, about escaping from the inevitable plunge into darkness. Love affairs, with men and women, cannot fill up the desolate spaces she describes in her more lyrical poems. The very fact of being in the world puts her into a state of existential anguish, and the only way out is through the mirror into the otherworld, into death.

In a poem entitled 'Infancia' (Childhood) published in *Los trabajos y las noches* (1965), Pizarnik refers to Alice, the protagonist of Lewis Carroll's stories for children, *Alice in Wonderland* and *Alice Through the Looking Glass*. Carroll's Alice enters one alternative world by falling down a gigantic rabbit hole, and the other by climbing through a mantelpiece mirror. Pizarnik's

[7] This passage is from the diary entry for 29 Dec. 1962, cited in Frank Graziano (ed.), *Alejandra Pizarnik: A Profile* (1987), 115, who notes that the extracts dating after 1961 have not been published in Spanish.

poem compares Alice to someone going into death with her eyes wide open. Like Alice 'en el país de lo ya visto', literally, 'in the land of the already seen', the land of what is not unexpected, Pizarnik's character goes into nothingness. Carroll's Alice enters a magical realm where extraordinary things happen, and danger is always dissolved into comedy, but Pizarnik's Alice has no such illusions. Her Alice is typical of the child figure who recurs in her poetry and prose, a fearful, suspicious child, haunted by images of women in red, bloodstained queens from the world of nightmares. Though she writes a great deal about childhood, it is never comfortable, safe, or pleasant, but always a time of fear, the moment of her realization of the terrors of living in the world.

Like Angela Carter, Pizarnik was fascinated by the darker side of fairy-tales, the wolf with fangs that drip blood, the murderous stepmother, the dolls with hearts of mirrors, that people the landscape of the Central European folklore of her ancestry. But, in contrast to Carter, the subtext of Pizarnik's writing concerns not so much the violence that crosses gender boundaries, but rather the violence perpetrated by women against women. One text in particular deals with extremes of female violence. Her story 'Acerca de la condesa sangrienta' (The Bloody Countess) (1975) is written in the fairy-tale mode, and consists of twelve short sections recounting the story of the sixteenth-century European aristocrat, Erzebet Bathory, the woman who has been the prototype of the myths of the Countess Dracula, who tortured over six hundred young girls to death in her castle to keep herself young with their blood.

Pizarnik's story opens with a preface, in which she refers to her source, a book about the Countess by the French Surrealist Valentine Penrose. In this way, she establishes her narrative as a story deriving from a book in another language about a historical character whose life has turned into legend—a series of texts meshing together in ways reminiscent of her fellow Argentinians, Borges or Bioy Casares. Penrose, she tells us in the preface, disregarded the Countess's obvious sexual perversion and madness, and focused instead on 'la belleza convulsiva del personaje' (the convulsive beauty of the character).[8] Starting

---

[8] 'Acerca de la condesa sangrienta', in *El deseo de la palabra* (1975), 179–98, 179. An English version by Alberto Manguel is included in his collection of stories by Latin American women writers, *Other Fires* (1986), 70–87.

with that notion of the convulsive beauty of horror, Pizarnik's version explores the linked question of the boundaries of freedom. Throughout, she intervenes in the narrative, commenting on the story she tells.

Luce Irigaray looks at what she terms 'the repressed female imaginary' that consists of an infinity of fragments in constant motion, where words are both ceaselessly embraced and simultaneously rejected. Asking what might happen if that female imaginary came into play as something other than fragments, she suggests that a phallic maternity would result, with woman losing the uniqueness of her pleasure in the race to power,

By diminishing herself in volume, she renounces the pleasure derived from the nonsuture of her lips: she is a mother certainly, but she is a virgin mother. Mythology long ago assigned this role to her in which she is allowed a certain social power as long as she is reduced, with her own complicity, to sexual impotence. (Marks and de Courtivron 1981: 104)

Pizarnik's Countess sutures other women's mouths; she chooses to torture to death young women, teenage girls, images of her own daughters whose shadowy existence remains an absent line in the narrative, or perhaps a reflection of herself, married at 15 to a brutal soldier husband. In his lifetime, the narrator tells us, she would torture for pleasure but not kill. After his death, when she assumed the power of ruler previously held by him, she began to take her sadistic pleasure-seeking to its logical conclusion, the death of her victims.

The first three sections of the story recount a series of examples of the Countess's methods of torture in gruesome detail. Section I, 'La virgen de hierro' (The Iron Maiden) describes the famous medieval torture device, a smiling clockwork doll that opens its arms and embraces its victims before impaling them on spikes. The Countess sits on her throne and watches as the doll's painted breasts burst open 'y aparecen cinco puñales que atraviesan a su viviente compañera de largos cabellos sueltos como los suyos' (and five daggers appear that pierce her struggling companion whose hair is as long as its own) (Pizarnik 1975: 181). In the ensuing sections a young girl is killed by having water poured over her naked body in the snow, another by being hung in a cage lined with sharp knives.

Here the Countess becomes more than a spectator. Sitting

below the cage that is suspended above her, the Countess is soaked in the blood of the victim. By the end 'han habido dos metamórfosis' (there have been two transformations): the living body is a corpse, and the Countess's white dress has turned red (Pizarnik 1975: 181). This is the first hint of what will later become explicit, that the Countess needs the blood of her victims in order to assure her own survival.

It is not until the fourth section that the narrator enters overtly into the narrative. She intrudes after describing the Countess's pleasure in the pain inflicted on other women, to recapitulate the basic features of the story so far. Later, she intrudes again to comment on the parallels between nakedness and death,

Desnudar es propio de la Muerte. . . . Pero hay más: desfallecimiento sexual nos obliga a gestos y expresiones del morir . . . Si el acto sexual implica una suerte de muerte, Erzebet Bathory necesitaba de la muerte visible, elemental, grosera, para poder, a su vez, morir de esa muerte figurada que viene a ser el orgasmo. (Pizarnik 1975: 185)

To strip naked is a prerogative of Death. . . . But there is more: sexual climax forces us into death-like gestures and expressions . . . If the sexual act implies a sort of death, Erzebet Bathory needed the visible, elementary, coarse death, to succeed in dying that other phantom death we call orgasm.

Having established the direct link between sex and death, the narrator goes on to suggest that the Countess chose to play the role of Death because she was so desperate not to grow old, and Death alone cannot die. Later, when the Countess starts to bathe in blood to preserve her youthfulness that connection between youth, beauty, and death is made yet more explicit. The Countess struggles to hold absolute power, understood in terms of controlling life and death and holding back time.

But there is also more than a suggestion that her actions are beyond any control, that the seeds of her destruction are contained within her own genetic make-up. The Bathory family history is briefly outlined, a destiny from which the Countess cannot escape. The narrator notes with irony that, by the time she reached 40, most of her family had been destroyed by madness or death. And yet, there is an order in the madness of the Bathory family, an order that the narrator invites us to read as both hereditary and learned. The Countess may have her bloodstained ancestry, but she also has her own desires as a woman and exercises those desires as soon as the social space that would permit her to enact them opens up.

Both Derrida and Irigaray use the image of the mirror, to illustrate the paradox of madness/not-madness, female/male, voice/silence. In some ways writing the mirror suggests for Pizarnik a solution to life's pain. The central episode of Pizarnik's story is fittingly entitled 'El espejo de la melancolía' (The Melancholy Mirror). Here the focus is again on the narrator, as she speculates on what the Countess might have felt as she sat for days in front of her great, dark mirror. The quotation that prefaces this section is from Octavio Paz: '¡Todo es espejo!' (Everything is mirror!). The dark, cold mirror before which the Countess sits is briefly described, but the mirror is itself a mirror of another reflection, that of the narrator and her murderous Renaissance predecessor. Nothing can satisfy the Countess, but equally she preserves her own secrets. The empty space of the mirror is one where the Countess can hide, sharing her melancholia with her own otherness, in a state where,

nada pasa allí, nadie pasa. Es una escena sin decorados donde el yo inerte es asistido por el yo que sufre por esa inercia. Este quisiera liberar al prisionero, pero cualquier tentativa fracasa como hubiera fracasado Teseo si, además de ser él mismo, hubiese sido, tambien, el Minotauro; matarlo, entonces, habría exigido matarse. (Pizarnik 1975: 190)

Nothing happens in it. No one intrudes. It is a bare stage where the inert I is assisted by the I suffering from that inertia. The latter wishes to free the prisoner, but all efforts fail, as Theseus would have failed had he been not only himself, but also the Minotaur; to kill him then, he would have had to kill himself.

Theseus is also the Minotaur; the narrator is also the Bloody Countess. This process of mirroring exposes the horror of the unconscious of the melancholic, for though she explicitly states that she has no interest in explaining the Countess, the narrator identifies her as suffering from melancholia. Writing the mirror for Pizarnik, then, is also a means of recording her anguished mutilation, albeit through a specious unification. Pizarnik's poetry and diary entries return over and over to descriptions of her own melancholy. In a poem entitled 'Historia antigua'

(Ancient History) she writes about the thoughts that come to her in darkness, 'el color infernal de algunas pasiones' (the hellish colour of certain passions) the 'sol negro de sus deseos elementales, excesivos, no cumplidos' (the black sun of elemental desires, excessive, unfulfilled) (Pizarnik 1965: 9). Beneath all that, in the place where she refuses to look, lies her inner Bloody Countess, obsessed with violence and madness,

> Alguien canta una canción el color del nacimiento:
> por el estribillo pasa la loca con su corona plateada.
> le arroyan piedras. Yo no miro nunca el interior de los
> cantos. Siempre, en el fondo, hay una reina muerta.
>
> (Pizarnik 1965: 9)
>
> Someone is singing a song the colour of birth;
> the madwoman with her silvery crown walks through the chorus.
> They heave stones at her. I never look inside songs.
> At the bottom, always, lies a dead queen.

The identification of the narrator with the Countess increases through the narrative, and the tone shifts significantly. Even as the Countess's crimes are catalogued and the number of her victims increases, so the narrator probes further to try to uncover her thought processes. What did she do with her lonely days and nights, we are asked, and we are told about the emotional dependence of the Countess on her two old female servants. She passes time with her jewels, her clothes, her mirror, like any other bored rich woman, though we are also told that she continued to administer her finances well, in order to provide for her absent daughters. She lives like a prisoner despite her absolute power and, once exposed by the Count Palatine, she is condemned to spend the remaining three years of her life a literal prisoner, walled up in her own castle.

Despite the reaffirmation of patriarchal order with the judgment against the Countess, the narrator insists that she showed no sign of repentance, no understanding that what she had done was in any way wrong. The end of the story brings the narrator and the Countess together in a state beyond feeling, a trance-like state in which perfect beauty consists of the horror of blood and broken female bodies,

> Ella no sintió miedo, no tembló nunca. Entonces, ninguna compasión
> ni emoción ni admiración por ella. Sólo un quedar en suspenso en
> el exceso del horror, una fascinación por un vestido blanco que se

vuelve rojo, por la idea de un absoluto desgarramiento, por la evo-
cación de un silencio constelado de gritos en donde todo es la imagen
de una belleza inaceptable. (Pizarnik 1975: 197)

She was never afraid, she never trembled. And no compassion, no
sympathy or admiration may be felt for her. Only a certain astonishment at the enormity of the horror, a fascination with a white dress
that turns red, with the idea of total laceration, with the imagination
of a silence starred with cries in which everything reflects an unacceptable beauty.

The Countess is compared to de Sade and Gilles de Rais, as
another example of someone who reached beyond all limits
and transgressed every social boundary. The story ends with a
rebuttal of the opening quotation from Jean-Paul Sartre, 'El
criminal no hace la belleza; él mismo es la auténtica belleza'
(the criminal does not make beauty; he himself is the authentic beauty) (Pizarnik 1975: 179), as the story of Erzebet Bathory
demonstrates that the absolute freedom of the human creature
is horrible. Ultimately, without the order imposed by reason,
the freedom of the human creature to express herself involves
unreflected, unrestrained murder.

Hypothesizing further on the unfolding of the female imaginary in a state of wholeness, Irigaray stresses the absolute self-
centredness of such a state:

Thus a woman's (re)discovery of herself can only signify the possibility of not sacrificing any of her pleasures to another, of not identifying with anyone in particular, of never simply being one. It is a sort of
universe in expansion for which no limits could be fixed and which,
for all that, would not be incoherency. Nor would it be the polymor-
phic perversion of the infant during which its erogenous zones await
their consolidation under the primacy of the phallus. (Marks and de
Courtivron 1981: 104)

Pizarnik's Bloody Countess is never one, she is reflected in her
dark mirror. But her universe is not incoherent; it is all too
coherent in the orderliness of its horror. The narrator follows
her into that universe, endeavouring neither to judge nor to
empathize, but the fusion between narrator and object of narration, and their mirroring, is all too apparent to the reader.
The story disturbs because of the increasingly close identification of the narrator with her subject and her refusal to condemn the atrocities she has described. Both women accept

their fate without question, both are condemned by their nature as melancholics. There is no sense of any freedom having been won even through excess, as the Surrealists claimed was the case of de Sade. The reader is placed in a similar position to that of the passive victims of the Countess's atrocities, appalled and yet unable to condemn or pass any moral judgment. The woman reader as voyeur is able to subjectify her self by speculating on the objectification of the other, but all ethical considerations have been abandoned; nothing remains but the aesthetic.

Pizarnik returns again and again to the problem of women's power and powerlessness. Her interest in fairy-tales and in the Alice stories is significant, for it is never clear whether Alice has any power or any control over the environment in which she finds herself. The child moves through a potentially threatening world protected only by her own innocence and her own ignorance. Just as Alice finds that size, shapes, and names constantly change, so Pizarnik writes about shifting perceptions and about the problem of naming things. Her little poem 'Nombre' (Only a name) plays with her own name:

> alejandra alejandra
> debajo estoy yo
> alejandra
> (Pizarnik 1976: 95)

The second line translates literally as 'underneath am I'. She is beneath her own name, buried under it. 'Este decir y decirse no es grato' (This saying and being named is not welcome), she says in 'Piedra fundamental' (Pizarnik 1971*b*: 13). 'Nombre' is more an epitaph than a celebration of naming, and recalls another poem, 'Mucho más allá' (Much further away) where she asks what use it is to go on hoping for something:

> Y qué da a mí,
> A mí que he perdido mi nombre,
> un nombre que me era dulce sustancia
> en épocas remotas, cuando yo no era yo
> sino una niña engañada por su sangre?
> (Pizarnik 1965: 73)

> And what is there for me,
> for me who has lost her own name,

> a name that nourished me sweetly
> in distant ages, when I was not I
> just a little girl deceived by her blood?

She goes on to ask what it is all for, and the poem concludes
with an image of a woman pursued, literally hounded to death
by unknown, violent assailants:

> Que mi realidad retrocede
> como empujada por una ametralladora
> que de pronto se lanza a correr,
> Aunque igual la alcanzan,
> Hasta que cae a mis pies como un ave muerta?
>
> > (Pizarnik 1965: 73)
>
> Why does my reality step backwards
> as if shoved by a machine gun
> then suddenly start to run
> though they catch her anyway,
> until she falls at my feet like a dead bird?

Patterns of imagery run through Pizarnik's writings, set out in
a series of binary oppositions. Light is contrasted with darkness, earth with water (the image of the shipwreck recurs frequently), silence with sound, solitude with crowds, the child
with the adult, the doll with the queen, the angel with death.
She uses the three symbolic colours of red, white, and black,
interlaced with green and lilac. What is perhaps most striking
about her poetry and her prose, however, is that these patterns
of imagery run through texts that might be described as anorexic, poems that are reduced to the bare minimum of words,
prose pieces that are so tight and condensed they are difficult
to assimilate. Compelled to write just as the Countess was
compelled to murder, Pizarnik stripped her texts down to the
bone. 'Porque una poesía como la de Alejandra no era para
comunicar, sino para incomunicar' (Poetry like Alejandra's was
not meant to communicate but to non-communicate) wrote
Inés Malinow, in a preface to some of her texts published in
1986.[9] And in her fragmentary 'Los pequeños cantos' (Little
poems), Pizarnik writes about the absence at the heart of writing, at the heart of life:

---

[9] Inés Malinow, preface to *Alejandra Pizarnik: Poemas* (1986), p. vii.

III
el centro
de un poema
   es otro poema
el centro del centro
   es la ausencia
IV
en el centro de la ausencia
mi sombra es el centro
del centro del poema
     (Pizarnik 1971*a*: 62–3)
III
The centre
of a poem
   is another poem
the centre of the centre
   is absence
IV
in the centre of absence
my shadow is the centre
of the centre of the poem

Borges too writes about the text within the text that goes on forever in an infinity of enclosures, but Pizarnik places herself in that space of nothingness. In her early poetry the sense of loss and sadness predominates, but the poetry of the late 1960s and early 1970s is much more violent. The posthumous collection 'La donante sagrada' that appeared in 1982 contains some of her drawings of monstrous creatures with gigantic almost plant-like heads and tiny stick-like limbs, and the prose-poems are full of images of wounds and dismemberment: 'Soy mi espejo incendiado' (I am my blazing mirror) she writes in one piece,[10] and elsewhere speaks of 'el martirio de beber en el espejo, el horror de ser dentro de mi propia sombra' (the torture of drinking in the mirror, the horror of being inside my own shadow) (Pizarnik 1982*b*: 27). Another fragment contains the phrase: 'No hay lenguaje para mi miedo como no hay guante para una mano cortada' (There is no language for my fear just as there is no glove for an amputated hand) (Pizarnik 1982*b*: 28). She writes of a universe peopled with 'ángeles violentos,

---

[10] 'La donante sagrada', in *Zona prohibida* (1982*b*), 25.

mutilados' (violent, mutilated angels) in love with words (Pizarnik 1982*b*: 31), of the 'lucha feroz entre sílabas y espectros'
(savage struggle between syllables and ghosts), of 'frases como
brazos amputados, deseos que nadie imaginó bajo el sol, estrellas
sin luz, olas sin mar' (phrases like amputated arms, unimaginable desires, stars without light, waves without sea) (Pizarnik
1982*b*: 32).

In these last fragments the sense of despair is overwhelming.
Earlier, in 'Piedra fundamental', she had asked where writing
could lead, and answered herself: 'A lo negro, a lo estéril, a
lo fragmentado' (To darkness, to sterility, to fragmentation)
(Pizarnik 1971*b*: 13). In this poem the dolls are torn to pieces
by an angry child in a passage that recalls the bloody Countess
and which links the violence of disappointment with her own
biography:

La muñecas desventradas por mis antiguas manos de muñeca, la de-
silusión al encontrar pura estopa (pura estepa tu memoria): el padre,
que tuvo que ser Tiresias flota en el río. Pero tú, por qué te dejaste
asesinar escuchando cuentos de álamos nevados? (Pizarnik 1971*b*: 13)

Dolls, torn to pieces by my ancient doll-like hands, the disappointment of feeling raw stuffing inside (raw steppes, your memory); a
father, who wanted to be Tiresias, floating in the river. But you, why
did you let them kill you as you listened to stories of snow white
poplar trees?

This passage, like the rest of the piece, shifts from *yo* to *tú* (I
to you) enigmatically. Is the first *tú* (of the 'memoria') her
father, the Russian emigrant with his memories of the great
open steppes of his own childhood, or is the *tú* herself, the I
speaker, who has been given that memory through childhood
stories? Certainly the second *tú* ('pero tú' (but you)) is herself,
and the storytelling signals the moment of her own death. The
following lines give further clues; using the image of piano
playing, she contrasts skimming across keys like a spider with
sinking in, diving, solidifying, 'para entrar adentro de la música
para tener una patria' (so as to enter music and get myself a
homeland) (Pizarnik 1971*b*: 13).

'Piedra fundamental' is one of Pizarnik's most explicit pieces
about cultural displacement, about not-belonging, and about
the inheritance of stories from another generation that are
transmuted into painful memories, recalling the linking of the

history of the Bloody Countess with her violent present. Pizarnik writes her own life constantly, though never explicitly, always through the signs and symbols of her own bleak, interior
landscape.

In his preface to Pizarnik's 1962 collection, *Arbol de Diana*,
Octavio Paz warns against attempts to analyse or decode Pizarnik's writing. Setting out his preface as an encyclopaedia or dictionary entry, he defines the tree of Diana by refusing to define
it,

(Quim.): cristalización verbal por amalgama de insomnio pasional y
lucidez meridiana en una disolución de realidad sometida a las más
altas temperaturas. El producto no contiene una sola partícula de
mentira ... debido a su extraordinaria transparencia, pocos pueden
verlo. Soledad, concentración y un afinamiento general de la sensib-
ilidad son requisitos indispensables para la visión. Algunas personas,
con reputación de inteligencia, se quejan de que, a pesar de su pre-
paración *no ven nada*.[11]

(Chem.): verbal crystallization through amalgam of passion-filled
insomnia and noontime clarity in a solution of reality exposed to the
highest temperatures. The product does not contain a single dishon-
est particle ... due to its extraordinary transparency, few people are
able to see it. Solitude, concentration and generally refined sensibility are indispensable prerequisites for seeing it. Some people, who
are considered intelligent, complain that despite all their learning
they *cannot see anything*.

Paz's hermeneutically coded praise of Pizarnik recalls the
dilemma set out by Derrida concerning the reading of madness. Reason is not enough, Paz suggests; what is required is a
special kind of sensibility that will enable the reader to enter
Pizarnik's universe, through a process of alchemical transformation, a journey through the mirror.

Arbol de Diana consists of thirty-eight tiny poems, some only
a few words long. Some poems are dedicated to friends, others
refer to paintings by Wols, Goya, and Paul Klee. The violence
of the later writings is absent here, but there are signs of what
is to come. The very first poem refers to the sadness of being
born, the next proposes images of breakdown, a hole or void,
a wall that trembles, and the third (which might be a love
poem) warns the beloved to be on guard against her,

[11] Octavio Paz, preface to 1962 edition of *Arbol de Diana* reprinted in *El deseo de
la palabra* (1975), 7–9.

sólo la sed
el silencio
ningún encuentro

cuídate de mí amor mío
cuídate de la silenciosa en el desierto
de la viajera con el vaso vacío
y la sombra de su sombra

(Pizarnik 1988: 11)

just thirst
silence
no meeting

care for me my love
care for the silent woman in the desert
the travelling woman with the empty cup
and the shadow of her shadow

In these poems, bones gleam in the night, flowers open up in the fog, dawn sees the speaker drunk on lilac-coloured light, precious stones fill up the throat of a petrified bird. But the woman, or women, that people this beautiful world of transparent light suffer and are afraid. The poems move from *yo* to *ella* (I to she) and back again,

miedo de ser dos
camino del espejo:
alguien en mí dormido
me come y me bebe

(Pizarnik 1988: 22)

fear of being two
pathway in a mirror;
someone sleeping within me
eats me and drinks me

The I/she is a traveller, a sleepwalker, a paper doll, a silken girl, a dead child, a sleeping woman eating her own heart. Poem 35 is an address to her life,

Vida, mi vida, déjate caer, déjate doler, mi vida,
déjate enlazar de fuego, de silencio ingenuo, de
piedras verdes en la casa de la noche, déjate caer y
doler, mi vida.

(Pizarnik 1988: 43)

Life, life of mine, let yourself fall, let yourself suffer,
life of mine, let yourself be bound with fire, with simple
silence, with green stones in the house of the night, let
yourself fall and suffer, life of mine.

In her diary entry for 15 April 1961, Pizarnik wrote about a
life lost for literature through the fault of literature: 'Por hacer
de mí un personaje literario en la vida real fracaso en mi
intento de hacer literatura con mi vida real pues esta no existe:
es literatura' (By making myself a literary character in real life
I fail in my intent to make literature with my real life since the
latter doesn't exist: it's literature) (Pizarnik 1986: 117). Pizarnik
constantly blurs boundaries, confuses the reflection in the
mirror with the image of the figure who looks into it, blends
past and present, memory, dream, and reality in texts that, like
a painting by Klee, whose style she greatly admired, refute
logical interpretation. Just as Paz insists in his preface that
poetry is to be received, rather than analysed, so Pizarnik wrote
texts that she abandoned to the reader, claiming she refused
to own them.[12] This abandonment recurs elsewhere in the image
of the drowning woman abandoned to the sea, or the child
who has been abandoned by the mother. In her diary entry for
30 April 1966, three months after her father's death on 18
January (tersely recorded in the diary with a single sentence:
'My father's death') she writes about being 30 years old and
knowing nothing of existence, adding 'to give up finding a
mother' (Graziano 1987: 123). Looking into the mirror, she sees
herself reflected back at herself as an adolescent, not as an adult.

Reading Pizarnik's writings is a moving and often painful
experience. The reader is drawn into her universe, led along
the pathways she creates through language, placed in a position that is both voyeuristic and vulnerable. For just as the act
of writing was paradoxically destructive for her and yet at the
same time served as a way of continuing to stay alive, so the act
of reading involves both bearing witness to Pizarnik's years
of pain and suffering and recognizing the inevitability of what
was to come. In 'Tangible ausencia' (Tangible Absence) she
addresses the reader directly,

Que me dejen con mi voz nueva, desconocida. No, no me dejen.
Oscura y triste la infancia se ha ido, y la gracia, y la disipación de los

---

[12] 'El poema y su lector', in *El deseo de la palabra* (1975).

dones. Ahora las maravillas emanan del nuevo centro (desdicha en el corazón de un poema a nadie destinado). Hablo con la voz que está detrás de la voz y con los mágicos sonidos del lenguaje de la endechadora. (Pizarnik 1982a: 29)

Leave me alone with my new, unknown voice. No, don't leave me. The childhood that has gone is dark and sad, grace and my gifts have been scattered. Now wonders are coming from a new centre (sorrow in the heart of a poem written for no one). I speak with the voice behind the voice and with the magical sounds of the language of mourning.

She yearns to be able to see light, not just to name it. Naming stifles feeling, the act of writing and of using language is slowly killing her. Creating poetry is an act of mourning, for a lonely childhood, a dead father, a missing homeland, an absence at the heart of things. Above all, writing is a continual reminder of the absurdity of trying to fit feeling into the constraints of grammar and syntax.

Her attempts to write about the prison house that is language and poetry recall Luce Irigaray attempting to define women's language:

It is continuous, compressible, dilatable, viscous, conductive, diffusible . . . It never ends, it is powerful and powerless through its resistance to that which can be counted, it takes its pleasure and suffers through its hypersensitivity to pressure; it changes—in volume or strength, for instance—according to the degree of heat, it is in its physical reality determined by the friction between two infinitely neighbouring forces —a dynamics of proximity and not of property. (Moi 1985: 142)

Both Pizarnik and Irigaray in different ways are struggling to define the undefinable, to find a way of articulating that which cannot be confined within the boundaries of language. Here Irigarary draws upon physics for her basic metaphor, contrasting the solid with the liquid. Pizarnik, similarly, contrasts the solid with the liquid, and one of her most central metaphors is the sea. Despite her stated aversion to all forms of explicit political involvement, she was nevertheless dealing with issues in her writing that feminist philosophers were also raising, albeit in very different ways. Cheris Kramarae, for example, writing in 1981 argued that 'those who have the power to name the world are in a position to influence reality' (Kramarae 1981:

165).[13] Pizarnik would have understood that statement, though what she explicitly did not want was to have that power. The difference between where she stood and where feminism stands is that she saw herself as damaged by the possibilities of having power, and, like the child that recurs through her writing, she tried to avoid taking the responsibility. In 'Tangible ausencia' she writes about being called from the other side of every mirror. Alice stumbled down her rabbit hole and crawled in pursuit of her kitten into the mirror, but Pizarnik describes the mirror as a compulsive thing that draws her into it, perhaps as it also drew the Countess.

In her insistence upon the fluidity of light and water as metaphors for the transparent state of eternal motion, which she contrasts with the horror of fixity, and in her sense of the restrictive power of naming things, Pizarnik touches on central concerns of late twentieth-century feminist thought. 'Las fuerzas del lenguaje son las damas solitarias, desoladas, que cantan a través de mi voz, que escucho a los lejos' (The strongest parts of language are lonely, desolate women singing out through my voice which I hear in the distance), she wrote in 'Fragmentos para dominar el silencio' (Fragments to overcome silence) (Pizarnik 1968: 32).

Pizarnik did not choose to exploit the mirror and hold herself apart from it; she disappeared into it, she made it her end rather than her means. Ultimately, Pizarnik gave up the struggle and stepped through the mirror into oblivion, but her writing is a testament to the terrible darkness against which she fought, an exploration of the impossible dichotomies of living in the world, where absolute freedom is horrible and the forces of rationality demand conformity and control over the individual. In a way, she collapses into her representations with the result that whereas Borges has the text *en abîme*, Pizarnik puts herself *en abîme*. The Countess with her dark mirror and her bloodstained clothes, the woman leaping with her shirt in flames, the lonely adolescent trapped in a woman's body are the images of woman's power and powerlessness that remain.

[13] Luce Irigaray, in *Sexes et parentés* (1987), 83, and *Ethique de la différence sexuelle* (1984), 122, also notes the extent to which language is sustained by blood, flesh, and materiality.

LIST OF WORKS CITED

BASSNETT, SUSAN (1990), 'Speaking with Many Voices: The Poems of Alejandra Pizarnik', in ead. (ed.), *Knives and Angels: Women Writers in Latin America* (London, 1990), 36–51.

DERRIDA, JACQUES (1978), *Writing and Difference* (London).

GILBERT, SANDRA M., and GUBAR, SUSAN (1979), *The Madwoman in the Attic: The Woman Writer and the Nineteenth-Century Literary Imagination* (New Haven).

GRAZIANO, FRANK (1987) (ed.), *Alejandra Pizarnik: A Profile* (Durango, Colo.).

IRIGARAY, LUCE (1974), *Speculum: de l'autre femme* (Paris).

—— (1985) *Speculum of the Other Woman*, Catherine C. Gill (Ithaca, NY).

—— (1981), 'Ce sexe qui n'en est pas un', in Marks and de Courtivron (1981), 99–106.

—— (1984), *Ethique de la différence sexuelle* (Paris).

—— (1987), *Sexes et parentés* (Paris).

KRAMARAE, CHERIS (1981), *Women and Men Speaking: Frameworks for Analysis* (Rowley, Mass.).

MANGUEL, ALBERTO (1986), *Other Fires* (London).

MALINOW, INÉS (1986), 'Preface', *Alejandra Pizarnik: Poemas* (Medellín).

MARKS, ELAINE, and DE COURTIVRON, ISABELLE (1981) (eds.), *New French Feminisms* (Brighton).

MOI, TORIL (1985), *Sexual/Textual Politics* (London).

PAZ, OCTAVIO (1975), ' "Preface" to *Arbol de Diana*', repr. *El deseo de la palabra* (Barcelona).

PIZARNIK, ALEJANDRA (1965), *Los trabajos y las noches* (Buenos Aires).

—— (1968), *Extracción de la piedra de locura* (Buenos Aires).

—— (1971a), *Los pequeños cantos* (Caracas).

—— (1971b), *El infierno musical* (Buenos Aires).

—— (1975), *El deseo de la palabra* (Barcelona).

—— (1976), *La última inocencia y las aventuras perdidas* (Buenos Aires).

—— (1982a), *Textos de sombra y últimos poemas*, ed. Olga Orozco and Ana Becciu (Buenos Aires).

—— (1982b), *Zona prohibida* (Veracruz).

—— (1986), *Alejandra Pizarnik: Poemas* (Medellín).

—— (1988), *Arbol de Diana* (1962) (Buenos Aires).

8

Cristina Peri Rossi's Gender Project
Rewriting Male Subjectivity and Sexuality in *Solitario de amor**

LINDA GOULD LEVINE

THE writings of Cristina Peri Rossi have long seduced the imagination of the critic in search of transgressive models of gender definitions and sexual roles. Brandishing an allusive and enigmatic literary style, her poetry and prose transport the reader to a metaphorical terrain where phallic power is decentred, sexual multiplicity is suggested, and boundaries of gender and identity are continually collapsed and expanded. Acutely aware of the constraints that fixed definitions place on the subject and well versed in contemporary theories which seek to destabilize phallocentric constructs, Peri Rossi offers her readers a complex body of fiction that inserts itself in a most compelling project for the woman writer: the reconfiguration of male subjectivity and sexuality. This is not to suggest that the restructuring of female subjectivity and sexuality in Latin American literature has been explored in all its possible dimensions, although certainly the writings of Sylvia Molloy, Diamela Eltit, Albalucía Angel, Isabel Allende, Elena Poniatowska, Rosario Ferré, Ana Lydia Vega, and Peri Rossi herself, among others, have greatly contributed to this endeavour. Rather, it is to recognize, as Kaja Silverman has forcefully stated in *Male Subjectivity at the Margins*, the degree to which ' "deviant" masculinities . . . represent a tacit challenge not only to conventional male sub-

* This paper was completed with the support of Separately Budgeted Released Time from Montclair State College. I am grateful to Ellen Engelson Marson for her perceptive comments and critical reading and to JoAnne Engelbert for her invaluable assistance with translations.

jectivity, but to the whole of our "world"' in that 'they call
sexual difference into question, and beyond that, "reality" itself' (Silverman 1992: 1).

Nowhere in Peri Rossi's body of writing is this claim more
powerfully realized than in her 1988 novel, *Solitario de amor*.[1]
Described by the author as the 'anatomía de la pasión' (anatomy
of passion) (Narváez 1992: 246) and narrated in the first person
by an unnamed male character hopelessly in love with the
enigmatic Aída, the text plays continual havoc with its readers.
Faithful to the author's disavowal of 'un mundo regido por
una sola lectura' (a world ruled by one reading alone) (Peri
Rossi 1981: 10) it can be interpreted on many different levels
which intersect with current theories of gender, myths of sexual
undifferentiation, critiques of compulsory heterosexuality, and
rewritings of Freudian premises. Central to all these readings
which suggest the full range of Peri Rossi's engagement with
theoretical concerns and issues crucial to feminist scholarship
is the author's implicit attempt to expand upon a Utopian project which has haunted her writings during the last twenty-five
years. *Solitario de amor* is, in essence, Peri Rossi's most carefully
conceived response to her desire to envision human sexuality
as a fluid spectrum of multiple preferences and options open
to the subject at all times.

If, in an interview published in 1985, the author decries 'the
sex which is socially imposed upon us' and expresses the longing for a 'multiple sex' to be used 'at liberty without society
feeling attacked and upheaved', her prose and poetry have
consistently provided the space for the realization of this libidinal multiplicity (Hughes 1985: 272–3). From the pages of *El
libro de mis primos*,[2] which call for a society where 'homosexuales,
heterosexuales' and 'hermafroditas' (homosexuals, hetero-
sexuals, and hermaphrodites) (1989: 147) have the right to
express themselves freely to the creation of the hermaphrodite
Alejandra in 'Gambito de reina' (*La tarde del dinosauro* (1985)),
and the poetic declaration in *Babel bárbara* that 'hay más de dos
sexos' (there are more than two sexes) (1991: 69), Peri Rossi's
transgression extends beyond the postulation of transvestism,

---

[1] Citations are from the third edition, published in Barcelona in 1989.
[2] Originally published in Montevideo in 1969. Citations are from the 1989
edition, published in Barcelona.

lesbianism, and homosexuality as viable sexual alternatives for her characters.[3]

Echoing and expanding upon Hélène Cixous's belief in the bisexual nature of each person, Peri Rossi's novel, *Solitario de amor*, provides the ultimate playground battlefield for her most extensive elaboration of the concept of androgyny. That she chooses a male narrator as the central focus of this Utopian endeavour is highly significant. Despite her claims that the narrator's sex is 'irrelevante' (irrelevant) because he is 'un símbolo del amor' (a symbol of love), his male gender and Peri Rossi's postulation, through him, of a 'nonphallocentric erotic economy' serve to 'dispel the illusions of sex, gender, and identity' which constitute heterosexual patriarchal society (Camps 1988: 42–3, 45; Butler 1990: 19).[4] Iconoclastically breaking down the boundaries which divide the sexes, Peri Rossi's narrator is simultaneously male and female in psyche and sexuality, a transgressive subjective space where heterosexual and lesbian experiences fuse together with dreams and fantasies common to both sexes.

To some degree, the narrator may be viewed as a contemporary version of the androgynous being whose duality is best captured by Plato in his *Symposium* (Buchanan 1959). In this lyrical tale of the origins of 'human nature' (1959: 143) Plato writes of three original sexes, 'man, woman, and the union of the two' (1959: 143) who were severed in half by a vengeful Zeus and destined to spend the rest of their lives in search of the other half which would then compose 'the whole . . . called love' (1959: 147). If, for Plato's speaker, Aristophanes, this myth explains the birth of male and female homosexuality, as well as

---

[3] For an analysis of the language of eroticism in Peri Rossi's early works, see John F. Deredita, 'Desde la diáspora: entrevista con Cristina Peri Rossi', *Texto Crítico*, 9 (1978), 131–42, and Hugo J. Verani, 'La rebelión del cuerpo y el lenguaje (a propósito de Cristina Peri Rossi)', *Revista de la Universidad de México*, 37 (1982), 19–22. For further commentaries on sexual ambiguity and plurality in Peri Rossi's novel *La nave de los locos*, see Lucía Guerra Cunnningham, 'La referencialidad como negación del paraíso: exilio y excentrismo en *La nave de los locos* de Cristina Peri Rossi', *Revista de Estudios Hispánicos*, 23 (1989), 63–74; Elia Kantaris, 'The Politics of Desire: Alienation and Identity in the Works of Marta Traba and Cristina Peri Rossi', *Forum for Modern Language Studies*, 25 (1989), 248–64; and Hugo J. Verani, 'La historia como metáfora: *La nave de los locos* de Cristina Peri Rossi', *La Torre: Revista de la Universidad de Puerto Rico*, 4 (1990), 79–82.

[4] For further discussion on the role of gender in narrative voice, see Gustavo San Román, 'Entrevista a Peri Rossi', *Revista Iberoamericana*, 58 (1992), 1041–8, 1045.

of heterosexuality, since the 'men who are a section of that double nature which was once called Androgynous are lovers of women' (1959: 146), Peri Rossi extends this tale beyond the limits of two prescribed and separate sexualities and seeks a fidelity to the original double nature of the human species. She achieves this end in *Solitario de amor* through a continual fluctuation of highly eroticized and lyrical scenarios which suggest, through their very ambiguity and fluidity, the postulation of a non-phallic heterosexual relationship with veiled lesbian connotations lived intensely by her narrator in search of unity with his other half. It is, indeed, no coincidence that the novel is situated in a city 'de cielos lánguidos . . . que diluyen los contornos' (of languid skies . . . that dilute contours) (1989*a*: 9); such is the constant slippage and erasure of fixed boundaries and sharply delineated spaces that characterize the novel.

From the very beginning of her text, Peri Rossi alerts her readers to her daring reconfiguration of male identity. As the narrator casts his 'múltiple mirada' (multiple gaze) (1989*a*: 11) upon the body of his beloved, he sees her through the eyes of 'mi avergonzado macho cabrío y desde mi parte de mujer enamorada de otra mujer' (my embarrassed maleness and from the vantage of the woman within me enamoured of another woman) (1989*a*: 11–12). This suggestive fusion of male and female is reinforced countless times in the text through the use of androgynous symbols which compare the two lovers with twins, parallel moons, and incestuous brothers and sisters. On still another level, the narrator experiences an acute split in his being, an inner division that is filled with clues and signs that refer exclusively and secretly to his love for Aída and which separate him from the rest of society and render him useless in his role as professor and intellectual, and, even more significantly, 'anormal' (abnormal) (1989*a*: 79). While the narrator attributes these characteristics to his overriding passion for Aída and the secretive nature of their love affair, the sheer intensity of the contradictory codes that constitute his identity—reminiscent of Juan Goytisolo's psychic battle with homosexuality in such works as *Coto vedado*—suggest a deviation from 'normal' manhood and further clues to Peri Rossi's destabilization of conventional male subjectivity.

The elaborate description of erotic play and the female body which, for Gabriela Mora, 'constituye uno de los aspectos más

extraordinarios del libro' (constitutes one of the most extraordinary aspects of the book), provides a concrete and metaphorical testing ground for the author's transgressive postulation
of sexual identity and gender (Mora, forthcoming 1996). Much
of the text reads, in fact, like a lyrical fictionalization of Luce
Irigaray's portrayal of 'female pleasure' as a vast and total activity centring on the breasts, the vulva, the lips, the vagina,
and the mouth of the uterus (Irigaray 1985: 28). Delicate and
sensual strokings of the breasts with fingers and mouth coexist
with ardent descriptions of oral sex plunging the narrator and
reader alike into a flow of bodily fluids and 'emissions' that
dispel the 'omissions' of woman's corporality from literary texts
so astutely observed by critics Sandra Gilbert and Susan Gubar
(1988: 232). The sheer oral nature of the narrator's sexual
activities: 'sorbo, chupo, bebo, beso, babeo . . . saboreo, absorbo,
relamo, paladeo' (I sip, I suck, I drink, I kiss, I dribble . . . I
savour, I absorb, I lick, I taste) (Peri Rossi 1989*a*: 88) not only
serve as a model for Jane Gallop's definition of *écriture féminine*
as a 'switch from the phallic to the oral sexual paradigm', but
also significantly repeat the patterns of eroticism seen in Peri
Rossi's previous writings involving both lesbian and heterosexual
relationships (Gallop 1988: 165).

Amy Kaminsky has perceptively noted in her analysis of Peri
Rossi's *Evohé* the presence of male speakers and a nonphallocentric sexuality which, although 'within the heterosexual
repertoire', can be read as 'lesbian poetry lightly coded' (Kaminsky 1993: 121). Within the context of the ambiguous codes of
Solitario de amor, the concerted attempt to decentre the male
sexual organ and provide a virtual panegyric of the 'pleasure
extending from male lips to female genitals' renders a similar
interpretation of sexuality (Silverman 1992: 368). Yet at the
same time as Peri Rossi leaves her text open to the possibility
of a homoerotic reading of the love relationship and the speculation that the male narrator is, in fact, a veiled representation
of a lesbian sexuality, she allows for still another reading which,
much like the 'multiple gaze' and 'parallel moons', suggests
the coexistence of a female and male soul, and a lesbian and
heterosexual continuum, within her male narrator.

Curiously, Peri Rossi reverts to a conventional code of binary
oppositions to communicate the heterosexual spectrum of
her novel. The narrator's penis is the 'llave' (key) which fits

perfectly in Aída's 'cerradura' (lock); he is continually situated on the 'outside' while she is the desired 'inside'; he is 'on top', while she is 'underneath'. Yet, beneath this somewhat clichéd recourse to stereotypical language lies a transparent reconfiguration of heterosexual lovemaking devoid of power and phallic supremacy. The narrator himself is acutely conscious of the unconventional nature of his sexual relationship. Lyrically describing his act of covering Aída not like 'los machos a las hembras . . . sino como las nubes al cielo' (males on females . . . but like clouds on the sky) (Peri Rossi 1989a: 127), he categorically reiterates that he experiences 'ninguna sensación de poder' (no sense of power) (1989a: 125), and merely seeks to respond to Aída's demands. Yet underneath this postulation of a non-phallic sexuality there lurks a complex web of emotions regarding male gender that haunts the narrator's unconscious. By expanding the scope of her narrator's subjectivity to the realm of his dreams, Peri Rossi not only delves anew into her familiar role of creator of allusive dreams and nightmares viewed as 'symbolic constructions whose task is to interpret reality', but also provides her text with an access point from which to critique psychoanalytical premises regarding the consolidation of male identity (Hughes 1985: 59).

The relationship between the castration complex and the formation of gender constitutes a thought-provoking terrain which has been discussed in great length by social scientists as well as by feminist critics. Disagreements concerning this psychological phenomenon encompass such areas as the cause of the castration complex, the role it plays with regard to the perpetuation of heterosexuality, and the disavowal of femininity and homosexuality, the actual nature of the threatened member as penis or symbolic phallus, and the identification of 'lack' as residing in the female or the male. While providing a detailed account of many aspects of this polemic, Kaja Silverman concurs with Serge Leclaire that 'classic male subjectivity rests upon the denial of castration' (Silverman 1992: 44). If one accepts this premiss as valid, the logical question that follows is: Does acknowledgement of castration hence constitute a refutation of 'classic male subjectivity' and the postulation of a new model of gender identification? *Solitario de amor* offers a fascinating window to this question as Peri Rossi vividly re-creates the castration anxiety that lurks in her narrator's unconscious.

Two main dreams provide the setting for the author's exploration of his psychological phenomenon. In the first one, the narrator describes himself as living in a house similar to Aída's in the city of this childhood. The house to the left is inhabited by his mother; the house to the right, by Aída. Centrally located between his mother and his lover, he is suddenly threatened by the appearance of a strange man, ugly, pimply, and myopic, who informs him that he is Aída's new lover and that, on Aída's request, he has come for the key to her house. Overcome with pain and distress, the narrator replies that he doesn't have the key, that, in fact, he never had it, but that if he did have it, he would never hand it over. The strange man decides to enter by the window, leaving the narrator alone with his mother, who declares: 'Es muy raro que nunca hayas tenido la llave de Aída' (It's very odd that you have never had Aída's key) (Peri Rossi 1989*a*: 64).

Before the reader has the chance to dissect the significance of this dream, the narrator himself offers his own version of its meaning after relating it to Aída and speculating to himself: 'Soy un hombre sin llave, es decir, un hombre sin sexo' (I'm a man without a key, that is, a man without a sex) (1989*a*: 64). What strikes this critic as even more interesting than the concluding acknowledgement of castration or the implicit association of 'sex' with 'el poder simbólico del falo' and 'el biológico del pene' (the symbolic power of the phallus and the biological power of the penis) as Gabriela Mora has suggested is the ambiguous suggestion of female identification that shapes the initial image of the dream and is carried throughout the entire text (Mora, forthcoming 1995). The comforting similarity of the two houses, or two wombs, of Aída and the narrator, serves to disrupt, on a very basic level, the 'repudiation of femininity' which is central to the Freudian notion of male 'gender consolidation' (Butler 1990: 59). Securely situated in a state of gender undifferentiation and pre-Oedipal comfort between mother and lover, it is only the intrusion of the strange man, the representative of the Lacanian 'symbolic order' or 'Law' of the 'Father' that disturbs the narrator's sense of harmonious union with woman and makes him long for a return to a protective female space instead of denying it as a component of his own subjectivity (Lacan 1977: 321).

The second dream, which serves as a foreshadowing of the

end of the novel and the termination of the love affair, also
functions to specify the precise meaning of the house of the
first dream. This oneiric sequence is described as a nightmare
in which the narrator dreams that Aída has expelled him 'de
su casa, de su útero, de su habitación, de su cuerpo' (from her
house, from her womb, from her room, from her body) (Peri
Rossi 1989a: 169). The conversion of nightmare to reality and
the ensuing sense of displacement from the female body marks
the narrator so severely that he acknowledges with even greater
force the full dimensions of his castration. Reversing his previous vision of himself as 'el tronco hundido en la matriz' (the
trunk submerged in the womb) (1989a: 98), he now declares
that Aída was his 'tronco' (trunk), his 'centro' (centre), and
that he is left 'un sexo fláccido' (a flaccid penis), 'un hombre
castrado' (a castrated man) (1989a: 178–81).

While clearly conveying the narrator's sense of despair at
losing his physical and symbolic access to Aída's womb, Peri
Rossi's novel provides a still more subtle enquiry into the narrator's conflicting feelings regarding his sexuality and identification with male gender. Rather than locating 'lack' in the
feminine spectrum—despite the enigmatic references to Aída's
'pequeño sexo' (small sex) (1989a: 95)—he consciously appropriates this lack for himself. To this degree, the very nature of
his fetishism, which is exhibited in his compulsive purchase
of sandals for Aída as well as in his frequent allusions to her
small feet (125, 143), responds less to his desire to find 'objects
chosen as substitutes for the absent female phallus' than to his
implicit recognition that the real subject of castration is not
Aída, but himself (Strachey 1973: 155). And yet, the sandal
itself, the displacement and replacement of the endangered
penis, is not the mainstay of security and protector of gender
identity as it is for the textbook fetishist. Rather, in a typical
Peri Rossian twist which negates the desirability of the threatened organ, the narrator continually displays an ambiguous
attitude toward the symbolic order that the penis/phallus has
come to represent.

In one of his romantic reveries that occurs while he and
Aída contemplate maps of 'paraísos perdidos' (lost paradises)
(Peri Rossi 1989a: 31) in the Cofradía de Ingenieros, the narrator feels transported back in time to the 'soledad del paraíso
anterior a la caída' (solitude of paradise before the Fall) (1989a:

34), where Aída becomes a symbol of the primeval woman, without a navel, without a husband, without children. As he savours his love for her in this eternal moment, he realizes that the paradise will be destroyed, lost forever, at the moment Aída's sandals cross the threshold of the Cofradía and plant themselves on the other side of the pavement, where she will once again become 'la mujer dotada de ombligo' (the woman endowed with a navel) (1989*a*: 34). Through this brief passage Peri Rossi fuses myths and theories of a diverse and heterogeneous nature to suggest that the original lost paradise was one of sexual non-differentiation erased by the emblem of the phallus (sandal) that separates the 'imaginary, where loss and difference are unthinkable' from the symbolic or patriarchal order (Eagleton 1983: 186).

Returning again to Plato's *Symposium* as an initial access point to address this speculation, the Greek philosopher offers a fascinating account of the construction of human form following the division in half of the original three beings that inhabited the universe. Desirous of fashioning a body that would serve as a reminder of their previous state, Zeus calls upon Apollo 'to heal their wombs and compose their forms' (Buchanan 1959: 145). Responding to this request, Apollo creates a belly with 'one mouth at the centre, which he fastened in a knot' leaving in that region various wrinkles 'as a memorial of the primeval state' before the skin was smoothed out and moulded (Peri Rossi 1989*a*: 145). The reference to both a state of paradise and to Aída as a woman who inhabits that terrain without a navel clearly reinforces Peri Rossi's multiple configurations of the desirability of an androgynous state untarnished by the imprint of the phallus/sandal or patriarchy/pavement on the terrain of paradise. The frequent appearance in the novel of images suggesting a primeval state—'lago antediluviano' (antediluvian lake) (1989*a*: 10), 'anterior a la palabra' (before the word) (1989*a*: 53)—further reinforces the mythical substratum of the novel as Peri Rossi combines Platonic theory with a re-creation of the prelapsarian paradise which suggests, in turn, an integral relationship between androgyny and the power of naming.

To clarify this relationship, Carolyn Heilbrun's *Towards a Recognition of Androgyny* provides a useful tool. In this classic study, Heilbrun offers provocative evidence for the postulation of 'the androgynous nature of God and of human perfection before the Fall' (Heilbrun 1964: p. xvii). Citing extensively from the literature of mysticism, she presents a compelling portrayal of 'God's conception of man' as 'a complete, masculinely feminine being', and suggests that 'Original sin is connected in the first instance with division into two sexes and the Fall of the andro-gyne, i.e. of man as a complete being' (1964: p. xvii). If one adds to this theory the concept of the 'original Logos' trans-mitted from God to Adam before the Fall, the complex dynam-ics of Peri Rossi's libidinal and linguistic politics acquires even greater significance (Steiner 1975: 58). Ever faithful to her belief that 'nombrar las cosas es imitar a Dios' (to name things is to imitate God) (Camps 1988: 47) or as Percival declares in *La nave de los locos*, 'apoderarse un poco de ellas' (to gain some control over them),[5] she bequeaths the power of naming and rite of linguistic baptism to Aída and the narrator alike, thus extending her concept of androgyny to the terrain of language.

Perhaps even more significant than this sharing of linguistic power, however, is the fact that naming becomes a vehicle by which the narrator is not only able to fuse himself anew with the desired body of his beloved, but also to claim for himself the primacy of birthing, of bringing forth words from his en-trails. Lyrically and powerfully shattering the exclusive identi-fication between women and birth, Peri Rossi presents a passage rich with connotations of an androgynous nature, where the narrator's body acquires and assimilates the texture of woman as he defines himself as both lover and midwife in possession of the creation of language and the word made flesh:

Voy poniendo nombres a las partes de Aída, soy el primer hombre, asombrado y azorado . . . Palpo su cuerpo, imagen del mundo, y bautizo los órganos; emocionado, saco palabras como piedras arcaicas y las instalo en las partes de Aída, como eslabones de mi ignorancia.
El lenguaje debió de nacer así, de la pasión, no de la razón. . . . Soy el primer hombre que, desde la oscuridad de sus vísceras, extrae a borbotones un grito gutural y profundo, un grito lleno de hilachas y de ramas, de sangre y de saliva para nombrar la pasión que lo acosa. (Peri Rossi 1989a: 18–19)

I am naming Aída's private parts, I am the first man, astonished and confused . . . I touch her body, image of the world, and baptize her

[5] Citations from this 1984 novel are from the 1989 edition, published by Seix Barral of Barcelona, 139.

organs; excited, I pull out words like ancient stones and I place them in Aída's private parts, as links of my ignorance.

This must be how language was born, out of passion rather than reason. . . . I am the first man to extract from the utter darkness of his entrails a deep, shuddering cry, a cry of tattered threads and branches, blood and saliva, to name the passion that haunts him.

Although the narrator clearly appropriates for himself in an androgynous fusion traditional female powers associated with the mystery of the womb and traditional male privileges associated with naming, this multitextured generation of words does not complete his identity. To exist, the narrator, too, must be named. Defining himself as both the womb and the space inside the womb, he portrays his own birth inexorably linked to the birth of words that shatter conventional language and create 'otras palabras, otros sonidos, muerte y resurrección' (other words, other sounds, death and resurrection) (Peri Rossi 1989*a*: 15). His need to emerge from the depths of Aída's entrails and the depth of her words is so great that, echoing his previous acknowledgement of castration but applying it now to the man/child in search of a lover/mother, he declares: 'Si ella no me nombra, soy un ser anónimo, despersonalizado, sin carácter, sin identidad. Soy un niño castrado' (If she doesn't name me, I am an anonymous being, depersonalized, without character, without identity. I am a castrated child) (1989*a*: 179).

This desire to have the word and identity emerge from the maternal body introduces still another reading, previously suggested, of *Solitario de amor* as a fascinating rendition of the pre-Oedipal phase and its relationship to the creation of language. Peri Rossi, herself, throughout her writings and interviews, has expressed her belief that 'el paraíso perdido del amor siempre es la relación intrauterina' (the lost paradise of love is always the intrauterine relationship), the sense of 'unidad umbilical' (umbilical unity), where one can disappear as a separate entity and fuse completely and totally with the body of woman (Camps 1988: 42). If her writings are continually filled with multiple symbols of the womb as well as of suggestive scenarios of exile from the lost paradise, *Solitario de amor* gives new meaning to this quest as the narrator longingly and desperately seeks to perpetuate 'este instante, sagrado . . . sacro . . . uterino . . . total' (this sacred . . . holy . . . uterine . . . total instant) (Peri Rossi 1989*a*: 98) when, as both lover and foetus, he feels united and fused with Aída and dreams of 'un paraíso donde nada cambia' (a paradise where nothing changes) (1989a: 146). The space of Aída's house, her symbolic womb, captured so well in the narrator's dreams, is the site of this pre-Oedipal paradise which holds at bay the symbolic order dominated by the imprint of the Father on social and linguistic practices.

In consonance with the shattering of gender boundaries that Peri Rossi has suggested throughout her entire novel, the fictionalized re-creation of the pre-Oedipal phase offers still another dimension to this theme. Pre-Oedipality has been conceptualized as a phase where the 'opposition between masculine and feminine does not exist' (Moi 1985: 165) and where 'semiotic' emerges as one of the 'two modalities' of the 'signifying process' whose 'drives' and 'energy discharges . . . connect and orient the body to the mother' (Kristeva 1984: 24). While Peri Rossi's novel does not reproduce the 'preverbal semiotic space' Kristeva writes of (1984: 27), it does capture the 'dissolution of difference' that Paul Julian Smith views as characteristic of this modality (Smith 1989: 27). This expression of a prime component of the semiotic within 'the syntactic language' of the symbolic—the other modality of the signifying process (Kristeva 1984: 22)—is most strikingly demonstrated when the narrator and his lover mirror each other in their lovemaking and erase the boundaries between their separate selves: 'Gime. Gimo. Grita. Grito. Jadea. Jadeo. Aúlla. Aúllo. Fricciona. Fricciono' (She moans. I moan. She screams. I scream. She pants. I pant. She howls. I howl. She rubs. I rub) (Peri Rossi 1989a: 125).

Just as the semiotic cannot ultimately replace the symbolic, Peri Rossi's narrator, too, is unable to safeguard the bond he shares with Aída and is ultimately expelled from his intrauterine paradise and forced to take up residence on the other side of the pavement. His attempt to recapture the contours of Aída's body through the act of writing ushers in further speculations on the complex nature of both language and androgyny in the novel. Lacanian theory postulates that, following the termination of the pre-Oedipal phase and the entrance of the male into the symbolic order, language is created as a substitute for an 'absence', a void that is particularly related to 'the primordial relation to the mother' (Lacan 1977: 286). As Judith Butler clarifies in *Gender Trouble*, 'the loss of the maternal body as an object of love is understood to establish the empty space out of which words originate' (1990: 68). But here, it must be noted that, in opposition to the plurality and fluidity of the semiotic and its intimate connection with the maternal, the language that marks the Law of the Father is one that implies hierarchical notions of power and the positionality of woman on the margins. Does this imply that once the narrator has been definitely expelled from Aída's womb/house/body he becomes a 'bearer or proponent of this repressive law' (Butler 1990: 79)? Or does the body of his writing and the words he generates approximate in such intensity the body of Aída that they enable him to expand the boundaries of the symbolic and experience anew a semblance of the semiotic or lost fusion with the maternal?

Peri Rossi's novel responds affirmatively to this latter question and ultimately substantiates Kristeva's claim that 'the subject is always both semiotic and symbolic' and hence, the 'signifying system he produces . . . is necessarily marked by an indebtedness to both' (Kristeva 1984: 24). The manner in which the narrator inhabits the two modalities is particularly clear at the end of the novel after Aída terminates her relationship with him. He embarks on a journey in the solitary space of a train compartment, a vehicle which represents a symbol of the womb according to the author's own account (Ragazzoni 1983: 235). In possession of a black notebook which reproduces the black mesh that covered Aída's naked body, and dressed himself in a dark suit that mirrors her own garb, he implicitly rests his fingers, once dipped in the milk that emerged from his lover's nipples, upon his notebook. Submerging himself in the symbolic 'white ink' of creativity which is bequeathed from mother to offspring as Hélène Cixous suggests (Cixous 1981: 251), but which also reinstates his former role as a man of letters, he writes Aída's body as he envisions her slowly and sensually masturbating to climax. Once again, he is aligned to the feminine sphere, as the multifolded contour of her clitoris shapes his fluid writing and the sibylline message she emits catapults him back to still another pre-Oedipal paradise. Responding to a Hebrew proverb's query about the destination of the lover blinded by passion, Aída suggests to the narrator that he seek his mother's house. His first dream is thus recast as his mother's house becomes the desired maternal womb that replaces the lost paradise. Residing simultaneously in a female and male terrain as he again appropriates the right of birthing his lover's passion and naming her body, the narrator sustains his dualistic nature up to the close of the novel.

Thus concludes Peri Rossi's audacious challenge to the limits of gender and her postulation of an androgynous subjectivity and sexuality as the centre of her male narrator. The implications of this work, which branches out in countless directions, collides with Freudian thought, rethinks Lacanian theory, intersects with French feminist's concept of language, reproduces themes from Platonic literature, and responds implicitly to serious enquiries on gender formation, are, indeed, enticing and daringly conceptualized. If gender may ultimately be viewed as a construct that responds to society's desire to perpetuate structures of power, Peri Rossi compellingly suggests in *Solitario de amor* that male gender can be reconfigured in the transgressive realm of fiction. By creating a male character intimately involved in the feminine sphere on many levels, she acknowledges the power of femininity as an integral source of human subjectivity which cannot be relegated to the margin or repudiated. To this degree, the fact that her narrator is nameless is, indeed, important. It is not to him *per se* that we must look for a new model of gender roles, but to what he represents for Peri Rossi: a blank page, or perhaps a black notebook on which to inscribe, in white ink, the contours of a radically different male subjectivity which could potentially restructure gender relationships and enable us to envision the impact of the written word on society.

LIST OF WORKS CITED

BUCHANAN, SCOTT (1959) (ed.), *The Portable Plato*, 6th edn. (New York), 121–87.
BUTLER, JUDITH (1990), *Gender Trouble: Feminism and the Subversion of Identity* (London).
CAMPS, SUSANA (1988), 'La pasión desde la pasión: entrevista con Cristina Peri Rossi', *Quimera*, 81: 40–9.
CIXOUS, HÉLÈNE (1981), 'The Laugh of the Medusa', in Elaine Marks and Isabelle de Courtivron (eds.), *New French Feminisms: An Anthology*, trans. Keith Cohen and Paula Cohen (New York, 1981), 245–64.

EAGLETON, TERRY (1983), *Literary Theory: An Introduction* (Minneapolis).

GALLOP, JANE (1988), *Thinking Through the Body* (New York).

GILBERT, SANDRA M., and GUBAR, SUSAN (1988), *No Man's Land: The Place of the Woman Writer in the Twentieth Century* (New Haven).

HEILBRUN, CAROLYN (1964), *Towards a Recognition of Androgyny* (New York).

HUGHES, PSICHE (1985), 'Interview with Cristina Peri Rossi', in Mineke Schipper (ed.), *Unheard Voices: Women and Literature in Africa, the Arab World, Asia, the Caribbean and Latin America*, trans. Barbara Potter Fasting (London, 1985), 255–74.

IRIGARAY, LUCE (1985), *This Sex Which Is Not One*, trans. Catherine Porter with Carolyn Burke (Ithaca, NY).

KAMINSKY, AMY K. (1993), 'Cristina Peri Rossi and the Question of Lesbian Presence' in *Reading the Body Politic: Feminist Criticism and Latin American Women Writers* (London and Minneapolis), 115–33.

KRISTEVA, JULIA (1984), *Revolution in Poetic Language*, trans. Margaret Walker (New York).

LACAN, JACQUES (1977), *Écrits: A Selection*, trans. Alan Sheridan (New York).

MOI, TORIL (1985), *Sexual/Textual Politics: Feminist Literary Theory* (London).

MORA, GABRIELA (1995), '*Solitario de amor* de Cristina Peri Rossi: una desmitificación del amor y otros retos', in JoAnne Engelbert with Dianne Bono (eds.), *Hacia un nuevo canon literario* (Hanover, NH, forthcoming).

NARVÁEZ, CARLOS RAÚL (1992), 'Eros y Thanatos en *Solitario de amor* de Cristina Peri Rossi', '*Alba de América*, 10: 245–50.

PERI ROSSI, CRISTINA (1981), *Indicios pánicos* (Barcelona).

—— (1985), *La tarde del dinosauro* (Barcelona).

—— (1989a), *Solitario de amor*, 3rd edn. (Barcelona).

—— (1989b), *El libro de mis primos* (Barcelona).

—— (1989c), *La nave de los locos* (Barcelona).

—— (1991), *Babel bárbara* (Barcelona).

RAGAZZONI, SUSANA (1983), 'La escritura como identidad: una entrevista con Cristina Peri Rossi', *Studi di Letteratura Ispano-Americana*, 15–16: 227–41.

SILVERMAN, KAJA (1992), *Male Subjectivity at the Margins* (London).

SMITH, PAUL JULIAN (1989), *The Body Hispanic: Gender and Sexuality in Spanish and Spanish American Literature* (Oxford).

STRACHEY, JAMES (1973), (ed.), *The Standard Edition of the Complete Psychological Works of Sigmund Freud*, 24 vols. (London), xxi. 147–57.

STEINER, GEORGE (1975), *After Babel: Aspects of Language and Translation* (New York).

9

Sonia Coutinho Revisits the City

LUIZA LOBO

ONE of the objectives of feminist criticism has been to challenge the view that women are socially or biologically handicapped in relation to men, thereby helping women break through the barriers imposed by patriarchy and phallocentrism. However, some feminist critics have flirted with versions of biological determinism when discussing the particular characteristics of women's writing:

Women's writing is a writing from the Inside: the inside of the body, the inside of the house. The writing of the return to this Inside, the nostalgia of the Mother and the sea. The great cycle of the eternal return, which naturally denies the masculine myth of technical progress and of faith in the future.[1]

Although many women's writings continue to centre on the space within—the body, the home, the mind, and the emotions—there is a new vein in women's writing which, while privileging the subjective, breaks out of the home both physically and stylistically, venturing into an epic mode and the tangled web of city streets.

This essay examines how the women characters in Sonia Coutinho's work break free from traditional dichotomies and adopt a postmodern coception of the city as a theatrical site in which forms of alterity can be enacted. Exiled from its construction and decentred, multilayered social life, women are able to reveal new ways of seeing and appreciating the labyrinthine city. They achieve this not as voyeurs but in pleasurable adventures and as the performers of their own futures. Their otherness allows them to see the postmodern city as a text

[1] My translation of Didier (1981: 37). For a discussion of this see Moi (1991: 163–7).

made up of complex new meanings, and thus to escape the metaphysical dualisms traditionally imposed on them: consumer/consumed, male/female, and cultural/natural. Starting from the notion of the city as text, this chapter explores the relationship between Coutinho's use of metafiction and intertextuality and the maze-like structure of the postmodern city.

Like other contemporary women writers in Brazil, Coutinho places her characters first of all in the home, in order to describe their hopes, fears, and inner thoughts.[2] The stream of consciousness technique that she observed in the work of Virginia Woolf and that of her compatriot Clarice Lispector (1925–77) is particularly well suited to this purpose. However, Coutinho's treatment of women's position in society differs from Lispector's, in that Coutinho's characters often escape their domestic space. *Uma certa felicidade* (A Certain Happiness) (1976) and *Os venenos de Lucrécia* (Lucrécia's Poisons) (1978) are particularly good examples of this. Her characters not only break out of their homes but at times even pursue erotic adventures.

Any analysis of how this writing invades the city streets needs to address the way in which women writers have focused on metropolitan life, and how a psychological dimension more prevalent in women's literature than men's has erupted from the traditional domestic space. Coutinho's work offers a striking example of this in Brazil, giving rise to what might be termed a new genre. She offers a kaleidoscope of images and self-images of women in the urban environment. Her characters create personae in search of identities, and present their stories in fictional but also autobiographical terms. It is through this autobiographical writing that the self-consciousness of her characters emerges. In the words of Florence Howe, it is in autobiography and the consciousness of one's life that 'the connection between feminism and literature begins' (Howe 1972: 255).

This kind of search does not come easily to Coutinho's characters, however. They oscillate between a sense of belonging to the external world of the patriarchal city and a sense of being set apart from it in a dream-like, narcissistic scenario which is usually within the confines of the home. The house or room is at once a 'refuge' and a claustrophobic space: 'the man's

---

[2] Sonia Coutinho was born in Itabuna, Bahia, in 1939. She moved to Salvador de Bahia with her family at the age of 7, and to Rio de Janeiro in 1968, where she became a journalist and translator.

world' outside it 'remains uncharted' (Sage 1992: 149).[3] These homes can become like the *huis clos* of Sartre's play, a personal hell peopled by the phantoms of failed relationships and intense imaginings. Yet Coutinho's characters are able to make sorties into the outside world because they tend to live on their own, with no children or husband.

There is also constant movement between the authorial voice and female characters' personalities and perspectives. Characters are prevented from attaining a measure of stability by the difficulty of representing their image, or of finding an existing representation within city life and society. When they do finally leave their apartments they are so immersed in their personal concerns that instead of stepping out purposefully they wander the streets as if lost.

There are, perhaps, similarities between the street wanderings of female characters in *Uma certa felicidade, Os venenos de Lucrécia,* and *O último verão de Copacabana* (Last Summer in Copacabana) (1985) and the autobiographical image of the *flâneur* (wanderer), as developed by Charles Baudelaire in *Les Fleurs du mal* and *Spleen de Paris* and explored by Walter Benjamin:

The crowd—no subject was more entitled to the attention of nineteenth-century writers. It was getting ready to take shape as a public in broad strata who has acquired facility in reading. It became a customer; it wished to find itself portrayed in the contemporary novel, as the patrons did in the paintings of the Middle Ages . . . To move in this crowd was natural for a Parisian . . . Far from experiencing the crowd as opposed, antagonistic element, this very crowd brings to the city dweller the figure that fascinates. (Benjamin 1976: 166–7, 169)

There are, nevertheless, several important differences between the inhabitants of Baudelaire's cosmopolis and those of Coutinho's. Baudelaire assumed the role of author-narrator-character in his poems, and although he was immersed in an age of emergent capitalism he could still maintain his privileged literary activity by writing for newspapers, publishing poems and critical essays, and intellectual literary discussions. Coutinho, by contrast, lives in a phase of capitalism which has alienated

[3] On the domesticity of the plots and on the 'feminine' rather than 'feminist' character of the literature of the 1970s see Lobo (1987: 49–54). See also García (1981).

individuals and their dreams much more dramatically than in the nineteenth century, and this makes her characters' positions more problematic. Moreover, as women these characters are doubly alienated by the city when compared with Baudelaire and his personae. Anyone performing creative tasks (such as Alice, who writes her memoirs in *O caso Alice* (The Alice Affair) (1991)) is rejected as fundamentally unproductive by a society which values only material profit.

With all these counts against them, Coutinho's women find it almost impossible to integrate themselves in society as it stands. Instead they must either stay within the confines of the home or wander the streets. Although the wandering of the *flâneur* offers them only random access to the surrounding environment, transgressing their personal 'walls' is represented as the only way of escaping their submission by/to a culture which oppresses them. Contrary to what one might at first assume—since 'woman is traditionally use value of man, exchange value among men. Merchandise, then' (Irigaray 1981: 105)—the act of buying empowers women and challenges the dominant binary oppositions subject/object, public/private. It allows a woman to extricate herself from the role of object (merchandise) by acquiring the goods of her choice. As Jean Baudrillard argues, only by overcoming the social symbolic 'can women escape the phallocentric order whose political expression condemns them to inexistence' (Baudrillard 1976*a*: 160).[4]

Awareness of the city and the significance of the *flâneur* is part of a long literary tradition which began with Baudelaire and was developed, in Brazil, by his contemporary Joaquim de Sousa Andrade (1832–1902). When Sousa Andrade moved to New York, he made Wall Street the setting for part of his epic poem *O Guesa*.[5] The move allowed him to explore the varied and changeable aspects of life in a modern metropolis. The contemporary cityscape also became very much in vogue in Brazil after Filippo Tommaso Marinetti's lectures and Blaise Cendrars's visit to São Paulo with his new Kodak camera in the

---

[4] For Baudrillard, 'the symbolic is neither a concept, nor an instance, nor a category. It is rather an act of exchange and a social relation' which brings about a 'compromise between the real and the imaginary' (1976*b*: 204). My translations.

[5] Twenty-one stanzas of the comic episode 'O inferno de Wall Street' (The Wall Street Inferno), from the long epic poem *O Guesa* (1876–1902), were translated by Frederick G. Williams in *From Those Who Wrote (Poems and Translations)* (1975).

wake of modernist poet Mário de Andrade. The latter made the multiple and fragmented city the central character in his book of poems *Paulicéia desvairada* (Maddened São Paulo) (1922), a landmark in Brazilian modernism.

The subjectivity of Coutinho's characters and their search for identity intensify the maze-like quality of the metropolis, where female characters become submerged, confused, and fragmented. Woman, objectified in such poems as Baudelaire's 'À Une Passante',[6] is now the conscious subject of this act of wandering, seeing and hearing the city for herself. With this awakening of a female gaze directed at the other, Coutinho's postmodern consciousness emerges, stimulated by her life in the decentred metropolis from the 1970s.

Elizabeth Wilson considers the city much more important for women's emancipation than rural life or suburban domesticity, and has suggested that it is time for a new vision and ideal of city life for women in the postmodern period (Wilson 1991: 11). Recalling the notion of the city as text, 'something to be read and interpreted', she proposes the circular maze as model for the postmodern city, one which provides women with 'settings for voyages of discovery' where they can stroll anonymously, loiter or play the adventurous *flâneur* (Wilson 1991: 10, 11):

This recurring image, of the city as a maze, as having a secret centre, contradicts that other and equally common metaphor for the city as labyrinthine and centreless. Even if the labyrinth does have a centre, one image of the discovery of the city, or of exploring the city, is not so much finally reaching this centre, as of an endlessly circular journey, and of the retracing of the same pathways over time. (Wilson 1991: 3)

For Frederick R. Karl, it is precisely in the rupture catalyzed by the maze-like geography of the city that a new decentred consciousness replaces the old monolithic gaze, bringing to an end logocentric, metaphysical, and eternal truths (Karl 1988:

---

[6] 'À Une Passante' is Poem XCIII of 'Tableaux Parisiens' in *Les Fleurs du mal:* 'La rue assourdissante autour de moi hurlait. | Longue, mince, en grand deuil, douleur majestueuse, | Une femme passa, d'une main fastueuse | Soulevant, balançant le feston et l'ourlet; . . . Moi, je buvais, crispé comme un extravagant, | Dans son oeil, . . . La douceur qui fascine et le plaisir que tue. . . . Ne te verrai-je plus que dans l'eternité? | Ailleurs, bien loin d'ici! trop tard! jamais peut-être!' It appears in *Œuvres complètes* (1975), ii. 92–3.

559).[7] Now statements are derived from the moment, and their verification from the course of events or from links in the linguistic chain. Karl notes how, in 'Structure, Sign and Play' (1966), Jacques Derrida uses the notion of decentralization to question the possibility of any fixed point in discourse from which to 'establish metaphysical limits for linguistic signifiers. This means that a chain of signs always leads to a new one, and that referentials are established in an arbitrary manner' (Karl 1988: 559).

Like discourse, the city seems to unfold itself infinitely, while decentralization and the possibility of an infinite chain of signifiers challenge the binary oppositions of metaphysical thought. These processes can be seen at work in some of Coutinho's short stories, particularly in the series of masks of Hollywood actresses after whom the female characters of *O último verão de Copacabana* are named. The cinematic mythology of mass culture, so typical of city life, lends meaning to the novel's protagonists as they wander through the streets of Copacabana. The constant use of masks as unstable signifiers in these short stories creates a web of intertextuality as Lola is identified with Mary Marvel or Mary Baston, Melissa becomes Lana Turner, Josete becomes Ann Margret; and Cátia takes on the suffering and mystery of Greta Garbo (Ralle 1986). Their glamorous masks allow these seductresses to walk in the city's artificial light as though it were limelight, while simultaneously disguising their fear of failure in patriarchal society. A similarly supernatural atmosphere surrounds Sofia in *Atire em Sofia* (Shoot Sofia) (1989) when Scott Fitzgerald turns up in a bar in Bahia, or Maria Callas, Rimbaud, and Humphrey Bogart make an appearance.

The changing forms of Coutinho's personae generate a multifaceted plot structure which recalls women's actual experiences and is found in earlier works by women writers. At the end of the nineteenth century, for instance, the journalist Carmen Dolores used similar resources in her short stories. In *O último verão de Copacabana* the heroines of the various short stories repeatedly change their names to suit their different attitudes and identities. There is, however, a subtle, but interesting difference between these two examples. While Dolores's

---

[7] See also Jacques Derrida's essays on the crisis of metaphysics, especially 'La Différance', 'Ousia et Grammé', and 'Le Supplément de copule', in *Derrida* (1972: 1–29, 31–78, 209–46).

character uses these masks to hide an illicit love affair, Coutinho's characters use them not to hide but to expose their fantasy selves and become integrated into city life.

Although it tends to be assumed that women are somehow inherently unsuited to urban life, they are in fact the most fit for it. Given the transformations witnessed in contemporary society —linking representations of cities to postmodern bricolage, challenging the limitations of Aristotelian and Cartesian designs to become collections of subcities rather than centred monoliths—women's changing masks have become an indispensable adaptive mechanism. Some male authors—Dostoyevsky with St Petersburg and Joyce with Dublin—have used the city setting as a sign of visibility; others, such as Breton with Paris, have used the city as sign of madness; Italo Calvino has used Babel as the representation of the invisible city. As Renato Cordeiro Gomes observes:

The representation of the city is linked directly to visual metaphors, and this is so recurrent as to have become a tradition. The scene of writing appears under the sign of visibility; writing figures as an act of 'giving sight to'. On the one hand, it is linked to the technique of the portrait when, in the act of producing the discourse, it refers to the reality that can be observed and is linked to the geography of the place: on the other hand, it is linked to attempt to build 'invisible cities', which the imagination makes visible. With both techniques the reader verifies the persistence of spatial metaphors in the description of the city, and understands it in visual terms. (Gomes 1984: 76, my translation)

Coutinho and other writers, such as Virginia Woolf in *Mrs Dalloway*, take this tradition further: the invisible cities that exist in characters' minds are themselves linked to a particular psychological orientation through the stream of consciousness technique which emphasizes metaphorical geography. While male authors view the city from the *outside looking in*, therefore, for women authors like Coutinho the city is seen from the *inside looking out*.

This emerges from the image of the city in *Mrs Dalloway*. The stream of consciousness technique allows the character to wander freely from the shop-windows on Bond Street to the clouds and back without abandoning her interior monologue. At the same time, the stream of consciousness allows for a stylistic shift in the character's axis of reality from realism to impressionism.[8] In this way 'a geography of space' becomes a 'geography of mind' (Gomes 1984: 76). Since Clarissa Dalloway many women characters have taken their first steps in the urban landscape as street 'hunters'. In an essay written five years after *Mrs Dalloway*, entitled 'Street Haunting: A London Adventure', Woolf muses on the act of wandering as an escape into the outer, public space of the street:

As the fox-hunter hunts in order to preserve the breed of foxes, and the golfer plays in order that open spaces may be preserved from the builders, so when the desire comes upon us to go street rambling the pencil does for a pretext, and getting up we say: 'Really I must buy a pencil', as if under cover of this excuse we could indulge safely in the greatest pleasure of town life in winter—rambling the streets of London. (Woolf 1964*b*: 23)

Gazing through shop-windows, these women characters have hunted down the consumer goods which enable them to assert their power to purchase and own property.

In books such as *Uma certa felicidade, Os venenos de Lucrécia,* and *O último verão de Copacabana*, Coutinho's women characters lose themselves while searching for their identity or while purchasing articles that symbolize the power of which they have been deprived:

A Avenida Nossa Senhora de Copacabana | Conheço o ronco desta rua e as janelas mil eu espio pensando | Milhares de janelas . . . Acordo de manhã, faço o café. Pela janela, uma nesga de céu e muitas paredes, isto é minha querida Copacabana. As vitrinas de tuas lojas mudam de três em três dias, teus bares abrigam gente de tantas partes, até velhas sozinhas de noite, com cara de eternamente honestas e calcando sandálias de borracha | O chope e as pizzas, Copacabana, e este esforço para viver, sobreviver... Zom, bum, trom, zum, dra, tchá, tchá, tchá, conheço todos os ruídos dos miolos deste bairro, máquina que amo por não pedir aos solitários que se identifiquem. Responde apenas ao dinheiro, e isto simplifica muito as coisas. Até oferece— desfile eterno de pessoas nas calçadas, vitrinas decoradas em constante variação, discussões sobre o tempo e obras públicas com garçons e choferes de táxi.

Avenue Nossa Senhora de Copacabana | I know the roaring of this street and the thousands of windows I spy while thinking | Thousands

---

[8] See the impressionistic style related to stream of consciousness in Coutinho's column 'Apontamento', *Jornal da Bahia* (1965–6). The style here resembles that of Clarice Lispector's chronicles later collected in *A Descoberta do Mundo* (1984).

of windows . . . I wake up in the morning, I make coffee. By the window, a fringe of sky and so many walls, this is my dear Copacabana. The windows of your shops change every three days, your bars shelter people from all parts, even old women alone at night, with their eternally honest features and their rubber sandals | Beer and pizza, Copacabana, and this effort to live, to survive . . . Zmm, boom, brrm, vroom, pah, cha, cha, cha, I know all the visceral noises of this quarter, a machine I love because it does not ask loners to identify themselves. It responds only to money, which makes things much easier. It offers an eternal parade of people on the pavements, the changing decorations of the shop-windows, discussions about the weather and public works with waiters and taxi drivers. (Coutinho 1976: 39, my translation)[9]

The spatial references to boulevards and streets are reminiscent of Baudelaire, and the concern about public building in the twentieth-century city recalls Woolf. Yet Coutinho's characters seem to seek themselves through memory, and consequently through time rather than space. In the short novel *O jogo de Ifá* (Ifá's Game) (1980) the protagonist Renato returns to Salvador da Bahia in order to recover memories of his distant past in that north-eastern part of the country. As the author-narrator explains in chapter 11 (with a quotation from Woolf's *Orlando*) Renato and another character, Renata, in effect form a single androgynous individual. Although the character fails to find the old family values he seeks, he finds himself in the uniqueness of each moment in the atmosphere of the city. The African rites that surround the cult of the Eguns (spirits of the dead) in Candomblé are an inextricable part of his past and an essential element of Salvador de Bahia's strangely anachronistic quality. It is a past alive and breathing in the present. However it is also here, where he sees himself in his past, that he searches for his future self by resorting to Afro-Brazilian prophecy. In chapter 37, the 'babalaô' (African priest) can consult the Ifá God, throwing shells in the 'jogo de búzios' (casting of the runes) to determine Renato's destiny. Unlike accounts in which the search for identity is undertaken strictly through space in the act of window-shopping, we have here a sort of vertical space through time. Meanwhile, Renato's counterpart, Renata, is often confined to an apartment in Rio de Janeiro,

[9] This is an experimental text, akin to a prose poem. I have inserted vertical lines to indicate the ends of unpunctuated lines.

as if waiting for something to happen. Initially, Renata remains nameless. She is a lonely woman unable to act. Renata's acute emotion is solitude. Time for her is slow, at first. Space is enclosed. Renata does not push for recollections as Renato does, but her initial questions are the same as his. (Quinlan 1991: 155)[10]

This recalls a moment in Walter Benjamin's essay 'The Storyteller' (1976: 85). Describing two types of oral narrator he refers to two metaphorical figures: one the sailor who travels in space; the other the peasant who tells his experience through time while fixed in space on his land. For Renato, the 'candomblé terreiro' (a sacred site where African rites are performed) becomes a privileged open space for the enacting of values that predate European patriarchal society. In his/her mind, this return to Salvador involves a mood of ritual that creates a kind of eternal present.[11]

The ambiguity of female characters towards the city and their memories of the past—which restrict their activities to the social order of domesticity—also figure in the author's first two novels, which have been published only recently: *Atire em Sofia* (1989), and *O caso Alice* (1991): 'Rio de Janeiro for Sofia does not mean the geography of independence. It means the geography of solitude' (Martins 1990: 8). Perhaps because of the increasing violence in Rio de Janeiro, where these novels are set, the author chooses to include elements characteristic of the underside of the city: assassination, mysterious disappearances, drug-dealing, break-ins, and theft. In both novels it is implied—albeit ambiguously—that the heroines are finally murdered. In *Atire em Sofia* the journalist, João Paulo, is writing a novel which parallels the main plot. Meanwhile Alice's story is told metafictively through her diary, which is stolen by a neighbour who takes up the narrative after Alice's mysterious disappearance. It is suggested that she is murdered by a Colombian drug-dealer acquaintance, while Sofia do Rosário is apparently murdered by João Paulo. Moreover Alice was herself a murderer, having killed her mother's second husband when she was an adolescent and, later, her estate-agent friend

---

[10] This quotation refers to *O jogo de Ifá*, 12–13.
[11] See Sonia Countinho's review of a book on this subject by Muniz Sodré, *Santugri: histórias de Mandinga e Capoeira* (1988), in Coutinho (1988). See, also by Muniz Sodré, *O terreiro e a cidade* (1993).

Dalmo Travassos. She behaves not as a murderer, however, but as a victim of her previous acts and recollections.

This constant self-pity on the part of female characters leads them to veer between violence and unconscious self-judgement, giving rise to a heightened awareness of the passage of time.[12] Sofia spends most of her time confined to an apartment where on one occasion she is unable even to locate her reflection in the mirror. Alice too vanishes from her apartment, and finds herself—perhaps only in her imagination or in an afterdeath state—in the Looking-Glass Hotel in a now devilish Salvador da Bahia. There she is taken prisoner by Kabbalistic demons with whom she has sex: the previously benevolent images of the Candomblé gods become terrifying European devils, in the form of members of a rock band. At the same time (and like Sofia) Alice is haunted by fearful images of harpies and destructive characters from the Greek of Hebrew Pantheon such as Lilith, the first rebellious Eve. The epigraph of *Atire em Sofia* seems to announce the appearance of a potentially cruel, self-destructive form of feminism: 'Quero experimentar um feminino terrível' (I want to experience a terrible feminine), a quotation taken from Antonin Artaud. In *O caso Alice* the epigraph—'Este é o tempo dos *Assassinos*' (This is the age of the *murderers*)—is taken from Arthur Rimbaud. As the reading of both of these novels progresses, the cruelty towards female characters becomes increasingly evident. The female images chosen by Alice represent the city as a 'mundo cão' (dog-eat-dog world) in which Alice is striving to survive, as it were, through the looking-glass but as a 'criança congelada (frozen child) (Argolo Estill 1992: 5):

Porque dentro de mim, dentro de você, Alice, ficou presa e sufocada uma menina ofendida. E dessas crianças congeladas são feitos os santos, os loucos e os assassinos. (Coutinho 1991: 141)

Because inside me, inside you, Alice, an offended girl is held and suffocated. And from these frozen children saints are made, madmen and murderers.

Thus, despite the high-action plot, we are still connected to the workings of the protagonists' minds. This is achieved

---

[12] Malcolm Silverman applies these expressions to the characters of *O último verão de Copacabana* in his review in *World Literature Today* (1988).

through the stream of consciousness technique and its emphasis on reflections, which creates a sense of ambiguity and uncertainty as the characters continue their search for identity in the postmodern cityscape. The combination of this technique with elements characteristic of the crime novel may signal the emergence of new genre.[13] This innovation is a consequence of the epic voyage, or *periplus*, experienced by many of Coutinho's characters who venture into the city: it follows the financial conquest of a room of their own. It may also signal a parallel between the present phase of Brazilian women's literature and the third 'female phase' of women's writing as described by Elaine Showalter in *A Literature of Their Own* (1991: 13).[14] Until this point most Brazilian women authors had lingered in what Showalter classifies as the 'feminine' phase of women's writing, barely approaching the second, 'feminist', phase.

This possible new genre prefigured in Coutinho's innovation remains linked to the description of women's experience inside their homes or bodies. This may reflect the fact that the domestic world is the one that women have known best and have identified with not because of their gender but because of their lifestyle. However, in the new literature that appears in Brazil from the 1970s, the patriarchal values that still structure women's social behaviour and feelings do not prevent women from venturing into the epic. The epic, in this case, may nevertheless consist of a mixture of adventurous journey and imaginary travel through time, in contrast with classical epics in which only the 'real' accomplishments of the hero in the 'real' mythological world are significant.[15]

The crime novel genre, initiated by Edgar Allan Poe, developed by R. L. Stevenson, and present in the gothic atmosphere of so many authors known to Coutinho, is echoed here in the

---

[13] Coutinho is aware of the crime novel genre practised by women, as can be seen in her latest book—an essay on the traditional development of the plot, the *roman noir*, and variations by women writers—*Rainhas do crime: ótica feminina no romance policial* (1994).

[14] Toril Moi calls attention to the confusion existing not only between the defining terms 'feminist' and 'female' but also between the terms 'feminine' and 'female', in Moi (1989).

[15] A small, imaginary *periplus* takes place in Clarice Lispector's *A paixão segundo G.H.* (1964), where the female protagonist ventures into her maid's room and the back area of her apartment apparently for the first time in her life. See also Luiza Lobo on *A paixão segundo G.H.*, in Marting (1993).

use of metafictional narration. In *O jogo de Ifá* the life story of Renato and Renata is taken up by an omniscient narrator, leading to conclusions which conflate both characters by the end of the short novel. The narrative of *O caso Alice* is intertwined with that of Lewis Carroll's *Alice in Wonderland* and *Through the Looking Glass*, with a constant play of mirrors and the merging of protagonists' names and actions. Alice's manuscript, filled with dream-like memories and references to the imaginary world encountered in her diary, is later replaced by the direct, police-like narrative of her neighbour Ciro, who even hires a detective to try to find her.[16]

Metafiction is a resource that reflects not only intertextuality as a feature of contemporary discourse—the image of the book as a microcosm is one of the most ancient examples—but also the maze-like quality of the city (Curtius 1957: 332, 339, 361). The recourse to metafiction and intertextuality and the attempt to see the city subjectively constitute a new woman's *paideuma*, or knowledge, In Coutinho's work this project was evident before *O jogo de Ifá* in a passage from the short story 'Amor, amores', from *Os venenos de Lucrécia*. Here a woman narrator duplicates herself first as a male film-maker and then as a male author-narrator-character, while continuing her confined existence in Copacabana:

O escritor—ele, afinal, o demiurgo sem identidade que, se soubesse quem era, provavelmente só escreveria sobre si mesmo mas, como se ignorava (consultando o espelho, via apenas o vazio, nenhuma imagem refletida) e precisava contentar-se com os múltiplos disfarces construídos, dia a dia, diante da máquina de escrever (uma personalidade por semana. (Coutinho 1978: 82)[17]

The writer—he, himself, a demiurgo deprived of an identity who, if he knew who he was, would probably only write about himself, but as he didn't know who he was (consulting his looking-glass, he saw only emptiness, not an image reflected in it) he had to be satisfied with the multiple disguises that he created each day, facing his typewriter (one personality every week).

---

[16] The contemporary Brazilian writer Márcia Denser in a review of *O caso Alice* (Denser 1978: 116), comments on 'cryptomnesia', the memories buried in the 'collective unconscious', which provoke a sense of displacement in time and space as well as in the structure of the text, resulting in a *mise en abîme* which is an extreme case of metafiction.

[17] 'Amor, Amores' (Love, Lovers) was republished in *O último verão de Copacabana* (1985), 116–24. My translation.

Here we have what Linda Hutcheon calls

a kind of fiction which began to run rampant in the 1960s. 'Metafiction', as it has now been named, is fiction about fiction—that is, fiction that includes within itself a commentary on its own narrative and/or linguistic identity. (Hutcheon 1990: 1)

In effect, Hutcheon sees the detective story as diegetic paradigm or model since the plot is based on the general pattern of the puzzle or enigma. The reader of a murder mystery comes to *expect* the presence of a writer within the story itself, be it Agatha Christie or Dorothy Sayers (Hutcheon (1990: 31):

I would not argue that in metafiction the life–art connection has been either severed completely or resolutely denied. Instead, I would say that this 'vital' link is reforged, on a new level—on that of the imaginative process (of storytelling), instead of on that of the product (the story told). (Hutcheon 1990: 3)

An existential, psychological reading is linked here to the fantastic or magic realist style of the author, rather than to the traditional Conan Doyle or Edgar Allan Poe police novel genre or the *roman noir*. At the same time, this psychological background is offset by realistic descriptions of settings, plots, and actions. Metafiction would seem to answer the need to produce a new focus in crime literature by women, one which is primarily on women's homes and everyday lives.

Life for women in the city can perhaps be seen as an 'anaclitic mode' of existence, after Jean-François Lyotard's notion of 'un procès en ana-', with which he seeks to overcome modernist and metaphysical dichotomies and to emphasize the way in which 'practices, and fragments rest upon, and lean on each other' (Lyotard 1986: 126).[18] Thus 'your own house [becomes] a tiny fleck in an everwidening landscape' and the body, house, and city become signifiers in an unending chain of new meanings (Rich 1994: 212). When these women wander the streets, as shoppers or *flâneurs*, they overcome the limiting dichotomies of metaphysical discourse and are able to make some kind of dialectical literary synthesis between place, time, and a new personal perspective. The fact that they have been excluded from the city's construction enables them to see it as 'other' and thus to grasp new meanings in this maze as centreless as

[18] See also Probyn (1990).

themselves. As subjects of an imaginary reading of the self and the cityscape, women can merge into the authoritarian, linear, dichotomously ordered space produced by the geography of city buildings, and create their own readings in a new geography of the mind.

LIST OF WORKS CITED

ARGOLO ESTILL, DANIEL (1992), 'O caso Alice de Sonia Coutinho', in *Jornal do Brasil*, 101/276 (11 Jan.), 5.

ANDRADE, MARIO DE (1922), *Paulicéia desvairada* (São Paulo).

BAUDELAIRE, CHARLES (1975), *Œuvres complètes*, 2 vols. (Paris).

BAUDRILLARD, JEAN (1976a), Le Corps manqué', in *L'Echange symbolique et la mort* (Paris), 155–60.

—— (1976b), 'L'Echange de la mort dans l'ordre primitif', in *L'Echange symbolique et la mort* (Paris), 202–15.

BENJAMIN, WALTER (1976), 'The Story Teller' and 'On some Motifs in Baudelaire', in *Illuminations* (New York), 83–100, 155–200.

COUTINHO, SONIA (1976; 1994), *Uma certa felicidade* (São Paulo; Rio de Janeiro).

—— (1978), *Os venenos de Lucrécia* (São Paulo).

—— (1980), *O jogo de Ifá* (São Paulo).

—— (1985), *O último verão de Copacabana* (São Paulo).

—— (1988), 'A lógica do Axé', *O Globo* (5 July).

—— (1989), *Atire em Sofia* (São Paulo).

—— (1991), *O caso Alice* (São Paulo).

—— (1994), *Rainhas do crime: ótica feminina no romance policial* (Rio de Janeiro).

CURTIUS, ERNST ROBERT (1957), *Literatura Européia e idade média latina*, 1st edn. 1946–7 (Rio de Janeiro).

DENSER, MÁRCIA (1978), 'Sempre', *Isto É* (8 Nov.), 116.

DERRIDA, JACQUES (1972), *Marges de la philosophie* (Paris).

DIDIER, BÉATRICE (1981), *L'Ecriture femme* (Paris).

GARCÍA, IRMA (1981), *Promenade femmilière: recherches sur l'ecriture féminine* (Paris).

GOMES, RENATO CORDEIRO (1984), *Todas as cidades, a cidade* (Rio de Janeiro).

HOWE, FLORENCE (1972), 'Feminism and Literature', in Susen Koppelman Cornillon (ed.), *Images of Women in Fiction* (Bowling Green, Ohio, 1972), 253–77.

HUTCHEON, LINDA (1990), *Narcissistic Narrative: The Metafictional Paradox* (New York).

IRIGARAY, LUCE (1981), *Ce sexe qui n'en est pas un*, in Elaine Marks and Isabelle de Courtivron (eds.), *New French Feminisms* (Brighton, 1981), 99–106.

KARL, FREDERICK R. (1988), *O moderno e o pós-modernismo: a soberania do artista 1885–1925* (Rio de Janeiro).

LISPECTOR, CLARICE (1988), *A paixão segundo GH* (1964), ed. Benito Nunes (Florianópolis).

—— (1989), *The Passion According to GH*, trans. Ronald W. Sousa (Minneapolis).

—— (1984), *A Descoberta do Mundo* (Rio de Janeiro).

LOBO, LUIZA (1987), 'Women Writers in Brazil Today', in *World Literature Today*, 61/1 (Winter), 49–54.

LYOTARD, JEAN-FRANÇOIS (1986), *Le Postmoderne expliqué aux enfants* (Paris).

MARTING, DIANE (1993), *Clarice Lispector: A Bio-Bibliography* (New York).

MARTINS, ANA MARÍA (1990), in *O Estado de São Paulo*, 111 (24 Feb.) 8.

MOI, TORIL (1989), 'Feminist, Female, Feminine', in Catherine Belsey and Jane Moore (eds.), *The Feminist Reader* (London, 1989), 117–32.

—— (1991), *Sexual/Textual Politics* (London).

PROBYN, ELSPETH (1990), 'Travels in the Postmodern', in Linda J. Nicholson (ed.), *Feminism/Postmodernism* (New York, 1990), 176–89.

QUINLAN, SUSAN (1991), *The Female Voice in Contemporary Brazilian Narrative* (New York).

RICH, ADRIENNE (1994), 'Notes Towards a Politics of Location', *Blood, Bread and Poetry* (London), 210–31.

SAGE, LORNA (1992), *Women in the House of Fiction* (London).

SHOWALTER, ELAINE (1991), *A Literature of Their Own: From Charlotte Brontë to Doris Lessing* (London).

SILVERMAN, MALCOLM (1988), Review of *O último verão de Copacabana*, *World Literature Today* (Spring).

SODRÉ, MUNIZ (1993), *O terreiro e a cidade* (Petrópolis).

—— (1988), *Santugri histórias de Mandinga e Capoeira* (Rio de Janeiro).

SOUSA ANDRADE, JOAQUIM DE (1975), 'O inferno de Wall Street' (The Wall Street Inferno), from *O Guesa* (1876–1902), trans. Frederick G. Williams, in *From Those Who Wrote (Poems and Translations)* (São Luís, Maranhão).

VALLE, DINORAH DO (1986), Review of *O Ultimo Verão de Coapacabana*, in *O Estado de São Paulo*, 107/34, 027 (1 Feb.), 10.

WILSON, ELIZABETH (1991), *The Sphinx in the City: Urban Life, the Control of Disorder and Women* (London).

WOOLF, VIRGINIA (1964*a*), *Mrs Dalloway* Harmondsworth.

—— (1964*b*), 'Street Haunting: A London Adventure', in *The Death of the Moth and Other Essays* (Harmondsworth), 23–36.

10

Cross-Cultural Homebodies in Cuba
The Poetry of Excilia Saldaña

CATHERINE DAVIES

STUDIES of Caribbean writing consistently draw attention to the polyphony, incompleteness, and ambivalence of its discourse. Similarly, they point to the precarious stance of Caribbean authors who are positioned at the crossroads of multiply interacting and hierarchically structured cultures and ethnicities. The resulting 'creative schizophrenia' is said to give rise to the split writer who bears the 'wounds of fragmentation' of the dissociated, alienated self (Gilkes 1986: 1). The situation is inevitably compounded when the author is a woman, when the problematic involves not only class lived through race but race and economics lived through gender.[1] In this essay I suggest that W. E. B. Du Bois's concept of double consciousness, or the double-voiced, 'two-toned' text referred to in African-American criticism (Gates 1984: 3), is inadequate to account for the fine shades of gendered ontological presence and hermeneutical practice in the work of Caribbean women writers, specifically black women writers in post-revolutionary Cuba. To engage with a feminist aesthetics of pluralism in a Caribbean context, a more subtle critical approach than that proposed by black essentialism and a more politically grounded approach than black deconstruction is needed.

I shall look to recent post-colonial approaches (rather than to African-American feminist criticism)[2] in a reading of the

---

[1] See Stuart Hall in Gilroy (1993: 85). See also Moore (1988: 9).

[2] African-American feminist criticism responds to a different agenda. For example, Mae Gwendolyn Henderson's valuable suggestion for theorizing racial difference within gender identity and gender difference within racial identity is limited not only by its elision of class but also by an almost Manichean black/white paradigm which does not hold for Cuba nor for much of the Caribbean (Henderson 1990: 18–21).

work of black Cuban poet Excilia Saldaña, whose two long confessional psychobiographies ('Monólogo de la esposa' (The Wife's Monologue) (1985), and *Mi nombre: antielegía familiar* (My Name: A Family Anti-elegy) (1991)) are particularly powerful and disturbing.[3] By focusing on *Mi nombre*, I hope to show that Saldaña's autobiographical poetry inscribes not only double-consciousness but also the multispeak of feminine subjectivity within a highly politicized post-colonial framework.

Post-colonial criticism has introduced innovative anti-essentialist concepts in an attempt to account for equivocal-ness and political agency in multicultural societies. Hence the ambivalent 'Third Space of enunciations' and the 'unhomely moment' of cross-cultural encounters in Homi Bhabha's work (Bhabha 1994) and in Paul Gilroy's study of the 'contact zones' between cultures and histories in an aesthetics of black Atlantic culture (Gilroy 1993: 15). According to Bhabha, the 'unhomely moment' is found in a 'borderline work of art' and is a 'paradigmatic colonial and post-colonial condition' (Bhabha 1994: 9–10). It is that disconcerting moment of a crosscultural encounter or initiation, the moment when the presence of alterity and hybridity makes itself felt. Gilroy's search for similar 'interme-diate concepts' (Gilroy 1993: 6) positioned between the local and the global, enabling a more 'transnational and intercultural perspective' (1993: 15) in cultural analysis, strongly rejects Afro-centric cultural nationalisms in favour of diasporic fragmenta-tion. Given the significance of positionality and location it is not surprising that 'home' has come to be a central trope for what are perceived as precarious identities: from R. D. Laing's notion of the divided self not being 'at home in the world', through placelessness, homelessness, unhomeliness, to home-place resistance and world-in-the-home, the figure of belonging or displacement recurs constantly in Caribbean and African-American critical discourse. But feminist reworkings of these ideas in a Caribbean context are scarce.

My aim is to explore the post-colonial trope of the 'home' with its cognate Freudian concept 'das unheimlich', the uncanny, and subsequent feminist inflections in Saldaña's work. Drawing on Ashcroft's intriguing correlation between post-

---

[3] Other works by Saldaña include, *Kele Kele* (Havana, 1987), *El refranero de la víbora* (Havana, 1989), and *La noche* (Havana and Berlin, 1989).

colonial creolization and feminist versions of the bisexual unconscious (the daughter's desire to return to the pre-Oedipal
mother replicates the post-colonial's desire to return to an
imaginary pre-colonial place of birth), I shall argue that for
Saldaña the mother/home is located in the hybrid female body.
'Writing the body' and 'writing out of a sense of place' thus
reconstruct both body and place as multicultural sites of difference (Ashcroft 1989: 30). A feminist critique which is informed
by a politics of location of this kind, involving not only geo-
graphical and cultural grounding but also the female body
and (black) women's 'authority of experience' (autobiography,
after all, has been considered a 'form of African embodiment')[4]
would seem to be particularly appropriate.

Contextualization, therefore, is in order. Reading for equivocal
traces of house and home in Caribbean women's writing implies focusing on family relationships, particularly grandmother–
mother–daughter affiliations in the extended family, forms
of female bonding, and African-American patterns of 'other-
mothering' (James 1993). It also implies working through
loaded metaphorical terms of gendered nationalist discourse
(mothercountry, mothertongue) in a post-colonial context. For
this reason, mainstream psychoanalytic theories of motherhood,
including feminist revisions of Freud and Lacan, can be as restrictive in a Caribbean/Cuban context as they are in an African-
American context.[5] The concepts of mother and mothering
are neither natural nor universal (Moore 1988: 23–30). Nevertheless, Hirsch's observation that most *feminist* psychoanalytic
theories of female subjectivity agree on women's fluid ego
boundaries, that 'women's being ... is continuous, plural, in-
process' (Hirsch 1990: 195) and her call for attention to be
paid to the linguistic and stylistic features associated with this
merging, reflection, and doubling in women's literature is
important in a reading of Saldaña's work (Hirsch 1990: 195).
These ideas on fluidity across boundaries are linked to the
concept of identity as process and mediation espoused by
post-colonial critics and they are entirely relevant to the study
of psychobiography. Conversely, ascribing importance to home

---

[4] 'Begin, though, not with a continent or a country or a house, but with the
geography closest in—the body' (Rich 1987: 212). See also bell hooks (1991: 29);
Baker (1989).
[5] See Abel (1990) and Spillers (1990).

space as well as to the mother-figure in the context of Cuban women's writing takes into account the specificity of Cuban household arrangements before and after the 1959 Revolution.

Saldaña was born in 1946 into a three-generation, black, Catholic, middle-class family which aspired to white cultural models. Ten years earlier, C. J. Zimmerman's 1935 study of the Cuban family underlined the marked differences between the wealthy (strictly homogamous) white families of Havana founded on the patriarchal, Roman Catholic models of the Spanish metropolis, and the less stable, more characteristically Caribbean, family organizations of the urban and rural poor. In the latter, consensual mixed unions rather than officially sanctioned monogamous marriages were the norm and children from such unions were officially illegitimate (Pérez 1980). The women in these families, often female heads of households without a co-residential male, worked for low pay as domestics (for the wealthy whites), peasants, or plantation workers; the male husband-fathers (surrogate or biological) were conspicuously absent. In Zimmerman's study there is no mention of the black and mulatto middle classes. Most of the (non-white) population in pre-revolutionary Cuba, therefore, could be said to be arranged in patterns associated with the Caribbean family, the salient features of which are matrifocality, flexible domestic arrangements, and indistinct household boundaries. The household (domestic unit) would not be coterminous with the kinship system (family).

What, then, does 'home' mean in this context and what gender roles are prescribed for women in the domestic sphere? What position does the female subject take up in a black, bourgeois household such as Saldaña's which is even more anomalous in as much as it is caught between the two models? Of course, the very domestic versus public dichotomy has already been questioned by feminists as has the Eurocentric premiss that society is the same thing as collective life (in contradistinction to private life) (Moore 1988: 21–4; Strathern 1993). In the plantation economy the slave co-residential unit (rather than the 'home'), formed around fictive (not blood) kin, was the in-between space of the female slaves' knowledge and resistance. It was here that African traditions survived (in religion, song, dance, and healing); 'within their own domains [slave] women were all-powerful' but, of course, ' "Mothering" in the modern sense of the word did not exist' (Bush 1990:

87). This points to a long Afro-Caribbean tradition of women's empowerment. However, so-called matrifocality and its possible origins (Africa, the plantation economy, unemployment) and the semi-mythical 'African-American-Father-Gone' (Spillers 1990: 127) are also, arguably, Eurocentric concepts suggesting deviation from nuclear family norms. Studies of twentieth-century Caribbean societies find that the relative status of members of the domestic group depend on age as much as gender and on how the household earns its living. Also, while men may not participate fully in family life they nevertheless enjoy a dominant position in society, 'physical presence is not necessary for the father-husband to fulfil his obligations' as head of the household (Remy 1973: 58). In both the two-generational (nuclear) and the three-generational (extended) Caribbean households, the senior males are usually the dominant members as fathers and grandfathers (Greenfield 1973). Thus the Caribbean norm is grand-patrifocality as a rule and grand-matrifocality as an alternative; the domestic unit is not usually constructed around the displaced mother or the father. This is certainly the case of the 1950s household portrayed in Saldaña's *Mi nombre*. Apart from the female speaking subject, the central figure in the poem is the grandmother (to whom the poem is dedicated); the mother is written out and the patriarchal grandfather/father figure is absent but all-powerful.

Mi nombre, written in the late 1980s, invents past family life from a contemporary position. If the concepts of motherhood, mothering, and home are complicated for pre-revolutionary Cuba they are no less so for post-1959 Cuba where state policies attempted to regulate family life and to change women's relationship to reproductive as well as productive labour (Pérez 1980: 246; Moore 1988: 139–43). In socialist Cuba women joined the work-force and handed over some of their mothering responsibilities to the state. The family was no longer conceived as a primarily economic unit, but it was still very much 'the basic cell of society', 'célula elemental de la sociedad' (site of socialization) and the 'centre of shared life', 'vida en común' (site of bonding and affection) (Wasmer Miguel 1977: 282–3).[6] Boundaries between the public and private spheres were

[6] The 1975 Family Code describes the socialist family as 'una entidad en que están presentes *e íntimamente entrelazados* el interés social y el interés personal' (an entity in which social and personal interests are present *and intimately interrelated*) (my emphasis).

thus gradually erased. But despite the radical reforms the average Cuban family structure changed very little.[7] One possible reason why 'kinship and marriage practices have proved highly resistant to change' is that public patriarchy has replaced private patriarchy (Moore 1988: 145) which is as much a reflection of the intermingling of private and public spheres in socialist Cuba as of Caribbean household patterns in pre-revolutionary days. As mentioned above, patriarchy seems to have functioned just as much at the level of the community before the revolution.

The dynamics of family life in Cuba, therefore, are traditionally complex and the boundaries between the public and private spheres consistently fuzzy. Home is an in-between space in which the position of the female subject is problematic. This upsetting of neat binary divisions, the process through which 'the private and public, past and present, the psyche and the social develop an intersticial intimacy' is a further example of the 'unhomely moment' (Bhabha 1994: 13). If the patriarchal home is thus unhomely and women socially and politically inscribed in it as displaced subjects of production *and* reproduction, what about female subjectivity?

By focusing on the subject-in-crisis inscribed in a poetic text which presents 'unhomely' moments of gendered subject formation, I hope to show that the split subject is most clearly visible in autobiographical poetry where 'self' and 'self-image' do not coincide, where a cohesive self-image is elusive (Benstock 1991). In a contemporary Cuban context, such texts are transgressive in as much as they do not present a centred subject nor a stable household-nation. They are noticeable among first-generation post-revolutionary black and mulatto women (born in the 1930s and 1940s) who stood to gain the most from the revolution. However, a political reading of disavowal of the home (that is, a rejection of the pre-revolutionary childhood

---

[7] Pérez Rojas (1979) noted that in 1970 25% of the female population was incorporated into the work-force (cf. 17% in 1953), just over half of the households were two-generational nuclear families, there were more female heads of household, about 30% of families were 'incomplete' (heads of household did not live with their partners), and more children lived with their (great) grandparents (probably due to housing shortages) (1979: 59–60). In 1989 over 80% of working women were still solely responsible for household chores *and* for raising children (resulting in the exhausting double-shift of working mothers) and almost as many considered this division of labour to be proper. See also Vilma Espín, *Cuban Women Confront the Future* (1991: 71).

home and/or the present-day home of the 1980s) is only one possible reading. A feminist critique may allow for a more nuanced interpretation, although reading along ethnic boundaries, as I have chosen to do, is fraught with problems. To show this I shall begin with an exception. *Richard trajo su flauta* (1967) written by Nancy Morejón (b. 1944) opens with three poems representing the subject's paternal grandmother, parents, and maternal grandmother respectively. In the first, 'Presente Brígida Noyola', the grandmother is inscribed through a series of natural images connoting energy, strength, and blackness. Blackness signifies exploitation and resistance. The grandmother of the third poem, 'Presente Angela Domínguez' is 'un poco más ligera' (a little lighter). A mulatta, her figure connotes Spanish troubadors and guitars as well as African bamboo ships and bracelets (Morejón 1967: 14). These, then, are two-toned woman-centred texts; but there is little sense of conflict. The intermediate poem, 'La cena', dedicated to the poet's parents, describes an evening meal at home from the subject's perspective. Once the working family is seated round the table the mother, who presides over the sacred scene, breaks the bread.[8] What is striking about this poem is its sense of family unity. No one speaks, but by means of a complex network of reciprocal looks, including looks between the poet and her mother, 'pidiendo con urgencia los ojos de mi madre | como el agua de todos los días' (looking urgently for my mother's eyes | as if for daily water) (1967: 12) the home circle exudes security and solidarity in the face of impending war (the missile crisis of 1962). There may be a sense of threat, but it emanates from elsewhere; there is no conflict in the home. Morejón's more recent collection, *Piedra pulida* (1986), contains a moving poem to her mother. The mother, a poor orphan in shackles lacked the luxuries of (white) colonial (domestic) culture (a garden, a room inlaid with ivory, a glass cabinet, a basket-work room), but she possessed hands like 'precious stones' which are the inheritance she leaves to her children ('Madre', Morejón 1986: 72). Thus the mother embodies black homeplace resistance. Seemingly, little is out of place in Morejón's poetry.[9]

---

[8] I owe this observation to Conrad James.

[9] The women of Morejón's family were certainly models of resistance. Her maternal grandmother, a mulatta of Chinese descendency, gave birth to twenty-four

Quite different is the poetry of Georgina Herrera (b. 1936) which presents a violent disavowal of the mother and the childhood home and seriously queries bell hooks's belief in African-American black mother worship (hooks 1991: 45). In the ironically titled 'Mami' (Herrera 1974) the adult poet addresses her mother in an attempt to redress past misunderstandings, but the initial gesture of good will rapidly fades,

> ¿Cómo pudo existir tan grande espacio
> entre las dos? ¿Cómo
> vivimos tantos años, sin que nada
> fuese a ambas común?
>
> (Herrera 1974: 36)
>
> How could a void so great exist
> between us two? How
> could we live together so many years, with
> nothing in common?[10]

Similarly, the mulatta poet Soleida Ríos (b. 1950) opens her book *Entre mundo y juguete* (1987) with the poem 'Casa'. But 'casa' (house) is no more than a word marking the fissure between discourse and life experience; 'Palabra dolorosa que no viví | no he visto' (Painful word I never lived | I have not seen) (Ríos 1987: 8).[11] There is an ethical element in the poetry of Herrera and Ríos; the split subjects in the poems above have no childhood home but clearly feel they ought to have had one. A (black, Cuban) woman's version of the 'unhomely', therefore, might be read as the disconcerting encounter of two cultures (African/European) figured in two types of corresponding domestic organization: the subculture of the flexible Caribbean household and the dominant culture of the middle-class or socialist nuclear family. The 'unhomely' could also be found where ideologically induced expectations of a comfortable

children; her paternal grandmother was registered as 'mother unknown' after being forcibly removed from her mother; Morejón's own mother was orphaned at 8 years old and, after marrying a docker (Morejón's father) she worked as a seamstress (conversation with the author, London, Oct. 1994).

[10] All translations are my own. See also the poems 'Escena familiar' and 'El patio de mi casa' (Herrera 1989) where the homeplace is shown to be both threatening and cosy.

[11] In the poem 'Agua de otoño' (Ríos 1987) Ríos again disavows the home yet it is clear from an earlier collection, *De pronto abril* (Ríos 1979), dedicated to her mother, Gloria, that the poet identifies closely with her mother.

family life (be they middle class or socialist) encounter women's real life experiences. Undoubtedly, the fissure between self and self-image runs deep.

It is the autobiographical poetry of Excilia Sadaña (b. 1946) which articulates a subject most clearly in crisis and rewrites the black, patriarchal home from a post-colonial feminist position. *Mi nombre* charts the trajectory of the poet's early life as a girl growing up in a stifling and oppressive family atmosphere, an exile in her own home. The poem, dedicated to her paternal grandmother, Ana Excilia, was one of five sections (including 'Monólogo de la esposa') in a former collection (also entitled 'Mi nombre') published in Mexico with a prologue by Cintio Vitier which was pulped because of the unacceptable level of errata. Both *Mi nombre* and 'Monólogo de la esposa' are confessional poems bordering on the schizophrenic. They instantiate the 'unhomely' moment, in so far as this 'relates the traumatic ambivalence of a personal psychic history to the wider disjunctions of a political existence' (Bhabha 1994: 10); their subtexts are concurrently the Cuban national crises and a traumatic personal experience (referred to explicitly in 'Monólogo de la esposa').[12]

What strikes the reader immediately about *Mi nombre* is the hybridity of the text. Written in Spanish, black print on brown paper, the poem swirls across the page with a rhythmic pulse reaching a crescendo reminiscent of the beating of African drums. In Gilroy's terms it constitutes a stereophonic (three-dimensional), rather than bi-focal 'contact zone' (Gilroy 1993: 3) marking the space between two cultures which are unassimilated yet not mutually exclusive. The intercultural positioning of the speaking subject makes this at least a 'two-toned' text; as speech act it attempts to represent symbolically what Homi Bhabha (drawing on Benveniste and Lacan) refers to as the 'Third space', the space of ambivalence, intercultural negotiation, and transference of meaning (Bhabha 1994: 36–7). Although it is an overtly autobiographical poem, in the process of writing the subject of the narrated events splits from the subject of enunciation as signifier (language) overrides signified (events).

---

[12] According to Saldaña (conversation with the author, Havana, Sept. 1992) her family did not welcome the revolution, so she left home and lived on the streets for seven years until her son was born. The subtext of her autobiographical poetry is the traumatic childhood experience of sexual abuse by her father.

Developing this idea, Bhabha's 'Third space' could be considered not just the space of non-syncretic hybridity but also the space of misrecognition, the only possible identity according to Lacan. The decentred speaker of *Mi nombre* is constituted through a series of gendered and racialized selves; subjectivity, sexuality, differences of gender and race, are played out in a performance which consistently resists closure.

The poem presents itself as a (Black) magic ritual uttered by a seeress possessing esoteric knowledge; she speaks a secret language and writes the hybrid, female body:

> Ejerzo otro idioma. Convoco otra dimensión.
> Indago
> por esta sangre
> de ahora y de aquí,
>   por esta piel
> a trechos
> manchada y áspera,
> a trechos
> fina como un madrigal
> o
> el suspiro de una niña
>
>   (Saldāna 1991: 4)

> I use another language. I summon another dimension.
> I search deep
> into this blood
> of here and now
>   in this skin
> in parts
> stained and sour
> in parts
> as fine as a madrigal
> or
> the sigh of a girl[13]

The cross-cultural poem thus presents the 'unhomely moment'. Bhabha, referring to Isabel Archer in James's novel *Portrait of a Lady*, describes how the 'unhomely moment' creeps up stealthily

---

[13] All translations are my own. It should be pointed out that *Mi nombre* opens up an intertextual dialogue with 'El apellido: elegía familiar' (The Surname: A Family Elegy), published by Nicolás Guillén in 1954 (later included in *La paloma de vuelo popular*, 1958). Indeed, Saldaña repeats whole lines from this poem, such as 'Un santo y seña | para poder hablar con las estrellas'.

on her as her own shadow and 'suddenly you find yourself taking measure of your dwelling in a "state of incredulous terror"' (1994: 9). He adds that feminist criticism makes visible the 'forgetting' of the unhomely by reconceptualizing space and questioning the public/private dichotomy resulting in the world-in-the-home (1994: 11). This poem does dissolve that dichotomy but it inscribes domestic space not so much as world-in-the-home as a hell-on-earth, 'la primera parada del infierno' (the first stage of hell) (Saldaña 1991: 7). What it gestures towards, as we shall see, is world-in-the-body.

The bounded space of the tyrannized home, the house-of-horror, 'todos tenemos miedo' (we are all scared) (1994: 12) where the omnipotent, possibly absent, patriarch glares down with a single eye of the Supreme Being, 'el ojo mágico del amo | ordena las rondas de la abuela y la madre' (the magic eye of the master | commands mother's and grandmother's rounds) (1994: 8) is disavowed in no mean terms. The bourgeois values and religious rituals (Christmas celebrations and the First Communion) of the 'sagrada familia y los reyes de oriente' (the sacred family and the Kings of the East) (1994: 19) are savagely mocked. 'Home' is disavowed; but contrary to Bhabha's view disavowal is not 'forgetting'. As Freud explains, negation entails recurrent affirmation, ongoing re-presentation.[14] In the poem, while one 'home' is negated another (unbounded, in-between) domestic space, neither public nor private, is tentatively re-presented. This is the hideaway of the maroons ('cimarrones'). The 'unhomely moment' creeps up on the speaker of the poem as the hybrid 'otherness' of her own pubescent body. By running away from the confines of middle-class institutions as a slave from the plantation, she enters another space, encounters a different tradition (maronage) and self-image:

> cimarrona de los parques,
> apalencada en el colegio
>
> .   .   .   .   .
>
> sin tierra en mi propia tierra:
> huyendo cada día del bocabajo
> y del cepo
>   (Saldaña 1991: 7–8)

[14] 'Negation is a way of taking cognizance of what is repressed', it is 'the intellectual acceptance of the repressed' (Freud 1958: xix. 235).

             runaway slave in the parks
             stockaded in the school
                 .   .   .   .
             with no land in my own land:
             fleeing each day the shackles
             and the stocks

The accumulation of references to African gods and rituals
further disturbs cultural boundaries, and thresholds other than
the domestic are transgressed: an initial series of binaries (past/
present, non-being/being, absence/presence, broadly corre-
sponding to negative black/positive white) are set up and at
the same time are dismantled. For example, the positionality
of the subject in the text and in time is shown to be unrepresentable, 'me camino I en todo lo que soy I o I que no fui I en lo
que dejaré de ser mañana' (I walk through I everything I am
I or I what I was not, I through what I will not be tomorrow)
(Saldaña 1991: 4). This way the poem inscribes disavowal of
the home while simultaneously affirming the homebody elsewhere as the text dissolves boundaries of time, space, and self;
it is poetry of the ontological 'unhomely moment', therefore,
but it reaches further.

The whirring pattern of words shifts the poem from the unhomely into the uncanny. The house spins round like a vortex
into whose centre the three women (mother, the daughter, and
the grandmother) are sucked:

             Mi madre y la madre de mi padre.
                 Y yo en el centro.
             Giran y rueda.
                 Y yo en el centro.
             Gimen y sufren.
                 Y yo en el centro.
             Todos se asoman. Todos las miran.
                 Y yo en el centro.
             ¿Dónde buscar cerrajero para esta reja?
                         (Saldaña 1991: 8–9)

             My mother and the mother of my father.
                 And I'm at the centre.
             Spin and turn.
                 And I'm at the centre.
             Suffer and cry.
                 And I'm at the centre.

Everyone peeps. Everyone looks.
And I'm at the centre.
Where can I find a locksmith for these bars?

The uncanny, 'das unheimlich', is fear of what is familiar and
should remain concealed; the uncanny moment can only be so
when positioned in what is and what is not at the same time.
'(Un)heimlich' is an ambivalent term meaning both cosy and
dangerous. It is closely related to negation; the prefix 'un' is
'the hall mark of repression' but it is 'with the help of the
symbol of negation [that] thinking frees itself from the restrictions of repression' (Freud 1958: xix. 236). In other words,
what is repressed constantly threatens with its presence. The
uncanny is this lack of differentiation, both the experiencing
of the repressed affect and the lifting of the repression by the
'doubling, dividing and interchanging' self, 'the subject [who]
is in doubt as to which his self is' (Freud 1958: xix. 234). The
speaker in *Mi nombre*, 'La que no soy—pero me usurpa por
costumbre y miedo—muerde' (The one [f.] who I am not—
but who usurps me by habit and fear—bites) (Saldaña 1991:
11), must try to construct an identity. She repeatedly recalls a
hidden crime, an enigma, something 'sospechoso' (suspicious)
which needs to be unlocked. Interestingly, Freud gives the Spanish translation of 'unheimlich' as 'sospechoso, siniestro' (Freud
1958: xix. 221) and Gilroy states that the 'grounded aesthetics
of the black Atlantic' is precisely 'a hermeneutics of suspicion
and a hermeneutics of memory. Together they have nurtured
a redemptive critique' (Gilroy 1993: 71). In this poem suspicion (from *su-specere*, to look under) means (as for Gilroy) query-
ing suspect cultural truths (racism, sexism). It also means (as
for Freud) searching for the object of repression. The attempt
at flight inscribed in the poem, 'apártense | que voy de prisa
y vuelo' (stand back | I'm in a hurry and I'm flying) (Saldaña
1991: 25), in fact confirms that repression (Freud 1959: xx.
153). But what is it that has been repressed? What is it that
must be queried? The negated object, now conjured up through
what Freud refers to as the 'heimlich' art (magic), are the
'heimlich' parts of the body (the pudenda) (Freud 1955: xvii.
221–7, 243) of black female sexuality.[15] The poem, then, is not

---

[15] In these writings Freud uses the term 'heimlich' to signify both 'heimlich'
and 'unheimlich'.

only about the alterity of cultures, but also about the unrepresentable alterity of the despised, miscegenated female self.

It is the complete and impossible rejection of the inseparable hybrid body that marks the 'massive and sudden emergence of uncanniness' which Julia Kristeva calls abjection (Kristeva 1982: 2).[16] The split subject, 'No soy yo—pero qué bien lo disimulo bajo la sonrisa tierna' (I am not me—but how well I hide it under my tender smile) (Saldaña 1991: 11) exhibits the shady 'hatred that smiles' (Kristeva 1982: 4); 'sin tierra en mi propia tierra' (with no land in my own land) (Saldaña 1991: 7), she is the 'exile who asks where' (Kristeva 1982: 8). For Kristeva the abject 'shatters the walls of repression' (1982: 15) so that what has been rejected but not shed is no longer negated. In the poem the abject emerges as what is and is not part of the dejected subject; her physical body, her hair, her skin. This otherness is inscribed in oxymora as both 'enemiga y gemela' (enemy and twin) (Saldaña 1991: 9); she is separated and yet unseparated from her body and cannot clean her skin 'hasta la transparencia' (to transparency) (1991: 10).

Mi nombre inscribes the black, slave experience in somatic terms. In this sense it is a woman version of the black Atlantic aesthetic. According to Gilroy memories of a slave past are construed as an instrument with which to critique bourgeois notions of modernity (Gilroy 1993: 71). But in *Mi nombre*, more importantly, they mark the encounter with the abjected female body and as such are essential to subjectivity. It is a precarious moment because the double-consciousness and hybridity much propounded by post-colonial critics actually threaten the female subject, balanced on the threshold of the symbolic, with complete self-dissolution.

The necessary process of autopoiesis begins in the poem at the point of total abjection when the speaking subject takes up a symbolic position by literally ingesting the symbolic sign. She receives the white wafer of the Christian God in Holy Communion. The biblical intertext, Gabriel's Annunciation to the

---

[16] For psychoanalyst Kristeva abjection is necessary for the formation of subjectivity and for the making of Symbolic sense. The abject (vomit, sweat, tears) is still part of the subject but must be expelled if the subject is to establish its separateness. The fact that the abject cannot be expelled means that it destabilizes both subject and object while, at the same time, its presence affirms their complete interdependence. It shows that notions of identity and corporeality are extremely tentative.

Virgin of the Immaculate Conception, is ironically subverted by its juxtaposition with an account of the girl's first menstrua- tion (the shift from first to third person marking detachment from the supposedly defiled self):

> y el fruto de la niña estalla en sangre y algodones
> salpica a su paso toda la casa
> riega la rosa,
> alimenta a la paloma
>
> (Saldaña 1991: 14)
>
> And the fruit of the girl explodes in blood and cotton
> it splashes the house as she walks
> it waters the rose,
> it feeds the dove

Confronted with the adored white baby boy (presumably Je- sus) she is overcome with anxiety, 'Yo sólo sé oirme la sangre I y la angustia I ante la belleza inevitable del niño de nácar' (I only know how to hear my blood I and my anguish I before the inevitable beauty of the mother-of-pearl boy) (Saldaña 1991: 15). In response, the repressed, hybrid female body (the abject) resurfaces not as the conventional subject of reproduction but as the process of production (the sugar mill), inseparable from the tradition (the memory of the plantation economy) which defines it:

> A través de la mulatez del melado
>   oteo un cuerpo:
> me regodeo
>   en el cañaveral inédito del pubis,
>   en el penacho de la cabeza,
>   en el desmoche de las axilas.
>   en el breve trapiche de los pechos,
>   en las piernas espesas,
>   en el tacho de bronce del ombligo,
>   en la centrífuga de los ojos,
>   en los dientes refinos.
>
>   (Saldaña 1991: 15)
>
> Through the mulatto mix of cane-syrup
>   I see a body:
> I take cruel delight
>   in the unwritten cane-fields of the pubis,
>   in the crest of the head,

in the cutting of the arm-pits,
in the small sugar-press of the breasts,
in the thick legs,
in the bronze boiler of the navel,
in the centrifugal eyes,
in the refined teeth.

Like many other Caribbean works, particularly those of Aimé Césaire, the search for self-formation is precisely this 'psychic re-memberment'; the poem performance 're-enacts the need to reintegrate the exiled subject in the lost body' (Dash 1989: 20, 22). *Mi nombre* signals recovery from the void of non-representable incorporeality by inscribing and transforming the female body and black history in the magic of language. 'Búscate una leyenda que en ella unan quien no soy | y quien serás ya para siempre' (find yourself a legend that unites who I'm not | and who you will be now forever) (Saldaña 1991: 16), the text announces with illocutionary force. Here the switch from 'I' to 'you' does not indicate dialogue with the self, the speaking 'I' is not the same as the 'I' spoken of. It indicates otherness now embodied in the double, the grandmother, who is given a name—Ana Excilia Bregante. The mother has been written out of the poem and is last referred to by the speaker, addressing the grandmother, as 'the wife of your son' (1991: 13).

For Otto Rank the double was 'an insurance against destruction' (Freud 1955: xvii. 235) and in *Mi nombre* it is the *alter ego* of the split subject, referred to early in the text as 'el enemigo' (the enemy), that redeems and in turn is redeemed by Ana Excilia, 'el enemigo | que te ama y te salva' (the enemy | which loves you and saves you) (Saldaña 1991: 13). 'Ana Excilia', then, is a polyvalent sign—with connotations of Santa Ana (the Virgin Mary's mother)—signifying fluid ego boundaries, hybrid female sexuality, African traditions, black women's history and secret knowledge, mothering incarnate. Ana Excilia is an African queen and an unknown warrior (1991: 26); the granddaughter's desire is to return to her as the embodiment of an imaginary pre-colonial African place of birth. In the final instance, Ana Excilia is recognized as the creation of the speaking subject, 'niña mía sin letras ni palotes' (my little girl without letters or strokes) (1991: 25) who writes the name and assumes the agency of the (illiterate) grandmother. By addressing 'Ana Excilia', then, the speaker is able to address and name her multicoloured,

performing, gendered self; by writing the grandmother's name
she handwrites all that was hitherto denied:

> voy a celebrar tu nombre
> en unas manos
> renegridas del carbón
> blanqueadas por la lejía
> amarillentas de resebo
>
> (Saldaña 1991: 26–7)
>
> I will celebrate your name
> in hands
> that are blackened by coal
> whitened by bleach
> yellowed by grease

In the process of naming the self as the other, the subject
position is temporarily filled by 'Ana Excilia' who now addresses
and names the former speaker:

> Excilia,
> tú,
>> siempre Excilia:
>> nombre de mi nombre:
>> nieta,
>> guardiana:
>> compañera.
>
> Excilia,
> you,
>> always Excilia:
>> name of my name:
>> granddaughter,
>> keeper:
>> companion.

Again we are reminded that identity is only possible in misrecognition. It is 'Ana Excilia' who is called on to deny the house,
the bourgeois values it represents, and even the speaker's name,
'niégame el nombre | si con él no alcanzo la totalidad de la
entrega' (deny my name | if with it I cannot give myself com-
pletely) (Saldaña 1991: 27).

Without a name or a house the female subject is finally free.
Her freedom is celebrated not in terms of employment, as
might be expected in Cuba, but in terms of freely chosen
motherhood. But this position is not stable either. The subject

gives birth to herself, and the boundaries of gendered identity and biological determinism collapse as she is reborn through her son, 'libre estoy en el espacio | de la libertad primera | para encontrarme el origen | en el hijo que me engendra' (I am free in the space | of first freedom | to find my origin | in the son that bears me) (1991: 30). As the daughter of her own son, she is impossible 'fictive' kin. She is, in the end, not a political or social subject at all, only a voice and never an identifiable, integral self.

What then does 'mi nombre' (my name) signify? The poem is an act of naming that resists closure. Social disorder (the revolution) creates the conditions for the birth of the new name, 'I see my name being born' (Saldaña 1991: 22), and this name will be left by the neonate to her son (1991: 30). But which name? The speaker rejects 'el nombre extraño | de los papeles oficiales' (the strange name | of official papers), the 'bastión de familia' (the pillar of the family), the seven-letter name made of 'miedo' (fear) (1991: 31). Is she referring to the patronymic, 'Saldaña', which is never actually mentioned in the poem? She also rejects 'el nombre que me dijeron | para poder hablar con las estrellas' (the name they gave me | to talk to the stars), the name of the dreamer. This indicates that she also rejects her given name, 'Excilia', which is also seven letters long and possibly linked to 'exile' (from the Latin *exsilium*, plural *exsilia*, meaning 'those who are banished'). 'Excilia', signifying exiled subject (ex-isle?), is not the new name either. The poem, therefore, ends ambiguously with an anaphoric coda repeating with drum-like rhythm an empty signifier 'mi nombre' which is filled not with an identity but with an accumulation of attributes:

> Mi nombre
> de pie y camino,
> mi nombre.
>   Mi nombre
> de yagua y cieno,
>   mi nombre.
>   Mi nombre
> de grasa y humo,
>   mi nombre
>
> (Saldaña 1991: 31)
>
>   My name
> of foot and path
> my name.

> My name
> of palm and mud
> my name.
> My name
> of grease and smoke,
> my name

The name (cotton, fire, alcohol, night, pot, thunder, river, honey, cave, sky, laughter, bow, moss, wind, seed, petal, glass, steel) signifies the universe and also Cuba. Is the subject, then, the universal female archetype, the fluid body-world described by Neumann out of which something is born and whose 'openings and skin are places of exchange between inside and outside' (Neumann 1955: 39)? The universal female body, symbol of the feminine, may be thus conceptualized as the ultimate boundary position, the 'unhomely moment' incarnate, the very site of the 'Third space'. For Jung, the archetype as figure of speech is precisely 'the unknown third thing' which remains unknown to the intellect (Neumann 1955: 17). But an archetype freezes the contents of the 'Third space', overriding the specificity of the text, and what the coda of this poem celebrates is the free play of multiple associations.

A different, more obvious, reading links the name with the nation; after all, on one level the poem is a panegyric to the Cuban Revolution—a point that should not be forgotten. Both subject and nation pass through moments of trauma—the crisis of 1956, for example, marks the Moncada rebellion and the girl's puberty, and they develop contemporaneously. The poem presents the subject clearly inserted in a social context of social upheaval. Indeed, the final lines of the poem leave no doubt as to the obviousness of this reading, 'Mi nombre | en el nombre de los que recién deciden su nombre | y sus recuerdos' (My name | in the name of those who have just decided their name | and their memories) (Saldaña 1991: 32–3). In a Hegelian sense, the poem would thus present a process of maturation. From a position of alienation and 'transcendental homelessness', nation and subject gradually acquire self-consciousness and self-recognition.[17]

In my view, closure is not so certain. The explicitly open signified of 'mi nombre' is constantly deferred; the poem itself foregrounds dissemination in the writing process. I prefer to

---

[17] I take this term from Georg Lukács, *The Theory of the Novel* (1971: 41).

read *Mi nombre* as an instance of post-colonial 'écriture féminine' which inscribes the aesthetics and the politics of the black Atlantic in terms of the fragmented, hybrid female body. Perhaps what this poem celebrates is the process of female subjectivity as the site of multicultural interaction freed from patriarchal formations and from familial and national constraints.

LIST OF WORKS CITED

ABEL, ELIZABETH (1990), 'Race, Class, and Psychoanalysis? Opening Questions', in Marianne Hirsch and Evelyn Fox Keller (eds.), *Conflicts in Feminism* (London and New York, 1990), 184–204.

ASHCROFT, W. D. (1989), 'Intersecting Marginalities: Post-colonialism and Feminism', *Kunapipi*, 11/2: 23–35.

BAKER, HOUSTON A., Jr. (1989), 'There is No More Beautiful Way: Theory and the Poetics of Afro-American Women's Writing', in H. A. Baker, Jr., and Patricia Redmond (eds.), *Afro-American Literary Study in the 1990s* (Chicago and London, 1989), 135–63.

BENSTOCK, SHARI (1991), 'The Female Self Engendered. Autobiographical Writing and Theories of Selfhood', *Women's Studies*, 20/1: 5–14.

BHABHA, HOMI K. (1994), *The Location of Culture* (London and New York).

BUSH, BARBARA (1990), *Slave Women in Caribbean Society 1650–1838* (London, Kingston, Bloomington, Ind.).

DASH, MICHAEL (1989), 'In Search of the Lost Body: Redefining the Subject in Caribbean Literature', *Kunapipi*, 11/1: 17–26.

ESPÍN, VILMA (1991), *Cuban Women Confront the Future* (Melbourne).

FREUD, SIGMUND (1955, 1958, 1959), *The Standard Edition of the Complete Psychological Works of Sigmund Freud*, ed. James Strachey, xvii, xix, xx (London).

GATES, HENRY LOUIS (1984), 'Criticism in the Jungle', in id. (ed.), *Black Literature and Literary Theory* (London).

GILKES, MICHAEL (1986), *Creative Schizophrenia: The Caribbean Cultural Challenge*, The Third Walter Rodney Memorial Lecture (University of Warwick).

GILROY, PAUL (1993), *The Black Atlantic: Modernity and Double Consciousness* (London).

GREENFIELD, SIDNEY M. (1973), 'Dominance, Focality and the Characterization of Domestic Groups: Some Reflections on "Matrifocality" in the Caribbean', in Stanford N. Gerber (ed.), *The Family in the Caribbean* (Río Piedras, Puerto Rico, 1973), 31–50.

HENDERSON, MAE GWENDOLYN (1990), 'Speaking in Tongues: Dialogics, Dialectics, and the Black Woman Writer's Literary Tradition', in Cheryl A. Wall (ed.), *Changing Our Own Words: Essays on Criticism, Theory, and Writing by Black Women* (London, 1990).

HERRERA, GEORGINA (1974), *Gentes y cosas* (Havana).

—— (1989), *Grande es el tiempo* (Havana).

HIRSCH, MARIANNE (1990), 'Mothers and Daughters', in Jean O'Barr, Deborah Pope, and Mary Wyer (eds.), *Ties that Bind: Essays on Mothering and Patriarchy* (Chicago (1979), 1990), 177–99.

HOOKS, BELL (1991), *Yearning: Race, Gender, and Cultural Politics* (Boston).

JAMES, STANLIE M. (1993), 'Mothering. A Possible Black Feminist Link to Social Transformation?', in Stanlie M. James and Abenia P. A. Busia (eds.), *Theorizing Black Feminisms* (London and New York, 1993), 44–54.

KRISTEVA, JULIA (1982), *Powers of Horror: An Essay in Abjection*, trans. Leon S. Roudiez (New York).

LUKÁCS, GEORG (1971), *The Theory of the Novel* (Cambridge, Mass.).

MOORE, HENRIETTA L. (1988), *Feminism and Anthropology* (Cambridge).

MOREJÓN, NANCY (1967), *Richard trajo su flauta y otros argumentos* (Havana).

—— (1986), *Piedra pulida* (Havana).

NEUMANN, ERICH (1955), *The Great Mother: An Analysis of the Archetype* (London).

PÉREZ, LISANDRO (1980), 'The Family in Cuba', in Man Singh Das and Clinton J. Jesser (eds.), *The Family in Latin America* (New Delhi, 1980), 235–69.

PÉREZ ROJAS, NIURKA (1979), *Características sociodemográficas de la familia cubana 1953–1970* (Havana).

REMY, ANSLEME (1973), 'Some Reflections on Caribbean Anthropology with Special Reference to the Family', in Stanford N. Gerber (ed.) *The Family in the Caribbean* (Río Piedras, Puerto Rico, 1973), 31–64.

RICH, ADRIENNE (1987), 'Notes towards a Politics of Location', *Blood, Bread, and Poetry* (London), 210–31.

RÍOS, SOLEIDA (1979), *De pronto abril* (Havana).

—— (1987), *Entre mundo y juguete* (Havana).

SALDAÑA, EXCILIA (1985), 'Monólogo de la esposa', *Casa de las Américas*, 152: 86–100.

—— (1991), *Mi nombre: antielegía familiar* (Havana).

SPILLERS, HORTENSE (1990), ' " The Permanent Obliquity of an In[ph]allibly Straight": In the Time of the Daughters and Fathers', in Cheryl A. Wall (ed.), *Changing Our Own Words: Essays on Criticism, Theory, and Writing by Black Women* (London, 1990), 128–9.

STRATHERN, MARILYN (1993), 'Making Incomplete', in Vigdis Broch-Due, Ingrid Rudie, and Tone Bleie (eds.), *Carved Flesh, Cast Selves* (Oxford, 1993), 41–51.

WASMER MIGUEL, GUILLERMO (1977) (ed.), *La Mujer en Cuba Socialista* (Havana).

11

Latin American Feminist Criticism Revisited

ANNY BROOKSBANK JONES

Texts open up when you talk to groups of others, which
often turn out to be classes, public audiences. Yet these
openings are not beginnings, for the staging of each such
talking is secured by politics.

(Chakravorty Spivak 1992: 55)

WITH these words Spivak (almost) begins revisiting French
feminism, in order to say something about the possibilities of
politicizing the theoretical and theorizing the political. This
chapter looks at how certain feminist critics have opened up
Latin American texts, revisiting, and re- and deconstructing
critical theory in the process. It considers the ethico-political
securing of these interventions, starting with the construction
of feminism itself in a Latin American frame.

Throughout the 1970s and early 1980s few signs of anything
resembling a home-grown Latin American feminist movement
were recorded. Reports in the last decade or so of emerging
feminist groupings in the region seem to suggest either an
important new development or the belated recognition of an
established one (Fisher 1993*a*, 1993*b*; Küppers 1994). Whatever their supposed origins, the Latin American Left has until
recently tended to see these groups not as allies but as a political irrelevance, diversion, or wooden horse (Carr and Ellner
1993). They have been partly supported in this by a certain
post-colonial feminist reading of 'Third World feminism' as a
First World construct, an epiphenomenon of hegemonic Western analytic categories (Talpade Mohanty 1991). This is a politically powerful reading, but it is weakened by a tendency to
homogenize Western feminist models and/or their effects rather

as those models are accused of homogenizing Third World women. Whatever Western means in this context, if Western feminist models are less homogeneous than suggested it is not clear why they should have homogeneous effects in Latin America or anywhere else. To recognize as much is to leave space for the agency of women who are never simply the victims or dupes of well-intentioned foreigners, however complexly asymmetrical the power relations that connect them. At issue here is representational power and its socio-cultural inscription in the lives of specific Latin American women. So, too, is the articulation of such questions with(in) feminist critical theory, an academic activity subject to its own relations of power.

The publication of Patricia Elena González and Eliana Ortega's influential *La sartén por el mango* in 1985 did not mark the birth of this activity in Latin American studies. 'Images of women' analyses and studies and anthologies of women's writing had been multiplying throughout the previous decade. In the absence of continental models these had tended to adopt (and occasionally adapt) northern radical feminist approaches. They questioned the objectivity of the canon and associated analytic and representational categories, linking the legitimation of knowledge claims to networks of exclusion and domination. With its focus on 'la existencia o no, definición o no, caracterización o no, de una escritura femenina' (whether a women's writing existed, and if so whether it could be defined or characterized), *La sartén* marked a shift in this debate (González and Ortega 1985: 13). From the early recognition that knowledge bears the marks of its producers critics now turned to precisely how women's knowledge and subjectivity might (or might not) be reflected in their cultural production. In her contribution to the volume Rosario Ferré was unwilling to assume a fixed women's nature deducible from, or reflected in, stable stylistic differences, but believed that women's experiences were sufficiently different from men's to generate specific women's themes (Ferré 1985). Josefina Ludmer's influential paper also rejected what she saw as a tendency to fix or homogenize women in notions such as 'lo femenino' (the feminine), or women's writing, preferring to trace discursive responses to specific instances of marginalization (Ludmer 1985). Rather different in its assumptions was Marta Traba's paper, which assessed particular instances of women's writing in terms of androcentric categories and criteria, and concluded that they met those criteria less successfully than did men (Traba 1985).

Ten years on, questions around women's experience and social and discursive construction remain crucial to the dynamic of feminist critical theory, and so too does the persistence of androcentric analytic categories. For while it remains politically essential for feminists to defend women as women to counteract patterns of oppression, it is not clear how this is to be done without recourse to the metaphysical framework which serves to legitimate that oppression. This dilemma, and the fact that despite all the texts produced by Latin American women writers 'todavía no hemos elaborado posiciones teóricas derivadas de la lectura de estos textos' (we have yet to develop theoretical positions based on readings of these texts), was the starting-point for Sara Castro-Klarén's contribution to *La sartén* (Castro-Klarén 1985: 36). In the absence of a properly Latin American theory, she maintained, the feminist critic who seeks to subvert patriarchal representational assumptions 'tendrá que enfrentar, no doblegarse o seguir, pero sí reflexionar y hacer mella con ... el nuevo feminismo francés' (will have to confront new French feminism, not in a slavish or uncritical way but by reflecting on and engaging with it) (1985: 36). This essay is of particular interest because, while Castro-Klarén is neither the first nor the last to reject the uncritical application of North American feminist criticism to Latin American texts, she is almost alone in basing that rejection on the supposed representational naïvety of its assumptions. She was also at that time one of very few Latin Americanists to recognize that, despite superficial similarities, 'new French feminists' such as Luce Irigaray and Julia Kristeva conceived of the subversion of the masculine Symbolic order, for example, the inscription of women's bodies, the paradigmatic status of psychoanalysis, and the work of difference in very different ways. At the same time she registered the implications for Latin American theory of a common anti-Enlightenment impulse in these women's discourses, observing that '[la] crítica literaria nutrida del neo-marxismo y el estructuralismo continental no puede dejar de lado la crisis del humanismo y su dialéctica' (Marxist- or structuralist-influenced literary criticism cannot ignore the crisis of humanism and its dialectic) (1985: 30).

Ten years on anti-humanist post-Enlightenment critiques are

more familiar, but their implications for feminism generally and identity politics in particular continue to be hotly debated. In a reference to 'la mujer y su posición universal' (woman and her universal position) Castro-Klarén obliquely underlined the fact that despite Kristeva's insistence on (psychic) difference within women and Irigaray's focus on differences between women and men, neither is primarily concerned with differences between women. Yet throughout the 1980s Latin American women were increasingly affirming their difference, as Latin Americans but also increasingly specifically, as non-white and/ or non-middle-class women from Mexico, for example, or Guadalajara, or Guadalajara's shanty settlements. If women figured as men's marginalized and excluded 'other', then these women figured as the 'others' of the predominantly white middle-class Anglo-European feminists who were purporting to speak on behalf of women in general. By the second half of the 1980s this presumption was increasingly being challenged by postcolonial feminist theorists attentive to these and other so-called Third World women's voices. However, by pressing the ethico-political claims of heterogeneity to their logical conclusion critics like Spivak also challenged the bases of identity politics. Feminism's 'discursive turn' meant that the subject— focus of the sense of self, authenticity, and integrity, and of the experience around which identity politics tended and continue to be constructed—was increasingly represented as 'more like a railway junction where signifiers, discourses and messages meet or flash past, than a source, origin or mirror' (Lennon and Whitford 1994: 4).

The influence of leftist analyses in Latin American cultural criticism from the late 1960s led many critics to focus less on the discursive construction or mediation of relations between women, men, and the social than on what are seen as the broader socio-cultural and politico-economic effects of those relations.[1] One of the very few Latin Americanists who have sought to articulate both focuses is Jean Franco. Her 1986

---

[1] Angel Rama and Beatriz Sarlo are influential examples of this. See Patricia D'Allemand's 'Hacia una crítica literaria latinoamericana: nacionalismo y cultura en el discurso de Beatriz Sarlo' in *Estudios: Revista de Investigaciones Literarias*, 1/2 (Caracas, July–Dec. 1993), 27–40, and, for a woman-centred view, Sarlo's contribution to Sara Castro-Klarén, Sylvia Molloy, and Beatriz Sarlo (eds.), *Women's Writing in Latin America: An Anthology* (Boulder, Colo., 1991).

'Apuntes sobre la crítica feminista y la literatura hispanoamericana' is particularly notable for its insistence on theory's
explicitly political edge. While criticism rescues lost texts or
re-evaluates forgotten ones, she claims, theory has a broader
political role in the exploration of power relations:

> tiene que partir de una crítica de las instituciones y antes que nada,
> del sistema literario en sí mismo . . . en relación con la jerarquización
> basada en la diferenciación entre lo masculino y lo femenino (y con)
> la manera mediante la cual la oposición masculino-femenino ha
> estructurado el conocimiento y ha enmascarado los propósitos de la
> evaluación académica. (Franco 1986: 32–3)

> has to start from a critique of institutions and above all of the literary
> system itself . . . with reference to hierarchies based on the masculine/
> feminine distinction (and) the way in which the masculine-feminine
> opposition has structured knowledge and obscured the aims of aca-
> demic evaluation.

For this purpose she is prepared to appropriate aspects of any
theories that might be serviceable: from Derrida's questioning
of limits and margins and examination of the power relations
that sustain the law of gender, to Marxist analyses of hegemony
and ideology in power relations. She does not dwell here on
the discursive status of such bricolage nor on precisely how
these elements might be brought together. However, she is
clear that feminism depends on such allies as Marxism and
deconstruction, and that they depend on feminism. While
observing that it has never been easier to dismantle the binary
systems supporting the crumbling master narratives, Franco
does not question the value for feminists of appropriating
theories (in whole or in part) which may themselves be on the
verge of collapse. Nor does she address how, in the absence of
master narratives, feminism as a political project grounded in
notions of justice and the rejection of patriarchally distorted
reality is to legitimate its own claims and competing notions of
reality, either among women or generally. She nevertheless
distances herself from radical postmodern positions by emphatically differentiating her bricolage model from varieties of
critical consumerism or liberal pluralism.

Two years later Franco published her influential full-length
study *Plotting Women*. It explored this double engagement in
detail, linking 'the contradictory claims between life practices

and textuality, political power and the virtues of marginality' in what she represented as the aftermath of the debate between Anglo-American and French criticism (Franco 1989: p. xxii). Her earlier writing had tended to present literary theory as political in institutional (or micropolitical) terms. Now she highlighted the links between theory, experience, and broader (macropolitical) activism, and she did this at a time when women's experience of a dislocated, 'improper' existence within male paradigms and on male terms was increasingly being seen as offering a standpoint for non-male-constructed knowledge. Experience does not figure in Franco's analysis as an unmediated engagement with the real, however, or as what happens to a pre-existent individual. Instead she uses Teresa de Lauretis's account of experience as the process by which subjectivity is constructed and supplements it with Foucauldian and Bakhtinian analyses of discourse, representation, exclusion, and transgression.[2] By this means Franco attempts to explore the dynamics of power and resistance in specific, gendered instances of 'the solitary struggle of isolated women' in Latin America and to demonstrate that the collective reality of 'women', as a site of resistance to ideology, is inherently political (Franco 1989: p. xxiii). Although, like de Lauretis, Franco does not dwell on the shift from critical reflection to politics this remains an important attempt to harness both micro- and macropolitical dynamics for Latin American feminist theory.[3]

This double engagement is possible because Franco, unlike many macropolitically focused Latin Americanists, is prepared to exploit theories constructed by and within non-Latin American contexts. Fourteen years earlier, Cuban critic Roberto Fernández Retamar had warned his Latin American readers against such cultural transposition on the grounds that 'una teoría de la literatura es la teoría de una literatura' (a theory of literature is the theory of a literature) (Fernández Retamar 1975: 48). Instead he advocated a home-produced theory of literary production, derived directly from Latin American writings. The end result was not a call for a cultural purge or exclusion zone, however. His own Marxist-influenced aesthetic

---

[2] See Teresa de Lauretis, *Alice Doesn't: Feminism, Semiotics, Cinema* (1984), ch. 6.

[3] For critiques of de Lauretis see Elizabeth J. Bellamy and Artemis Leontis, 'A Genealogy of Experience', in *The Yale Journal of Criticism*, 6/1 (Spring 1993), 163–84, and Joan W. Scott's 'Experience', in Butler and Scott (1992), 22–40.

was justified implicitly by its descent and distillation through key figures in Latin American criticism and by his acknowledgement that such assumptions form part of a shared Western intellectual tradition. Latin Americans cannot simply reject this tradition, he maintained, but must engage with it critically. Writing as he was in the early 1970s, Fernández Retamar underestimated the way in which academic globalization would compound the effects of historical imbrication. Nor could he predict the extent to which psychoanalytic, post-structuralist, post-colonial, and feminist writings would in their different ways also help problematize the site from which criticism emanates.

In 1989 Hernán Vidal edited the proceedings of the 1988 Minnesota conference on Hispanic and Luso-Brazilian feminist criticism. In the introduction he too is preoccupied with what he represents as external influences on the elaboration of Latin American theory. Above all he deplores the uncritical application of French and Anglo-Saxon feminist theory without regard either to cultural contexts or to the contribution of the exercise to the feminist cause (Vidal 1989). For him, the crucial task for Latin American feminist criticism is 'la concertación de esfuerzos que por sobre las differenciaciones ideológicas consensualmente establezca tareas comunes bien delimitadas' (a concentrated effort to overcome ideological differences and agree clearly defined common objectives) (1989: 17). This failure to achieve consensus he attributes not to ideological and other differences but to the rhetoric which underpins a certain feminist discourse of unity and identity. For Vidal, this rhetoric is a barrier to self-criticism and open exchange with opposed theories, and he advocates in its place:

una interpenetración de las diferentes lógicas [formando] un caleidoscopio de diferentes perspectivas sobre un mismo objeto [y] una organicidad totalizadora de su visión de mundo. (1989: 15)

an interpenetration of different logics [forming] a kaleidoscope of different perspectives on the same object [and] a totalizing, organic world-view.

The fact that this vision of kaleidoscopic, organic totality owes more to Martí, for example, than Foucault, both licenses his pronouncements and accounts for their failure to register the power relations that operate within any consensus. However, his sensitivity to northern imperialism makes him quick to detect the workings of power behind certain recurring themes in the conference's papers. The search for an essentially feminine literary discourse, for example, is characterized as a projection of 'la técnica y teorías [relacionadas con] el desarrollo de los programas de estudio de la mujer de los Estados Unidos... sobre la producción literaria de otras culturas' (techniques and theories [associated with] the development of US Women's Studies programmes... on the literary production of other cultures) and contrasted with 'una mayor preocupación política entre las latinoamericanistas' (a greater concern with politics among Latin Americanists) (1989: 8). Interesting though they are, Vidal's observations are rather undermined by generalizations which evoke a more monochromatic than kaleidoscopic critical totality. Universals (if not totalities) may have a limited, strategic value for feminist theory but this needs to reflect the key role of Latin American women precisely in challenging universalizing and totalizing pretensions in feminist thought.

In 1992 Debra Castillo published her own brilliantly original sketch for a Latin American feminist criticism, based on very different priorities and assumptions. Castillo positions her study as a response to Castro-Klarén's account of the continuing crisis of humanism and of the need for a properly Latin American literary criticism. She refuses to impose specific critical models or an overarching theoretical framework on 'the diverse, shifting and often contradictory voices of Latin American feminist writers' (Castillo 1992: p. xxii). Instead she offers 'something like a recipe ... the general conditions of possibility for at least one type of Latin American feminist criticism' (1992: p. xiv). In place of 'a single overspecific theoretical model' her list of ingredients offers a 'continually self-questioning theorizing' anchored in a number of strategies—the exploitation of marginality, for example, negation and appropriation, superficiality and subjunctive mood—each derived from 'Latin American feminist writing' (1992: p. xxii). This recipe is elaborated with reference to the work of a range of Latin American and Chicana women writers, after which the Conclusion 'comes back to the role of the Latin Americanist as feminist critic in this postmodern, postcolonial scene' (1992: p. xxiii).

Clearly there is much here that Vidal would not approve of, although like him Castillo confronts and attempts to unsettle asymmetrical north/south power relations. Like Franco she uses elements from a range of models for this purpose, including deconstruction, postmodernism, and post-colonial theory. Castillo resists the binary oppositions that would have cast her intervention as something like a bridge between the US and Latin America. Instead she assumes a complex double-voicing in an attempt to enact what has been called 'the serious heteroglossic play of dominant and marginalized discourses', in which the split feminist subject seeks to engage both simultaneously in a space proper to neither (Butler and Scott 1992: p. xv). She is thus able to displace the difficulties of following up the feminist critique of identity with a constructive moment, in which some form of identity must presumably be established, by offering an exceptionally flexible model for construction. Some of the elements Castillo selects for her model are remotivations or mimetic redeployments of charges often levelled against women writers, such as negativity or superficiality. This intensifies the sense of a complex critical invagination.

Castillo offers a confidently polemical repudiation of the iconization of Rigoberta Menchú, Domitila Barrios de Chúngara, and others as hegemonic figures of truth in a certain macropolitical discourse. However, it may be that she is unnecessarily defensive when asserting the claims of the micro- over the macropolitical in an academic context. A concern for the micropolitical operations that construct the field within which positions emerge differentially, an attention to the exclusions that sustain those positions, and a persistent questioning of the givens of political discourse (its appeal to Enlightenment notions of the origin, the fixed and unified political subject, ethical grounding, and so on) do not after all imply a rejection of macropolitics. As Franco has demonstrated, however, their analytic articulation is unlikely to be straightforward. For example, the deconstructive procedures used to unsettle hegemonic centre/ periphery and colonizer/colonized oppositions have an endlessly affirmative quality that is not easily reconciled with the subaltern's need to reject brutal or otherwise repressive measures.

Castillo's study highlights rather different articulation problems within what I have rather loosely characterized as the micropolitical itself. By emphasizing the play of power in discourse she is able to evoke its diffusion, to seem to displace it from the white middle-class US academic or powerfully hegemonic icons of unpower towards nameless and inaudible Latin American women. Referring her text to a 'postmodern, post-colonial scene' goes some way to licensing the kind of mobility and bricolage needed for this masterful renunciation of mastery. Yet there is no indication of how the postmodern and post-colonial elements of this 'scene' are to be articulated, particularly in what is represented as a feminist context. Like feminism, post-colonial theory has a political charge that is broadly underpinned by notions of justice and, often, progress which are the explicit focus of postmodern Enlightenment critiques. The difficulty of articulating any position (including a refusal to take up positions) with such critiques is underlined in postmodern writing's own dependence on more or less explicit general rules and values.[4]

The breadth and energy Castillo brings to this exceptionally complex project and her brilliant textual analyses makes this study the high-water mark of one kind of feminist criticism. A rather different set of preoccupations is increasingly making itself heard in Latin American feminism, however, and one which questions from a new perspective the appropriateness of directing the big guns of alien theory at emergent Latin American cultures. To claim that alien theories do not reflect Latin American experience, for example, need not imply an appeal to untheorized notions of authenticity or propriety, however, or an ignorance of debates around identity. Nor need it signify a refusal to accept that no theory is entirely original or produced in a vacuum, or that a process which is not simply transculturation enables elements of exploited theories to acquire new, local meanings in new combinations.[5] However, this new perspective on theoretical imposition arguably owes as much to the increasingly high profile throughout the 1980s and 1990s of Latin America's new social movements—particularly that of women and so-called feminist groups—as it does to developments in feminist criticism.[6] Writing in 1992 Jean Franco

[4] See e.g. Linda J. Nicholson (ed.), *Feminism/Postmodernism* (London, 1990), especially Linda J. Nicholson and Nancy Fraser, 'Social Criticism without Philosophy: An Encounter between Feminism and Postmodernism', 19–38.

[5] This combination of concerns was highlighted by Susan Frenk in a paper on Latin American feminist theory at the Cross-Currents in Latin American Gender Theory conference at Brimingham University, UK, Mar. 1994.

[6] This has attracted considerable international feminist attention. In addition to works cited see: Elizabeth Jelin, 'Citizenship and Identity: Final Reflections' in ead. (ed.), *Women and Social Change in Latin America* trans. J. Ann Zammit and Marilyn Thompson (London, 1990), 184–207; *NACLA: Report on the Americas*, 27/1 (1993); Sarah Radcliffe and Sallie Westwood (eds.), *Viva: Women and Popular Protest in Latin America* (London, 1993); Sarah Radcliffe, '(Representing) Post-colonial Women: Authority, Difference and Feminisms', *Area*, 26/1 (1994), 25–32.

underlined the growing importance for international feminism
and feminist cultural studies of these social movements, noting
that 'the woman intellectual cannot claim unproblematically
to represent women and be their voice, but she can broaden
the terms of political debate by redefining sovereignty and by
using privilege to destroy privilege' (Franco 1992: 80). This
shift of emphasis from the ethico-political difficulties of representing the other in her/his difference towards a more prag-
matic (if inevitably more normative) focus on finding some
means of engagement illustrates the dynamics of the enlarged
debate. In a full-length study of Latin American feminist criticism published a year after Castillo's, Amy Kaminsky broadens
this debate in a slightly different, though familiar, direction.
Like Vidal, she starts with Latin Americanists' macropolitical concern for social relations, as read off through dominant, apparently natural, analytic, and interpretive categories (Kaminsky
1993: p. xv). This she contrasts with a micropolitical, in her
account apolitical, North American feminist focus on the
discursive construction of these categories and relations. In
Kaminsky's account the 'political' and the 'aesthetic' have been
constructed as antithetical in the US academy and the 'political'
marginalized in its literary discourse. Suggesting that sexuality,
and particularly lesbian sexuality, has been similarly marginalized in Latin America she attempts to bridge these differences
by undertaking 'the feminist demetaphorization of the language
of sexuality for Latin Americanists and the Latin Americanist
derhetorization of the language of politics for feminists' (1993:
135). Kaminsky sees her study as a response to the demands of
both a radical materialist feminism and an oppositional politics,
and advocates a Latin American feminist criticism which addresses 'gender oppression (closely tied to issues of sexuality)
while interacting with the material effects of political and
economic dependency and considering the resistance to all of
these' (1993: p. xii).

Unlike Vidal, Kaminsky accepts the importance of the US
feminist linking of the personal and the political, but insists
that any response to this link must reflect its own positioning.[7]

[7] I am indebted here to the work of Dr David J. Woods and in particular his
contribution to a paper we presented to the Day Conference on Latin American
Women's Writing, Institute for Latin American Studies, London, June 1994, 'Big
Guns and Suffering Bodies: Present Problems in Latin American Feminist Criticism'.

In her view criticism needs to be able to participate in 'the transformation of repressive cultural practice' not only within the institution but in specific social contexts (Kaminsky 1993: p. xiv). Kaminsky sets her concern with the material oppression of women and their agency through action against post-structuralist accounts of women as a sign of alterity or the bodily. She offers no blanket rejection of post-structuralist premises, however, since if its undermining of identity politics is unquestionably uncomfortable, post-structuralism's questioning of supposedly universal categories has been crucial for feminism. Kaminsky's project is notable first for the centrality she accords feminist practice, second for her insistence on the link between this practice and the social context that generated it, and third for her assumption that within this context conflict may be resolved in a spirit of solidarity. Clearly the delimiting of contexts is less simple or innocent than Kaminsky suggests and, while solidarity may be an essential starting-point, the work of power relations and the determination of identity by exclusion cannot be ignored. The organizing metaphor for her project is nevertheless a startlingly suggestive one:

when victims of repression are honoured in Latin America, be they disappeared students or murdered archbishops, their names are called out as if in the rolls, and the collectivity responds '*Presente* present', often eliciting the response, '*ahora y para siempre* now and always'. (Kaminsky 1993: 24–5)

Presence is 'a notion that posits the sense of self in the quest for transformation' resulting in a 'conscious positioning, enabling choice and agency' (1993: 25). This suggests coherent political subjectivity, and the self in quest of transformation within the community as an intersubjective source of individual identity.

It could be argued that Kaminsky's untheorized distinctions between theory, practice, pure theory, and material reality, her treatment of experience, race, class, and gender as givens, and her undeconstructed references to presence would be easier to deal with if she did not draw on post-structuralist insights elsewhere. Yet this tension between micropolitical and macropolitical concerns remains one of the most characteristic features of the enlarged Latin American feminist debate. Among these features are: a desire for an appropriately and specifically Latin

American and more broadly materialist critical theory, but also
a questioning of identity and appropriateness/appropriation
in this context; a rejection of binary oppositions but also of the
over-hasty metaphorization of material and social bodies in
such notions as hybridity; an acknowledgement of both the
inevitability of theoretical mediation and the need for greater
openness to innovative local practices which might otherwise
be dismissed as theoretically naïve; a concern for the social and
material other but also for the status of distinctions between
the other and the same, the material and the theoretical, critical
theory and social practice. Academic feminists are accustomed
to tracing the operations which construct the field in which
gender, literary, and other relations emerge, and to seeing these
operations as political. We know that such a politics cannot
assume a stable and unified subject or object, be it 'woman',
'text', or 'Latin America'. Nor can it assume unproblematic
access to what Spivak terms 'the impossible intimacy of the
ethical' (Chakravorty Spivak 1992: 81). Yet there will continue
to be moments and fields in which any engagement with these
mobile and heterogenous subjects, as individuals or collectively,
seems contingent precisely on the strategic treatment of context as given, and of identity as the stable and unproblematic
rallying point of self-conscious political subjects. We know that
the ethico-political purchase of such strategies is questionable,
particularly when they harden into routine; this is only one of
the tensions which currently 'secure' our critical work and with
which we have undoubtedly become too comfortable. Critics
who seek a sustainable articulation of macro- and micropolitics
cannot afford to ignore or exaggerate these tensions, but nor
can we allow ourselves to be held in check by them any longer.

LIST OF WORKS CITED

BUTLER, JUDITH, and SCOTT, JOAN W. (1992) (eds.), *Feminists Theorize the Political* (New York and London (1993).
CARR, BARRY, and ELLNER, STEVE (1993), *The Latin American Left: From the Fall of Allende to Perestroika* (Boulder, Colo.).
CASTILLO, DEBRA (1992), *Talking Back: Toward a Latin American Feminist Literary Criticism* (Ithaca, NY).

CASTRO-KLARÉN, SARA(1985), 'La crítica literaria feminista y la escritura en América Latina', in González and Ortega (1985), 27–46.

CHAKRAVORTY SPIVAK, GAYATRI (1992), 'French Feminism Revisited: Ethics and Politics', in Butler and Scott (1992), 54–85.

DE LAURETIS, TERESA (1984), *Alice Doesn't: Feminism, Semiotics, Cinema* (Bloomington, Ind.).

FERNÁNDEZ RETAMAR, ROBERTO (1975), *Para una teoría de la literatura hispanoamericana y otras aproximaciones* (Harana).

FERRÉ, ROSARIO (1985), 'La cocina de la escritura', in González and Ortega (1985), 137–54.

FISHER, JO (1993*a*), 'Women and Democracy: For Home and Country', in *NACLA: Report on the Americas*, 27/1: 30–6.

—— (1993*b*), *Out of the Shadows: Women, Resistance and Politics in South America* (London).

FRANCO, JEAN (1986), 'Apuntes sobre la crítica feminista y la literatura hispanoamericana', in *Hispamérica*, 15/45: 31–43.

—— (1989), *Plotting Women* (London).

—— (1992), 'Going Public: Reinhabiting the Private', in George Yúdice, Jean Franco, and Angel Flores (eds.), *On Edge: The Crisis of Contemporary Latin American Culture* (Minneapolis, 1992), 65–83.

GONZÁLEZ, PATRICIA ELENA, and ORTEGA, ELIANA (1985) (eds.), *La sartén por el mango: encuentro de escritoras latinamericanas* (Rio Piedras).

KAMINSKY, AMY (1993), *Reading the Body Politic: Feminist Criticism and Latin American Women Writers* (Minneapolis).

KÜPPERS, GABY (1994), *Compañeras: Voices from the Latin American Women's Movement* (London).

LENNON, KATHLEEN, and WHITFORD, MARGARET (1994) (eds.), *Knowing the Difference: Feminist Perspectives in Epistemology* (London).

LUDMER, JOSEFINA (1985), 'Tretas del Débil', in González and Ortega (1985), 47–54.

TALPADE MOHANTY, CHANDRA (1991), 'Under Western Eyes: Feminist Scholarship and Colonial Discourses', in Chandra Talpade Mohanty, Ann Russo, and Lourdes Torres (eds.), *Third World Women and the Politics of Feminism* (Bloomington, Ind., and Indianapolis, 1991), 51–80.

TRABA, MARTA (1985), 'Hipótesis sobre una escritura diferente', in González and Ortega (1985), 21–6.

VIDAL, HERNAN (1989) (ed.), *Cultural and Historical Grounding for Hispanic and Luso-Brazilian Feminist Literary Criticism* (Minneapolis).

12

Response
Cutting/Edge

DEBRA CASTILLO

ANNY JONES's essay elegantly articulates a concern that has been exercising many of us for some time now about the role of the Western or Western-trained academic in relation to Third World cultural expressions and artefacts. As she points out, in *Talking Back*, I focus on questions of theoretical appropriation and on specific critical readings of (mostly) fictional texts that help me explore these concerns. I try to look at questions of knowledge production and the normalization of certain institutional practices. At the same time, one of the things I want to show in that book is how issues of curriculum, pedagogy, and politics unfold in tense imbrication with issues of cross-cultural, interclass, and sexually charged exchanges. Particularly insidious in the academy is the all too common substitution of a Latin America invented by and for other academics for interaction with the Latin America that lies outside the purview of academic discourse. Jones's essay centres on the opportunity for both cross-Atlantic and cross-hemispheric dialogue—and the inevitable misprisions involved in such limited cultural exchanges—in which First and Third World intellectuals meet in their appreciation of the same overdetermined and highly constructed critical object. For despite a generalized recognition that old categories and old verities are no longer able to account for the world, there is a parallel recognition among traditional as well as resistant academics that Eurocentrism is inextricably built into the very structure of 'our' critical and fictional narratives, at the same time binding these narratives into a restrictive syntax that conforms itself around such simplistic binaries as the one noted above, and validating precisely these simplistic and restrictive narratives as the critical discourse that wins us plums in both First and Third World academies. Deborah McDowell would go even further: 'There's a lot of radical criticism that gets the grammar right, but we have become much too comfortable with radical language and not sufficiently committed to radical action', and she concludes, 'We're in an era that privileges oppositional criticism, and yet this criticism can sometimes be an act of substitution' (McDowell 1989: 25). Oppositional criticism, in other words, substitutes for oppositional action. To the degree that post-colonialist theories and the Western-trained 'subaltern' intellectual both allow us to think these catachreses and at the same time to hold on to the rejected binary logic of Eurocentrism, they too participate in this crisis. And to listen to us here in the universities, it is hard to imagine how the crisis can get much worse.

I would like to move out of this specular tautology if I can, by going back to Adrienne Rich's seminal and much commented-upon 1984 essay, 'Notes toward a Politics of Location' and to a companion essay of Rich's even more pertinent to my objective here, also from 1984, 'Blood, Bread, and Poetry: The Location of the Poet'. In 'Notes toward a Politics of Location', Rich grounds her struggle for understanding and for accountability in the world in her own body, as a white, Jewish, lesbian, feminist, US citizen and poet speaking (at that particular moment) in Europe. The physical location of this multiply culturally traversed body becomes the centre of her discourse, but, she reminds us, her centre is not *the* centre (Rich 1986: 231). She is a white woman in a country that, despite a white male political and theoretical establishment, is not white and not particularly sympathetic to females. As she puts it 'The United States has never been a white country, though it has long served what white men defined as their interests' (1986: 226). Furthermore, at the same time as Rich notes that her interests, insofar as they intersect with dominant white male perspectives, inevitably intersect also with her race, she remembers the circumscribing nature of whiteness as a gendered racial, poetic, and political location (1986: 219).

Rich carries this acknowledgement of a moving location, centred on the body, into 'Blood, Bread, and Poetry' as well. For Rich location is not just academic, and it is both politicized and personalized in multiply intersecting forms. The opening paragraph is worth quoting in its entirety:

The Miami airport, summer 1983: A North American woman says to me, 'you'll love Nicaragua: everyone there is a poet.' I've thought many times of that remark, both while there and since returning home. Coming from a culture (North American, white- and male-dominated) which encourages poets to think of ourselves as alienated from the sensibility of the general population, which casually and devastatingly marginalizes us (so far, no slave labour or torture for a political poem—just dead air, the white noise of the media jamming the poet's words)—coming from this North American dominant culture which so confuses us, telling us poetry is neither economically profitable nor politically effective and that political dissidence is destructive to art, coming from this culture that tells me I am destined to be a luxury, a decorative garnish on the buffet table of the university curriculum, the ceremonial occasion, the national celebration—what am I to make, I thought, of that remark? *You'll love Nicaragua: everyone there is a poet.* (Do I love poets in general? I immediately asked myself, thinking of poets I neither love nor would wish to see in charge of my country.) Is being a poet a guarantee that I will love a Marxist-Leninist revolution? Can't I simply travel as an American radical, a lesbian feminist, a citizen who opposes her government's wars against its own people and its intervention in other people's lands? And what effectiveness has the testimony of a poet returning from a revolution where 'everyone is a poet' to a country where the possible credibility of poetry is not even seriously discussed. (Rich 1986: 167–8)

In this comment, the relation of First and Third World intellectuals is almost precisely reversed from the information retrieval and appropriation model. From her own particular location, Rich occupies what might otherwise be defined as the traditional space of the Third World intellectual, marginalized in relation to the Anglo-Eurocentric establishment, while the Nicaraguan poet curiously moves to a First Worldish position of influence and prominence. Rich marks and restates several times her own marginality to hegemonic political/cultural establishment of the US, and seems to long for participation in a country such as Nicaragua where poetry is taken seriously outside the limited purview of the academy, where as a matter of course poets like Ernesto Cardenal take on major responsibilities for shaping their government. This use-value of poetry in its proper location separates it irremediably from the deracinated poetic object abstracted from its proper place in Latin American reality and inserted into the Western university. Furthermore, the seriousness and centrality of poetic work in Latin America contrasts vividly with Rich's sense of her merely decorative function, her merely academic appeal in the US, a country where poetry is seen as so trivial that not only is poetry *not* considered a sufficient qualification for political office, but poets are almost entirely ignored. With conscious perversity, Rich leans nostalgically towards the manifest oppressions of Latin America where poets are taken so seriously in the political realm that they are disappeared and murdered for their writing, at the same time as she contemplates her politically disempowered location in a US where her most radical political pronouncements will be met with 'dead air'.

'You'll love Nicaragua: everyone there is a poet' frames this enquiry and injects it into a personalized cultural analysis in terms of an explicitly feminist and geographically situated poetics *and* politics of location. The implicit statement underlying her friend's enthusiasm for Nicaragua is a shared perception that poetry is shockingly undervalued in the US and that the situation is quite different in Latin America. 'We both love poetry,' the woman is telling Rich, 'therefore, we love Nicaragua.' It is precisely this untheorized craving for poetics as political praxis that recasts Rich's ingenuous interlocutor as an oppositional 'I' to Rich's more nuanced reflections—and yet the 'we' that frames the discourse remains intact and is reinforced by repetition. For while Rich rejects the naive form of this statement, the yearning for an authority grounded in poetry remains, and so does Rich's implicit question: Where, and on what grounds, does the feminist poet locate her political agency? Rich's question goes beyond the concerns of professional disciplinary dynamics and more directly concerns itself with two other questions: Who cares? What social reorganizations are effected?

Following Rich, then, I would like to speak specifically from my own narrow arena of action as a feminist Latin Americanist located in an élite, north-eastern US university. First of all, calls for the transformation of society and for a more nuanced ideological awareness of educational stakes, like Rich's, Jones', and mine, work from within a common understanding of the educational process and a recognition of the value and importance of the Humanities in maintaining and policing the nation's sense of itself and its cultural heritage. Increasingly, however, both popular and academic presses in the US describe a student body for whom traditional liberal arts education in general, and literary studies in particular, has become increasingly marginal and unappealing, and who find profoundly irrelevant the attempts by literary critics of both the Right and the Left to grapple with cultural issues. Not only do proportionately fewer students enter traditional Humanities fields, but Humanities courses are more and more marginally represented in the typical student's curriculum. Furthermore, among our students there is an abundance of conflicting understandings about social and cultural circumstances. When a classroom includes, for example, a first-generation Dominican-American female engineering student from the Bronx and a fourth-generation Chinese-American male pre-med student from an exclusive western prep school, where does a white, feminist scholar from the midwest begin to approach questions of authority, of class, of gender, of race, and of cultural forms? Unsurprisingly, in this context, to borrow a phrase from Gerald Graff:

the literature teacher stands before the class not as a member of an identifiable collective engaged in modes of thought that most students might see themselves as internalizing, but as the representative of alien requirements which tend to be seen as obstacles to be circumvented with as little damage to the students' career ambitions as possible. (Graff 1989: 257)

And yet, imagining an intellectual debate in a classroom of such relatively successful and confident young people remains possible. Despite what Graff sees as the cutting edge of incomprehension between humanists and technocrats, both groups share the privileged space of a post-secondary education that makes for viable argument, that allows teachers to categorize students as alternately resisting, indifferent, or engaged, even across the power and authority differentials that make discussions sometimes seem artificial.

By way of contrast, let me refer you back to a Latin American view on the imbrication of literature, pedagogy, and politics. At one point in *Talking Back*, I write briefly about María Luisa Puga's 'El lenguaje oculto'. In that essay, Puga proposes to explore the values and social interests presumably served by the classical curriculum of study and to propose a more appropriate vehicle for exploring the range of Latin American responses to a diverse and self-questioning Latin American reality.

The Mexico City novelist and intellectual defines the themes of a series of thirty-four lectures she proposes to give in a tour of the north of the country. She will focus on 'the appropriation of language', which, in her definition, is how language acquires a voice of its own when literature begins to appropriate the history of the nation; 'how we are taught to read', in which she delineates a general practice of miseducation, since language and culture are presented in schools as alien objects of detached study rather than as integral components in the ongoing construction of the self; 'what we read', and disconcertingly she finds that what 'we read' in school are classics from Spain like *El mío Cid* complemented by a diet of American best sellers at home; 'how language colonizes', the examination of how people are taught to speak 'correctly'; 'identity through language', that is, the manner in which a personal self-concept is created in stories told us and stories we tell about ourselves (Puga and Mansour 1987: 12).

This listing of issues will undoubtedly sound familiar, even commonplace to readers of this volume. It is also clear from her discussion of Mexico, and of the operation of the Ministry of Public Education, that Puga sees clearly that any 'national' curriculum, defined from the centre of the country, will inevitably do violence to the diverse cultures of its citizens. At the same time, she sees no real alternative; the US, she comments at one point, is powerful precisely because it has been able to impose successfully upon its citizens a single national image. Her comment about the US is, of course, highly debatable. I am less interested in debating it, however, than in noting the tension between a rejection of that perceived cultural imperialism (so like Mexico's, though more successfully imposed) and her wistful acknowledgement of an empowering structure that works to the benefit of the national project.

The situation is even worse than she imagines, however. Her series of lectures is not only reductive in terms of the curricular machine grinding away in Mexico City; it is deeply irrelevant to the provincial towns she visits in the north of Mexico. Puga is prepared to fill the time allotted to her, to tell her audience what she knows or suspects about the political stakes in the struggle between the use of classical Spanish vs. modern Latin American texts as the vehicles for the construction of a modern literate citizenry. In either case, however, the discussion is premissed upon the attendance of a group of people who share a sophisticated ability to read and whose values and social projects are served by one set of texts or the other. She implicitly expects to share her concern about an appropriate curriculum for Mexican schoolchildren with people who, presumably like herself, have been forced to read Spanish classics, and found them alienating, people who read canonical Latin American literature for personal pleasure, people who have had the money and leisure to purchase the glossy translations of American best sellers sold in upmarket department stores like Sanborns as well as the cheap and colourful comic books ('fotonovelas,' 'historietas') hawked by street vendors. Instead, she finds indifferent administrators, empty rooms, incorrectly copied phone numbers, cancelled events, or lectures rescheduled with groups of bewildered students herded into inappropriate rooms to provide her with an audience.

In the small provincial town of Vícam, for example, she prepares to give her talk to the junior high and high school children, who have been bussed in, many without breakfast, for the occasion, thus providing her with an ample, although not entirely enthusiastic, audience. She wants to converse with the students; they hesitate and hide their faces. Puga assumes this action shows a reluctance to speak and further assumes the reluctance to speak is due to shyness; in any case it blunts her attempts to create an atmosphere of open discussion. One of the teachers reminds her of yet another problem; the students are Yaqui Indians, many of whom have only a rudimentary knowledge of Spanish (Puga and Mansour 1987: 16). Puga is a well-intentioned, well-dressed, well-connected, well-fed woman from the centre of the nation. Between her and these young people of Vícam there is an absolute lack of a common ground for discussion. Puga struggles on valiantly:

Eran no sé cuántos. Estábamos en la biblioteca del CBTA de Vícam, en donde lucen sus lomos los libros de siempre, ya saben: Sor Juana, Alfonso Reyes, Octavio Paz, Carlos Fuentes . . . gracias a ellos somos internacionales, pero no logramos que la gente de nuestro país nos lea. A los chavos de Vícam eso no les servía. Clases de literatura habían tenido, sí. Algunos recordaban haber leído *La Celestina, El cantar del Mío Cid*. . . . Con razón odiamos tanto leer. Nos ocuparon el lenguaje; lo llenaron de gestos que no son nuestros, que no nos dicen. (Puga and Mansour 1987: 17)

I don't know how many were there. We were in Vícam's CBTA library, where the splendid spines of all the usual volumes were on display: Sor Juana, Alfonso Reyes, Octavio Paz, Carlos Fuentes . . . thanks to them we are international, but we can't get people from our own country to read us. For the kids of Vícam it was a waste of time. They'd had literature classes and some remembered reading *La Celestina, El cantar del Mío Cid.* . . . No wonder we hate reading. They took over our language, filled it with gestures that are not ours, that do not speak [to] us.

Puga's difficulty with the Yaqui students is captured succinctly in the morasses of her pronoun references: 'we' (the students and Puga) were in the library, 'we' (Mexicans) achieve an international presence in the works of our most famously exported writers, 'we' (the best writers: Puga implicitly includes herself in the canonical role call) are not read in Mexico. Then, more distanced: 'it' (the library, this lecture) has no relevance to Yaqui speakers from Vícam; it is not a space they frequent, and reflects no recognition of their culture or their language. 'They' (the students) have been compelled to read canonical Spanish works even more distant in time and space from their realities and found them incomprehensible and hateful; 'we' (the students and ex-students) find them boring: worse, 'they' (such works) are imperialistic. Such national masterpieces do not feed Yaqui souls; they seem written for external consumption only. In these works, says Puga, shifting ground once again, 'our' (Spanish) language has been occupied as if by an invading force. Yet, still, the specific case of the Yaquis has been left unaddressed. Even granting that the Spanish of canonical texts rather than 'our [Mexican] Spanish' occupies the space of learning, with all the available interstices filled in with roughly translated versions of American best sellers, Puga has still not focused on the central issue. Spanish is a foreign tongue for the Yaqui schoolchildren; Mexico is a colonial power. The implications of this half-unacknowledged internal colonization of Mexico's own people are vast, if unexplored. In Puga's own words, the 'they' who have taken over 'our' language includes all the Spanish speakers, prior to Independence as well as up to the present day, whose national project is served by defining Spanish as the common language, and who glorify in abstract terms the Indian past and mestizo present through a misleading appropriation. 'They' filled the imposed language 'with gestures that are not ours, that do not speak [to] us' although they make ritual signals in that direction, and do so without acknowledging or appreciating the still vital, still silenced Indian present. Even in the presence of the Yaqui children, the Indians enter into the equation reduced to props in their own drama of identity. All of the struggles Puga describes among the competing cultural traditions of Spain, Mexico, and the United States remain irrelevant to these young people since they have left no place for the Yaquis, who not only must read *El mío Cid*, but must also awkwardly translate it into their own language. And without breakfast. In this context, her ambiguous rejection of the United States as the country that 'understood that in order to become powerful it had to colonize its own people' (Puga and Mansour 1987: 39) seems highly ironic.

Puga's dilemma with respect to the Yaqui youths in Vícam throws into relief a concern common to many of us as the university increasingly diversifies its student body. Puga, in her presentation to the silent young people of Vícam, describes a very different cross-section of society in which the material and linguistic conditions for dialogue are completely absent, and not just on the grounds of a power differential. Thus, I feel compelled to note that all of the foregoing discussion, and whatever is yet to follow, depends on a cultural heritage shared by Puga, myself, Jones, and you, the reader, premissed on a model of education whose goal is, in Jeffrey Sammons's words, 'the cultural formation of the self so that it might reach the fullness of its potentialities' (Sammons 1993: 14). It is this shared heritage from which we cannot distance ourselves that makes this discussion possible, even as the (silent) presence of the Yaquis denounces it.

In her reading of J. M. Coetzee's *Foe*, Gayatri Spivak suggests that 'there can be no politics founded on a continuous overdetermined multiplicity of agencies' (Spivak 1991: 166), and she continues: 'perhaps that is the novel's message: the impossible politics of overdetermination (mothering, authoring, giving voice to the native "in" the text; a white male South African writer engaging in such inscriptions "outside" the text) should not be regularized into a blithe continuity' (1991: 174). 'We' the readers may resist co-option into the cultural community of a given text's value system on various grounds. Clearly, alternative knowledge systems, including those of women-centred and non-Western determined texts, are still among those excluded from the expansive, universalizing 'us'. In our Western textual universe the silent lesson of the Yaquis still has limited consequences for our revisionary intellectual projects. They cross the field of interpretation not as resistance to reading, but as a discursive product that offers too many readings, and yet has been consistently under-read, from both sides of the violent, divisive cultural cut.

What is breaking down, say Sánchez-Tranquilino and Tagg in an article on another figure of the borderlands, the *pachuco/a* (the snappy dresser or 'zoot-suiter'), 'is the discursive formation of a discipline—the conjunctural effects of its practices, institutions, technologies, and strategies of explanation' (Sánchez-Tranquilino and Tagg 1992: 557). This unravelling is particularly noticeable in such borderline presences as those haplessly evoked by María Luisa Puga. The Yaquis, like the '*pachucos/as*', cannot be easily accommodated within the cultural histories of either nation. To paraphrase Sánchez-Tranquilino and Tagg again, these figures not only mark, but provoke, a certain kind of internal cultural crisis in the narrowly conceived imaginations of the nation, just as they mark, but refuse to inhabit, the gender roles, subject positions, and nationalistic spaces limned out for them in the violent conflicts of cultural miscegenation. These wounds, these transgressive cuts, characterize a practice in which the conjunctural describes only one side of the seam.

I do not imagine that I can address the problems of a US pedagogical practice, much less resolve them, in these few pages. The kinds of suggestions I might make for curricular reform must likewise seem obvious, and would hardly appear disinterested ones to any audience, even (especially?) myself. Today, as I look around my upstate New York classroom, I am more than ever certain that, whatever my book achieved, there is much more to be done. What continues to intrigue me, however, is Puga's evocation of the silent Yaqui youths and her inability to communicate with them on any grounds. The point of this essay, accordingly, is not to posit a model for contemporary change, but rather to uncover the constructed nature of ethics-talk and ascriptions of agency. The point is to re-examine the question of supposedly universal values involving the most basic relations of agent, process, and object. Puga poses a crucial question about how individual relations in the pedagogical situation all devolve into relations of oppression, making clear the link between discourse and the strategies of oppression. Once the Yaqui youths have become visible, their major effect upon the reader is to make visible the invisible modes of operation of a mainstream Western culture which, if it takes cognizance of their presence, cannot remain the same. Puga's dilemma may not be a new one, but in discussions about micro- and macropolitics set in, and deriving from, the First World academy, it necessarily defines a cutting/edge.

LIST OF WORKS CITED

GRAFF, GERALD (1989), 'The Future of Theory in the Teaching of Literature', in Ralph Cohen (ed.), *Future Literary Theory* (New York, 1989), 250–67.
McDOWELL, DEBORAH (1989), Interview with Susan Fraiman in *Critical Texts: A Review of Theory and Criticism*, 6/3: 13–29.
PUGA, MARÍA LUISA and MANSOUR, MÓNICA (1987), *Itinerario de palabras* (Mexico, DF).
RICH, ADRIENNE (1986), *Blood, Bread, and Poetry: Selected Prose, 1979–1985* (New York).
SAMMONS, JEFFREY (1993), 'Squaring the Circle: Observations on Core Curriculum and the Plight of the Humanities', in *Profession 86*, 14–21.
SÁNCHEZ-TRANQUILINO, MARCOS, and TAGG, JOHN (1992), 'The Pachuco's Flayed Hide: Mobility, Identity, and *Buenas Garras*', in Lawrence Grossberg, Cary Nelson, and Paula Treichler (eds.), *Cultural Studies* (New York, 1992), 556–70.
SPIVAK, GAYATRI (1991), 'Theory in the Margin: Coetzee's *Foe* Reading Defoe's *Crusoe/Roxana*', in Jonathan Arac and Barbara Johnson (eds.), *Consequences of Theory* (Baltimore, 1991), 154–180.

Afterword
From Romance to Refractory Aesthetic

Jean Franco

WOMEN's writing in Latin America is known primarily to the rest of the world thanks to a group of best-selling titles—Isabel Allende's *La casa de los espíritus* (*House of Spirits*), Angeles Mastretta's *Arráncame la vida* (*Mexican Bolero*), and Laura Esquivel's *Como agua para chocolate* (*Like Water for Chocolate*).

Success, however, has its price. Just as English and American women at the end of the nineteenth century were accused of flooding the market with cheap romance—leading witty writers like Oscar Wilde to ridicule them and 'serious' writers like Henry James and Thomas Hardy to revise their craft (Huyssens 1986)—so these popular writers have met with a certain scepticism, particularly at a time when literary evaluation is increasingly measured in terms of sales.

A recent article published in *Confluencias* notes the runaway success in Germany of Allende's *La casa de los espíritus* and Mastretta's *Arráncame la vida* (translated into German as *Tango Mexicano*), both of which were on the best-seller lists for weeks. Esquivel's *Como agua para chocolate* may now be better known than García Márquez's *One Hundred Years of Solitude*. Judging by the book blurbs the main attraction of these books abroad is still that stale sales cliché, 'magic realism'—a code word for 'exoticism'. However, this does not explain their success in Latin America nor the fact that the writers are widely accepted as feminist.

They do indeed represent a version of feminism, whether by portraying women's liberation from victimization or by creating strong women characters such as Alba in *La casa de los espíritus*, Catalina in *Arráncame la vida*, or Jesusa in *Hasta no verte*

Jesús mío (by Elena Poniatowska) who take power into their own hands. Sara Sefchovich, in whose novels protagonists are empowered by female erotic fantasies which lift them out of their humdrum lives, describes herself as a militant feminist, wife, and mother, and a voracious reader. In her novel, *La señora de los sueños*, women find sexual liberation, intellectual knowledge, political activism, or religious enlightenment through dreams inspired by their reading.

These novels all belong to the category of art romance. Romance has strong defenders, among them Fredric Jameson who, in *The Political Unconscious*, invented the category of 'art romance' to describe novels such as Alain Fournier's *Le Grand Meaulnes* or Stendhal's *La Chartreuse de Parme*, so the term is not a derogatory one. The back-cover blurb of Angeles Mastretta's *Arráncame la vida* compares her heroine to Stendhal's passionate women, thus associating her novel with this particular canon.

Commenting on Northrop Frye's discussion of romance, Jameson observes that he 'insists on the essential marginality of the most characteristic protagonists of romance, slaves or women, who, by their necessary recourse to fraud or guile rather than to sheer physical power, are more closely related to the Trickster than to the Solar Hero' (Jameson 1981: 113). We should keep in mind that what is seductive about the Trickster's guile is his or her use of the system rather than any desire to destabilize or overturn the status quo.

Popular romance—that is, Harlequin and Mills and Boon romances as opposed to art romance—also has its defenders, among them Janice Radway, who claims that, contrary to élitist criticism, the readers of Harlequins are not simply passively seduced by the form but rather enjoy and play with its conventions (Radway 1984). The game in the Harlequin is limited to the single goal of trapping a man higher in social rank and wealth. In art romance, the trickster role of woman has a different outcome. In Angeles Mastretta's *Arráncame la vida*, for example, Catalina's marriage to Andrés Ascencio (who eventually rises to the position of Governor of Puebla and right-hand man of the President of the Republic) begins the story of a long struggle in which Catalina gradually uncovers the vast system of greed, brutality, and corruption which constitutes local and national politics and is only provisionally liberated by the death of Andrés. Mastretta's narrative inverts the structure of popular romance; like other art romances, however, the story evolves chronologically over time and culminates in personal liberation at Andrés's graveside. Although women's oppression is equated with political repression, what beguiles us in the novel is Catalina's wiles both as seductress and as deflator of macho pretentions. In another vein, Elena Poniatowska's *Juchitán de las mujeres* (*The Women of Juchitán*)—an essay that accompanied photographs by Graciela Iturbide—inverted the notion of strong, dominant males by describing powerful females who hold economic and political power in that area.

There is, however, a growing divergence between the international best-selling writer (and a feminism of equality), on the one hand, and the neo-avant-garde for whom the seduction of romance merely reproduces the seduction of commodity culture under neo-liberalism. For this neo-avant-garde it is a new aesthetic which is also 'political' in the broadest sense of the term that is now urgently needed.

The neo-avant-garde emerged in those countries that went through the experience of dictatorship; they claim that to revert to traditional narrative is to leave the 'house in order'— (a phrase which was uttered by Alfonsín at the end of the military regime). To state that the house is 'in order' not only accepts the premisses of neo-liberalism (i.e. that it 'saved' countries from chaos) but also evades the challenge of those premisses, one of which is the mystical appeal to the market as an index of value. Tununa Mercado, for example, comments on the irony of her own surname—'mercado' (market), 'the unavoidable new sign of Menemist Argentina which corrodes urban life, and clouds and nullifies consciousness' (Mercado 1994*b*). She goes on to criticize the pluralism of neo-liberal societies, which practise a formal rather than a participatory democracy: 'Pluralism makes ideas, divergencies, anger, confrontation disappear merely by invoking (the threat to) economic stability.' Women's literature that relies on the seduction of traditional narrative despite its 'feminism' thus becomes a literature of accommodation with narrative seduction analogous to the seduction of the commodity.

The requirement of a 'refractory aesthetic' (to use Nelly Richard's phrase) is that it should undermine the values of the market-place and bring to crisis older structures. Thus in her book, *Masculino/femenino*, Nelly Richard, who belongs as a critic to the neo-avant-garde, shifts the meaning of 'feminine' drastically so that it is no longer associated with the limited feminist goal of equality nor with the inversion in the positions of power (Richard 1989; 1994). Rather, the feminine includes everything—transvestite performance, certain artistic practices, some by male artists—that destabilizes the discursive structures of media-dominated societies whose discourse she describes as monumental, pluralist, and massive. By monumental she means the obliteration of ambiguities; by massiveness, she means the substitution of quantitative criteria (for example, sales or polling) for evaluation; and by pluralism she means diversity of opinion without acknowledgement of real differences. Like several other contemporary writers and critics, Richard is concerned with the inequalities between centre and periphery although, in her view, centre and periphery are not necessarily geographic areas since there is a periphery in the US and a centre in Chile. Rather the terms are used to distinguish a hegemonic discursive formation which constantly reproduces market criteria of evaluation from 'marginal discourse' where the validity of this discourse breaks down or turns into nonsense. The most interesting illustration of this is Diamela Eltit's pastiche of the testimonial, *El padre mío* (Eltit 1989).[1] This tape-recorded interview with a schizophrenic homeless man presents the reader with the fragmentary monologues that arbitrarily string together newspaper headlines, paranoid sensibility, and popular conspiracy theories which, while they cannot be put together to form a narrative, mark the fracturing of sense at the margins with paranoia as the only common denominator.

Now this disruption of meaning may seem reminiscent of the avant-garde of the 1920s, except that Eltit is writing in a radically different environment, one in which revolution is no longer a possibility, in which neoliberalism is triumphant, and the exclusion of vast sectors of the population from education and from health care and adequate living standards has become ever more flagrant. Some opposition to this state of affairs comes from social movements such as the Mothers of the Plaza de Mayo and the Retired Workers' movement in

[1] See also Nelly Richard's discussion of *El padre mío* in Josefina Ludmer (forthcoming, 1996)

Argentina. However, political parties and the social sciences which had formerly analysed and acted on behalf of those suffering social injustice are for the most part seen as compromised by their accommodation of neo-liberalism.[2] While the more radical of the social movements elaborate new political strategies, the neo-avant-garde engages in the critique of neo-liberalism at the level of value. This involves a revaluation and a repoliticization of the aesthetic on new lines as a force for destabilization, a force that derives its impulse from its marginality.

One aspect of this is the focus on sexuality, both lesbian and heterosexual, in contemporary poetry, since poetry is the most marginalized form of writing at the present time. In general this kind of poetry—the poetry of Carmen Ollé and Carmen Berenguer, to cite just two writers—is not confessional poetry but a far more radical disruption of gendered language.

But the connection between the emergence of a neo-avant-garde and the experience of authoritarian regimes is perhaps best appreciated in the novel, especially in those novels which propose a redefinition of the 'aesthetic'. Let me refer again to two authors who approach the question of the aesthetic in somewhat different ways—Tununa Mercado of Argentina and Diamela Eltit of Chile. Mercado, a native of Cordoba (Argentina), lived in exile in Mexico. Diamela Eltit began to write during the Pinochet regime in Chile and formed part of an activist vanguardist group, CADA (Colectivo Acciones de Arte), which took part in unconventional acts of protest against the dictatorship. With redemocratization in both Argentina and Chile the post-dictatorship state declared a *punto final* (a full stop) to investigations of repression, inaugurating a deliberate policy of putting the past behind and obliterating memory.

Memory thus became an important topic in the literature of the *cono sur*, particularly in women's fiction. One thinks, for example, of Luisa Valenzuela's story 'Cambio de armas', in which a woman tries to recuperate her memory obliterated by torture. But what particularly interests me in Mercado's and Eltit's writing is their radical rethinking of writing itself and, in particular, their hostility to what one might term the story—by which I mean a plot structure and 'characters'. For Mercado, writing is different from literature and occurs 'in that much

[2] See the critique of the social sciences in Richard (1994).

maligned place—the ivory tower which is a far from literature and so near to writing' (Mercado 1994*b*).

This may seem surprising and even shocking at first glance until we realize that the tower is a place that women have had to conquer. Elsewhere I termed this 'reinhabiting the private', pointing out the way the term 'private' covers so many contradictory meanings—in classical political thinking it refers to the feminine space of reproduction as against the masculine space of production; it refers to private life as the space of the self as against social space, to private enterprise against the state, domesticity as against action in the world, a household or private space as against the public sphere (Franco 1992). For Mercado, however, both everyday life and *escritura* (writing) are powered by eros. The domestic is not an inferior compartment of existence but a tactile, sensuous relationship with things. One of the stories in *Canon de alcoba* (1988), which were widely characterized as 'erotic' texts, describes a housewife going about her daily tasks with such rapt attention that they are converted into a form of *jouissance*.

What characterizes Mercado and Eltit is that they reorganize these meanings on new lines: Mercado disassociates the private sphere from the family, both writers disassociate affect from family romance, and body from self. Mercado's theory of the minimal and Eltit's marginality are awkward, not easily categorizable concepts (Mercado 1994*b*). What both authors attempt is to make of 'the private' a kind of reserve energy from which the so-called public sphere can be destabilized, allowing for an 'eros' that is not simply tied to romantic love. In this sense, they engage in a transvaluation of values from market values to the investment of eros in all aspects of life.

In her critical writings, Tununa Mercado deliberately blurs the compartmentalization of the aesthetic as if it only applied to art, music, and literature. In her view, there is no discontinuity between perception in the service of literature and perception in the service of everyday life. 'Just as contemporary feminist theory linked the private and the political, thus clearing away the dichotomy that had been detrimental to women, so the political dimension can no longer be considered a supplement' (Mercado 1994*b*). She describes her project as nothing less than 'a politics for the end of the century'.

Mercado believes that opposition to the massivity of the media is expressed as 'La letra de lo mínimo'—that is, a minimalist concept of writing that eschews the pleasures of the grandiose. She declares that she has never been able to interest herself in character, plot, or the normal rules of novel-writing and that her writing does not easily fit into conventional genre categories. In a talk she titled 'The Tidy House' ('La casa en orden'), she pointed out that the metaphor of the tidy house, cleaned up after the dictatorship, was symptomatic of the euphemisms that prevailed even after redemocratization and which for the returning exile was particularly alienating (Mercado 1994*a*). Her one novel, *En estado de memoria* (1990), depicts the violence of the separation of past and present that produces a vacuum in the protagonist's life which is filled by meditations, evocative images, and incidents randomly brought together through memory and observation both during exile in Mexico and after her return to Argentina. What is striking is that for this narrator most experiences are vicarious. She wears second-hand clothes, buys second-hand furniture, and has a number of second-hand experiences. This abstraction of affect and its arbitrary relocation is illustrated by a description of her membership of a reading group which embarks on a thirty-year reading of a cult book of the exiles, Hegel's *The Phenomenology of Mind*, a philosophical enquiry into mind which ignores the body completely. The experience of reading Hegel does not open up universal knowledge for the narrator and her friends but becomes a teasing and fragmentary process, a 'distracted' reading of a text, chosen almost at random.

On her return from exile, the protagonist becomes obsessed with a *linyera* (a homeless man, 'linyera' being a word that suggests 'línea' or boundary). The *linyera* sleeps on a bench in the park, his head resting on a copy of *The Story of Perón*. The *linyera* is of course an outsider, an outcast. He is also a male intellectual who still inhabits public space if only as a derelict. Mercado's protagonist recognizes a fragile and tenuous fraternity in marginality. It is this which finally allows her to write; it is not what she writes but where she writes that is significant, however, for she writes on a wall that bars the view from her study and as she writes the wall begins to crumble and gradually slips out of view 'like paper through a crack'. It is as if the barriers between self and other, inner and outer, private and public, are paper barriers which it is the work of writing to destroy while avoiding the establishment of new certainties.

The comparison and contrast with Virginia Woolf is both tantalizing and striking, for in Mercado's case there is a kind of necessary ascesis or withdrawal from a society whose values are alien to her and which, while reminiscent of *fin-de-siècle* modernism, is directed *against* society's self-forgetting. Mercado's ivory tower is not a place of privilege or protection but a Utopian space where boundaries that are hindering social and political innovation can come down.

In very different fashion, a series of novels by Diamela Eltit implicates gender and the aesthetic in the project of reconfiguring the periphery within global capitalism. Her novels, her performances of self-mutilation during the dictatorship, her testimonial recording of a schizophrenic in *El padre mío*, her collaboration in a photo essay on love among the lunatics of Putaendo, all hold up the distorting mirror of the marginal to reflect the monstrous image of the classical centre (the West). Her first novel, *Lumpérica* (1983), must surely be regarded as one of the great works on the military regime. In *Lumpérica* a woman sits on a park bench under an illuminated sign in the centre of Santiago; the entire novel is about the different movements of this woman's body under the vigilance of an illuminated advertisement. What the novel enacts is the disassociation of self from body, and of subject from the somatic, an experience often associated with torture and its 'attempt to deterritorialize the meanings of the body'.[3] However, Eltit is never referential or overtly allegorical. To read one of her novels—*Lumpérica, El cuarto mundo* (1988), *Vaca sagrada* (1991), *Por la patria* (1986), and most recently, *Los vigilantes* (1994)—is to share in this radical experience of disassociation.

Eltit's first four novels were written under the dictatorship, an experience which she describes as 'pasional y personal,' and as a gesture of survival (Eltit 1993). For Eltit the danger of thinking in terms of women's writing or feminist writing is that it ghettoizes: 'A novel that declares itself as feminist or feminine or by a woman, would not be subversive merely because it referred to real dilemmas' (Eltit 1993). She also specifically criticizes art romance:

the space of the romance is not the only possible one for woman, nor is unlimited sacrifice, nor anecdotal references to sexual liberation [the only theme]. It seems more important to me to uncover the

---

[3] Marcial Godoy, unpublished thesis.

constellation of conscious thought which connects the individual to
the public sphere, the subjective to the social. (Eltit 1993)

Eltit works 'with fragments of material, with scraps of voices',
in order to explore 'nomadically' ('a la manera vagabunda')
'genres, masks, simulacras and verbalized emotion' (Eltit 1993).
Like Mercado, she underscores the limits of public discourse
and attitudes; for her, literature is disjunctive rather than

an area of responses that leave readers happy and content. The (ideal)
reader to whom I address myself is more problematic, with gaps,
doubts, a reader traversed by uncertainties. And here the margin, the
multiple possible margins mark, among other things, pleasure and
happiness as well as turbulence and crisis. (Eltit 1993)

Julio Ortega aptly describes her work as 'putting into crisis
the masculine and the feminine as biological destiny, social
roles, discursive economies, fables of identity and confirmations
of power' (Ortega 1993). Her most recent novel, *Los vigilantes*,
takes to the limit a problem of French feminism: whether
women can speak within the symbolic order. The protagonists
are a woman and a child who live in virtual isolation partly
because of the hostility of the neighbours. The child whose
monologues open and close the novel is certainly 'abnormal'.
He has a dissonant laugh, bangs his head against the wall, and
plays incomprehensible games. The bulk of the novel consists
of the woman's written missives addressed to a masculine third
person, a kind of personified regulator who apparently reproves,
threatens, and admonishes since the woman's letters in response
are complaining, defensive, intermittently angry, submissive,
or defiant. The addressee may be the child's father, or a guard-
ian figure but he is also a more abstract entity—the name-
of-the-father, or the divine. The child's expulsion from school
which occasions the first letters marks the initial sign of stigma-
tization which in turn arouses paranoid fears—of a lame neighbour who keeps the woman under constant surveillance, of the
visits of her mother-in law (who exemplifies 'Western perfection'), of the fact that the 'father' is threatening to sue her.
These external mandates drive her to desperation and they
gradually acquire a public dimension when she transgresses
the 'senseless' laws promulgated by her neighbours.

Instead of openly repressive rule, this society works through
the internalization of regulations on the part of citizens who

act as vigilantes. The city is described as 'in decadence'; the most powerful citizens have fled to the slopes of the cordillera. Although the powers-that-be court 'the loving gaze of the other side of the West', this 'Other West' is described as 'terribly indifferent to any kind of seduction and regards the city only as a worn-out theatrical performance' (Eltit 1994). During a period of intense cold, the woman takes in homeless people despite society's prohibition. For this 'plot against the West' she is denounced and eventually expelled from her home. This expulsion is, as it were, from the Western episteme itself; the novel closes with the child's monologue which is on the margins of cultural intelligibility.

Despite the impression that may have been given by this brief summary this is not simply a transcription into narrative of Kristeva's presymbolic 'langage poétique'. Rather, Eltit's method is to stage two possibilities—either Woman reacts to the rules that she cannot alter, or she is outside rational thought. The novel brings both these possibilities into crisis. Eltit is not in the business of suggesting solutions, though her novel suggests that the self-regulatory norms of neo-liberalism exacerbate the marginalization of Woman.

In a photo-essay *El infarto del alma* (1993), written in collaboration with the photographer Paz Errazuriz, Eltit explores another kind of marginality, that of the mentally sick who are confined to a remote asylum in Putaendo. The asylum had formerly been a tuberculosis hospital. Commenting on this change from one form of isolation to another, Eltit writes

the poverty of lungs was replaced by mental poverty . . . the liberatory loving romantic dream by the strait jacket to restrain this forbidden, unintelligible delirium. The patients are outsiders, deprived of citizenship yet still hungry for love. (Eltit and Errazuriz 1993)

Paz Errazuriz's photographs, therefore, focus not on the solitude of madness or the freakishness, but on the loving relationships that have been formed in the asylum. These are photographs of couples evidently from the lower classes—the faces are of the *huaso* or lowest rung in that class-conscious society but always photographed together. Eltit's text is part commentary, part travel description, part pastiche, an enquiry into love, sickness, and marginalization. Most of all it is a meditation on that form of affect in which the imaginary plays

so intense a role and which has been likened to madness because of the loss of the sense of self. It goes without saying that
El infarto del alma is not a sociological tract. As in *Los vigilantes*
Eltit pushes a commonplace to the productive limit—in this
case the romantic association of love and madness is transformed into an enquiry into the loving of the mad.

Although Mercado and Eltit are very different writers, they
clearly endorse a feminism which is neither one of equality nor
of difference. Latin American women have often expressed
their discomfort with theories that exclude feminism from other
political struggles and make it only a matter of concern to
women. What is interesting is that both of them appeal to a
new aesthetic, one that is rooted in marginalization. The modern Latin American novel has often been written as an allegory
of national identity. Underlying that allegory was an unexam-
ined notion of subjectivity that took gender for granted and
made nation or community the love object. What these women
writers show us is that 'nation' and 'community' cannot be
rethought without first exposing the limits of a system in which
gender has been implicated in social control. At those limits
the Enlightenment narrative disintegrates into the language of
the mad, the outcast, or the child. And it is here that these
women position themselves.

LIST OF WORKS CITED

ALLENDE, ISABEL (1982), *La casa de los espíritus* (Barcelona).
ELTIT, DIAMELA (1983), *Lumpérica* (Santiago).
—— (1985), *Por la patria* (Santiago).
—— (1988), *El cuarto mundo* (Santiago).
—— (1989), *El padre mío* (Santiago).
—— (1991), *Vaca sagrada* (Buenos Aires).
—— (1993), 'Errante, errática', in Juan Carlos Lertora (ed.), *Una
poética de literatura menor: la narrativa de Diamela Eltit* (Santiago 1993).
—— (1994), *Los vigilantes* (Buenos Aires).
—— and ERRAZURIZ, PAZ (1993), *El infarto del alma* (Santiago).
ESQUIVEL, LAURA (1994), *Como agua para chocolate* (Barcelona).
FRANCO, JEAN (1992), 'Going Public: Reinhabiting the Private', in
George Yúdice, Jean Franco, and Juan Flores (eds.), *On Edge: The
Crisis of Contemporary Latin American Culture* (Minneapolis 1992).

GARCÍA MÁRQUEZ, GABRIEL (1969), *Cien años de soledad* (Barcelona).

HUYSSENS, ANDREAS (1986), 'Mass Culture as Woman', in *After the Great Divide: Modernism, Mass Culture, Postmodernism* (Bloomington, Ind.).

JAMESON, FREDRIC (1981), *The Political Unconscious: Narrative as a Socially Symbolic Act* (Ithaca, NY).

LERTORA, JUAN CARLOS (1993) (ed.), *Una poética de literatura menor: la narrativa de Diamela Eltit* (Santiago).

LUDMER, JOSEFINA (1995) (ed.), *Fin de siglo* (forthcoming).

MASTRETTA, ANGELES (1985), *Arráncame la vida* (Mexico, DF).

MERCADO, TUNUNA (1988), *Canon de alcoba* (Buenos Aires).

——— (1990), *En estado de memoria* (Buenos Aires).

——— (1994*a*), 'La casa en orden', unpublished talk given at Bryn Mawr, US.

——— (1994*b*), *La letra de lo mínimo* (Buenos Aires).

ORTEGA, JULIO (1993), 'Diamela Eltit y el imaginario de la virtualidad', in Lertora (1993).

PONIATOWSKA, ELENA (1969), *Hasta no verte Jesús mío* (Mexico, DF).

——— (1989), *Juchitán de las mujeres* (Mexico, DF).

RADWAY, JANICE (1984), *Reading the Romance: Women, Patriarchy and Popular Literature* (Chapel Hill, NC).

RICHARD, NELLY (1994), *La insubordinación de los signos (cambio político, transformaciones culturales y poéticas de la crisis)* (Santiago).

——— (1989), *Masculino/femenino: prácticas de la diferencia y cultura democratica* (Santiago).

VALENZUELA, LUISA (1982), 'Cambio de armas', in *Cambio de armas* (Hanover, NH).

Index

love 106, 117 n., 235–6
  in Allende 70, 74, 77, 80–1
  in Bombal 121–2
  erotic 113–15
  in Gambaro 17, 27
  narcissistic 125
  Platonic 112
  in Rulfo 124
  'love in the feminine' 5, 115
Ludmer, Josefina 202
Luna, Rafaela 54–5, 58–9
Lyotard, Jean-François 7, 176

McDowell, Deborah 216
madness 6, 115, 127–8, 142, 235–6
  city as sign of 169
  in Pizarnik 132, 134, 136
  in Rulfo 114
magic 79–80
  in Saldaña 188, 191
magic realism 66, 76, 78–80, 226
Malinow, Inés: *Alejandra Pizarnik:
  Poemas* 130 n.
man, as spectator, in Gambaro 14, 20 n.
Marechal, Leopoldo 30 n.
Mares, Pablo 59–60
marginality 56, 86, 206, 208, 211,
  217, 227, 230, 236
  in Eltit 90 & n., 97, 231, 233, 234,
  235
  Ludmer on 202
Marinetti, Filippo Tommaso 166
marriage 33, 38
  in Allende 68
  in Bombal 115, 116, 119–20
Martí, José 207
Martín Fierro 30 n., 44
Marxism 205, 206–7
  Campobello's sympathy with 59 n.
  criticism, literary 203
  in dialectics 59
  feminism and 205
masculinity 76, 77
Masiello, Francine 31
  Between Civilization & Barbarism 58
masks 168–9, 234
masochism, female 87–8, 93
master(ing) eye/I 14 & n., 16, 18,
  19
Mastretta, Angeles: *Arráncame la vida*
  (Mexican Bolero) 226–8
maternal body 158
  fear and 88
  horror and 102

loss of 159
menstruation and 96
matrifocality 182–3
melancholia 6, 135, 138
memories 230, 232
  in Eltit 95–6
  in Pizarnik 141
Menchú, Rigoberta 48 n., 209
Menemist Argentina 228
menstruation 96
  in Allende 81
  in Eltit 85–6, 88, 93, 94–5, 96,
  99–100
  in Saldaña 193
Mercado, Tununa 8, 69, 228, 230–3,
  234, 236
  Canon de alcoba 231
  En estado de memoria 232
  'Tidy House, The' ('La casa en
  orden') 232
  view of writing 231–2
mestizaje 75 & n.
metafiction 7, 164, 172, 174–6
metaphysics 168, 176
Mexican Revolution 4
  distortions of 49, 50, 61 & n.–2
  music and 60 & n.–61, 62
  novels of 46–8
Mexico:
  indigenous dances 50 & n.
  Ministry of Education 50 n., 220
  National School of Dance 50 n.
  military repression 92 n.
Mills and Boon 227
Ministry of Public Education, Mexico
  50 n., 220
Minnesota conference, on Hispanic
  and Luso-Brazilian feminist
  criticism 207–8
mirrors 128 n.
  in Allende 82
  in Bombal 117–18, 119–20
  in Coutinho 173, 175
  in Eltit 92–3
  in Gambaro 12, 14, 15, 17, 18, 19,
  24, 26
  in Lange 38–41, 42
  in Pizarnik 6, 131, 132, 135, 136,
  137, 140, 142, 143, 144, 146
misogyny 67–8
modernism 30 n.
Molloy, Sylvia 4, 51, 58, 148
money 15, 17–18
Mora, Gabriela 72, 151–2, 154

psychoanalysis:
  Classical Western 107–9, 110–11:
    see also Freud and Freudianism
  Lacanian 120
  theory 5–6
psychobiography 180, 181
public space 231
  in Mercado 232
Puga, María Luisa:
  'lenguaje oculto, El' 219–21
  national curriculum and 220–5

Quiroga, Horacio 30 n.

race 7
racism 15–16
Radway, Janice 227
rape 72, 80
rational discourse 127
reading 144
  theory of, in Lange 3, 34
  strategies 43
  as subversive act 128
realism 26
reappropriation, of female body 67,
    70, 73
reductionism 128
religion 189, 194
repression 191–2, 230
  economic 97
  political, women's oppression and
    228
reproduction, feminine space 231
resistance literature 4
Retired Workers' movement 229–30
Rich, Adrienne 216–18
  'Blood, Bread and Poetry: The
    Location of the Poet' 216–17
  'Notes toward a Politics of
    Location' 216
Richard, Nelly: *Masculino/femenino*
    228–9
Rimbaud, Arthur 173
Ríos, Soleida: *Entre mundo y juguete*:
  'Casa' 186
romance 4, 73–4, 78, 226–8
  politics of 67
romance literature 75
roman noir, see novels: crime
Rosenfeld, Lotty 90 n.
Rowe, William 79–80
Roxlo, Nalé 32 n.
Rulfo, Juan: *Pedro Páramo* 5, 105–10,
    112–14, 115, 120, 123–5

Russia 59 n.
Russian Formalists 12
Rutherford, John: *Annotated
    Bibliography of the Novels of the
    Mexican Revolution, An* 47

sadism 133–4
sado-masochism 5
Saldaña, Excilia 7
  Mi nombre: antielegía familiar (My
    Name: A Family Anti-elegy) 180,
    183, 187–8, 191, 192, 194, 198
  'Monólogo de la esposa' (The
    Wife's Monologue) 180, 187
Sammons, Jeffrey 223
Sánchez-Tranquilino, Marcos 224
Sarmiento 51
Sartre, Jean-Paul 113 n., 165
Sayers, Dorothy 176
sea, in Pizarnik 139, 141, 144, 145
Sefchovich, Sara: *señora de los sueños,
    La* 227
self-love, women's 76–7
self-mutilation 233
sense of self 20, 89, 93, 212
  nation's 218
sex, death and 134
sexism 15–16
sexual abuse, of Saldaña 187 n.
sexual ambiguity 74–5, 77, 149–52
  in Peri Rossi 149–52
sexual binarism 36–8
sexual freedom 33 n.
sexuality:
  ambiguity of 74–5, 77, 149–52
  human, definition of 149
  marginalization of 211
  in poetry 230
  reconfiguration of, in Peri Rossi
    6
sexual multiplicity 6
Showalter, Elaine: *Literature of Their
    Own, A* 174
silence 71, 80, 106, 127, 129
  in Pizarnik's poetry 139, 143–4
Silverman, Kaja 153
  Male Subjectivity at the Margins
    148–9
sisterhood, in Allende 77, 78
Smith, Paul Julian 159
Smith, Sidonie 52
Song of Songs 113
Sousa Andrade, Joachim de: *O Guesa*
    166 & n.

women (*cont.*):
  as spectators 19
  as writers, expectations of 33
women's movements:
  development of in 1980s 68–9, 72,
    76
Woods, Richard O., on Mexican
  'life-writing' 47
Woolf, Virginia 7, 164, 171, 233
  Mrs Dalloway 169–70
writing 169, 197
  death and 85
  defilement and 100
  as destructive 6, 129, 131, 144–5
  horror and 102

importance of 230–1
as life-sustaining 6
menstruation as an alternative form
  99–100
Mercado's view 231–2
Pizarnik's view of 129, 130, 139,
  141
as political act 90
politics of 8
as reconstruction 181, 188, 194–5
strategies, invention of 43
as subversion 128
theory of, in Lange 3, 34

Zimmerman, C. J. 182